Banker's
Guide to
Financial
Statements

Other books on lending from Bankers Publishing Company:

Accounts Receivable and Inventory Lending by David A. Robinson
Commercial Problem Loans by Robert H. Behrens
Lending to Agricultural Enterprises by Thomas L. Frey and
   Robert H. Behrens

Thomas J. O'Malia

Banker's Guide to Financial Statements

SECOND EDITION

Bankers Publishing Company
Boston

Text design: David Ford
Typography: DEKR Corporation
Production Editor: Nancy Coleman
Copyediting: Celeste Ronciglione
Indexing: Donald Chaffee
Printing and binding: R. R. Donnelley & Sons Company

First Edition 1976; Second Edition 1982

Printed in the United States of America

Library of Congress Cataloging in Publication Data

O'Malia, Thomas J.
   Banker's guide to financial statements.

   Includes index.
   1. Financial statements.   I. Title.
HF5681.B204 1982   657′.33′024332   82-8786
ISBN 0-87267-038-4   AACR2

To Carole   My wife, my lover, my friend

To Erin, Molly, and Megan   May your cup always be half full

About the Author

Thomas J. O'Malia is a financial consultant with experience as a corporate treasurer, commercial lending officer, and public accountant. He has been involved in commercial banking on the east and west coasts.

He has lectured nationally on how to deal with financial institutions, and has been a guest lecturer at the University of Southern California Graduate School of Entreprenurial Management.

He holds a BS in accounting from King's College and an MBA from the University of Scranton. He has attended the ABA National Commercial Lending School at the University of Oklahoma and regional seminars of the Robert Morris Associates. He has also served as an instructor for courses sponsored by the American Institute of Banking.

Contents

Exhibits

Preface to the Second Edition

This revised and updated edition of BANKER'S GUIDE TO FINANCIAL STATEMENTS follows an immensely successful first edition. Published in 1976, the first edition was enthusiastically adopted by several banking schools and many bank training programs for use in introductory courses on financial statement analysis. In addition, thousands of bankers purchased copies and used them to acquire and sharpen their skills.

The preparation of the second edition was undertaken after a survey revealed that many readers were interested in a revised edition. Subsequently the entire text was reviewed, revised, and updated as necessary, edited for clearer presentation of its concepts, and then completely reset in type. Material has been added on new subjects such as inflation accounting and accelerated cost recovery. Many of the surveyed readers told us that a glossary and an index would be valuable. Both have been added to this edition.

One of the popular features of this text is its extensive use of sample documents to acquaint readers with material they are likely to encounter on the job. All of the samples of financial statements, tax forms, accountant's letters, and other documents have been reviewed and updated or replaced as necessary.

The numerous exercises that provided an opportunity for readers to practice their new skills were another popular feature of the first edition.

These exercises were updated and new ones added. Fifteen exercises, many of which contain complete financial statements for review, will be found in the new edition.

In all of our work on the new edition however, we have been careful to retain what made the first edition such a remarkable success. The scope and purpose of the book remain unchanged. The new edition continues to be a basic and down-to-earth introduction to the fundamentals of financial statement analysis written specifically from the lender's point of view.

Preface to the
First Edition

The role of banking historically has been to invest depositors' funds in various enterprises and receive a fee for this extension which, in turn, is used to reward both depositors and shareholders with interest and dividends. The primary form of such investment is the extension of credit known as a loan.

Contrary to popular belief, the difficulty of making a loan does not increase proportionately with size. A loan of $5,000 is not necessarily easier to make than one of $500,000. As a matter of fact, a good case can be made that the $500,000 loan is the simpler of the two. Why? Most companies that would approach a bank for a large loan probably have been in business for a number of years, have statements prepared by reputable accountants, have forecasts of their future plans and earnings, have developed a continuing management team, and understand their own financial needs.

As a rule, some or all of these factors are missing in a $5,000 to $25,000 request. Often the client only knows that he needs funds. Cause and effect are not only unknown, but also not really understood. There are other factors that make it increasingly difficult to make a good small loan. One of these is the bank's desire to service clients promptly. Another is that, in most institutions, requests of this nature are presented to branch or general bankers who have had little opportunity to learn the art of commercial lending, and even fewer opportunities to practice what they have learned.

Most branch personnel are trained to make what commercial lending officers call ''gut'' loans — loans without supporting data that are usually made on the strength of one's ''gut reaction'' to the client during the interview. Although this is probably the best way to make personal loans or car loans, it usually spells disaster for commercial loans.

Surveys on the subject of loan losses consistently point to this fact. The annual Robert Morris Associates survey of commercial charge-offs show that 97 percent of all loans charged off originated under $50,000, and many can be traced to loans that started at $25,000 or less.

The methods for solving this problem generally boil down to two. The first is to staff branches with commercial loan officers capable of handling difficult commercial loans. Of course, the cost would be prohibitive and many would argue that the results would not be substantially better. Lending smaller amounts of money still depends, in part, on ''gut'' character evaluation. Many senior people have not developed this skill to the same degree of proficiency that some branch lenders have.

The alternative is to create a system that builds on the branch banker's strengths. The system would vary from institution to institution, but it would always involve both education and review. For too long education of branch personnel to handle small commercial loans has been neglected. In banks of all sizes there continues to be a lack of sympathy for the branch banker in his role as a commercial officer. How often have we as senior officers said, ''It's only twenty grand. If Jones can't handle it, then we have the wrong guy out there.''

The review phase is not as involved as one may think. Branch officers who have gained expertise in commercial lending will, on occasion, see situations that are not familiar to them. In such cases they need a sounding board. They should have access to senior, full-time commercial officers who can understand their problems, effectively listen to a concise, informed presentation of a problem, and offer guidelines or checkpoints for review. If the system is working properly, the bank can deliver a full complement of talent for the critical moment of decision. The result should be a healthy loan portfolio.

This text is written to serve as a guideline for self-education and to be used in connection with a lending review program. Only by having a good grasp of the basics will the front-line lending officer be able to use the help of the bank's senior officers.

A number of excellent programs are available for education on all levels of management in commercial lending. The most outstanding is the Robert

Morris Associates commercial lending course. The American Institute of Banking also continues to offer many courses dealing with various aspects of commercial lending.

Unfortunately, most programs have not been designed to tackle the practical problem of analyzing financial statements. The many excellent texts available today seem to be geared more to the *academic* than the *practical* world.

This is a strong but defensible statement. Most branch officers are not technically trained, and many of the best officers are not college graduates. A lengthy discussion on such subjects as working capital adequacy is not important to them. They need practical guidelines.

Beyond this, a large number of small business borrowers have *no* financial statements. If there is one, it usually is what commercial officers refer to as a "greasy brown bag" because it is written on old scraps of brown lunch bags or on the back of a used envelope. In those rare cases where a statement exists, it is prepared by a brother-in-law or a cousin once removed. Handling this sort of statement is the challenge a small-loan officer faces.

Most academic approaches to analyzing financial statements fail to recognize one very important fact: every time a loan officer sees a financial statement and then starts to analyze it, *he is analyzing it in the context of the loan request*. It's one thing to read and dissect a statement if you are preparing a general market report on a large company for distribution to prospective stockholders. Their interest is general. A loan officer reviewing a $25,000 request for a piece of milling equipment, on the other hand, can get right to the practical aspect of reading the statement to see how repayment will be made. This difference is his one great advantage.

After all, the purpose of analysis as done by a bank is to determine the ability of the borrower to meet the conditions of a loan. What is his repayment ability? What is the risk to the bank? To analyze a statement in the context of a particular request does not take hours of academic review. If one is considering a short-term loan for working capital because of an inventory build-up, then the review of financial data is limited to a certain few, select areas.

This is the message of this text. Analyzing statements to make loans requires a practical, common sense approach. We hope this text will aid in the development of the necessary skills.

Because experience and exposure are necessary to develop skills, fifteen exercises have been included in the text. These provide opportunities to put into practice some of the concepts we will cover. In some instances they will be mechanical exercises in which you are asked to work a problem. You are urged not to pass these without completing them. Do not dismiss them as being too easy or too difficult. In other instances the exercise will be in the form of a financial statement that you are asked to review. Comments will follow each. For greatest effectiveness, you should jot your comments on a separate sheet first and then compare them with the composite of observations by other readers of the same statement.

Throughout this text, we will attempt to achieve three major goals. The first is to make the loan officer feel *comfortable* when dealing with financial statements as part of the loan decision process. Second, the text seeks to expose the *types and sources* of statements available. Finally, a major effort will be made to develop an understanding of and to develop the ability to use *source and application* of funds data.

To accomplish these goals, five major subject areas will be covered. They are the composition of a statement; the mechanics of analysis; ratios — their meaning and use; comparisons and trends; and finally, changes in financial position.

Acknowledgments

There have been so many individuals who have done so much to make this work a reality that it is impossible to publicly thank each one of them. Their ime and talents have been most generously given and are deeply appreciated.

There are some who have not only assisted but who are really part of the work. Without their efforts the project would never have materialized. A special public thank you is sent to each of them: William E. Epperson, *First Alabama Bank*; George W. Frank, CPA, *Management Control Associates*; Robert C. Heim, *First Eastern Bank, N.A.*; Horace E. Kramer, *First Eastern Bank, N.A.*; Frank P. Orlando, CPA, *Parente, Randolph & Co.*; Robert D. Richardson, *First Eastern Bank, N.A.*

The author is indebted to the following firms for the many statements which are contained in the text: Haskin & Sells, *John McHale, Partner*; W. H. Johnson and Company, *William H. Johnson, CPA, Partner*; Laventhol & Horwath, *David L. Murzin, Partner*; Parente, Randolph & Co., *Frank P. Orlando, Partner*; Peat, Marwick and Mitchell, *Mort Erlich, Richard Nimmons, Partners*.

The revised edition has many changes in the content of the book and some contributions from new sources. The efforts of the contributors are greatly appreciated. A special thank you to M. B. Scott and Charlie Bird for adding new dimensions to the author and to Mort Erlich and Dick Nimmons of Peat, Marwick and Mitchell for their assistance in updating the tax and financial statements.

Part I   The Statements

1   The Role of Statements

Before any actual discussion of financial statements can begin, a number of preliminary items should be reviewed briefly as a refresher.

The financial strength of a company is but one of many aspects to be considered when making a loan decision. Consideration must be given to the time tested Cs of credit. The *character* of the applicant may overshadow his or her financial strength or make up for its weakness. The *capital* of the prospect is the first point of financial review. Banks seek to share in opportunities, which means that there should be some reasonable relationship between what the banks and the creditors will invest and what the ownership will risk. The third of the historical Cs of credit is *capacity* of the company to perform. To consider a loan which triples the company's volume raises serious nonfinancial questions regarding the company's ability to produce at that level.

In today's world, the historical three have been expanded to five. The newcomers are self-explanatory. They are *conditions* and *collateral*. If you listen to our marketing professionals, the sixth C is *checking account* — can we get it?

Organizations

A rose is a rose is a rose, but a statement is not a statement is not a statement. Not only is each statement unique, but each *type* of organization is by its nature different from others. A partnership, a proprietorship, and a corporation are forms of organization that differ in many respects. A review of their structures is not necessary here, but it is appropriate to remember that their reasons for being in business are different. Proprietors are in business for personal salary. They cannot be compared with a public corporation that bears the responsibility of paying dividends. Nor can a public corporation be confused with a privately held corporation that seeks the same goal as a proprietorship while using a different tax vehicle. A partnership may be a simple combination of two proprietors or it may be more formal than a large corporation.

The important thing to remember is that both the type and purpose of the organization must enter into your analysis. The nature of a business should be considered. Is the company a manufacturer or part of a service industry? Obviously, the statements of manufacturers and sellers of services will be completely different. Does the company sell wholesale or retail? Is it part of a seasonal industry? How large an area does it cover? All of these questions temper the pre-analysis portion of the decision.

Types of Loans

A major item to consider before reviewing the statements is the loan request itself. When you know about the business and then review the request, you can look at the statement in the *context* of the loan.

In our bank, we talk about all loans having to meet what is affectionately known as "Kramer's Law." The law, named after a retired president of the bank, simply states that two things are necessary to have a good loan: first, know where the money is going; and second, know how it is going to be paid back. Of course, this means more than just asking the obvious questions: How much do they need? Is it enough? For how long do they need it? It also means more than asking the not-so-obvious questions: Why are they coming to me? If they've been in business for a while, why not go to their present bank?

Essentially, you are asking if what the client proposes is feasible and if the past record supports it. Analysis is the tool you will use to measure repayment ability.

The answers to your questions will, of course, not be clear. Judging the situation correctly is how lending officers earn their pay. One key to determining the probability of success is to be certain we know what type of loan we are reviewing. There are only two types of loans. No, not secured and unsecured; and no, not time and demand. These are not types, they are terms. The two types of loans are those that are paid by *asset conversion* and those that are paid by *profit distribution*. The difference is probably best shown by two simple examples.

In the first, a man operates a candy store and seeks to borrow funds to purchase additional inventory for his Easter business. The funds are obtained and the product becomes inventory. The inventory is then displayed and sold. Sales are completed and become accounts receivable. When they are collected, the cash has completed the cycle, and the loan is repaid.

In the second example, the same candy vendor approaches you for the same amount of money, but this time it is to be used to purchase a candy counter. The counter, unlike the candy, will not be sold. Repayment, then is not dependent on asset conversion, but is dependent on the ability of the owner to make a profit on this equipment. The profit must be sufficient to meet your payment as well as return a reasonable portion to him.

In the first example, the analysis of the statement would be general. Provided a past record existed, and provided the company had reasonable balance (equity to debt), then one would assume the business would continue and that you could and would follow the asset through the cycle to repayment. In the second case of buying the counter, the analysis shifts to profitability. Does this expenditure increase profits? Are they increased in sufficient amounts to make the expenditure worthwhile for the client as well as to produce enough to meet your retirement payments? Is the past record one of reasonable profits? How much equity is there in the business to absorb an unforeseen loss? Will the company be profitable three years from now when the loan is still being repaid?

Without stating it directly, we have been discussing short-term and long-term borrowing, or, as the difference is more commonly stated, single-payment notes versus term notes. The differences are many. What is important to us is that the type of loan will determine just how you will read a statement.

There are, of course, other methods of repayment besides asset conversion and profit distribution. Among these are loans which will be retired by the investment of additional capital or which can be refinanced by another institution. They will not be reviewed here. It will suffice to say that the loans being examined here should not be dependent on these latter sources of repayment. A loan that depends on one of these methods should be referred to a seasoned loan specialist.

Summary

The one advantage a loan officer has in reviewing and analyzing financial statements is that he can do it in the *context* of the request before him. If you keep in mind the nature of the company, its structure and purpose, and answer the basic question of how the funds are to be used and how they are going to be repaid, then statement analysis becomes a matter of common sense. The "academics" of analysis are not as overwhelming as they seem.

2   What Is a Financial Statement?

It is commonly understood that a financial statement is composed of two major parts — the balance sheet and the income statement. But this definition leaves out a third and fourth part. These are the statement of stockholders' equity and the statement of change in financial position. For a banker, this fourth part is the most important.

This section is devoted to a complete review of the composition of the first three parts of the statement. A later section will be devoted to the change in financial position.

Before delving into the individual components of the financial statement it is important to know the purpose of each. This chapter will provide an overview of the parts of the statement and a brief summary of each one's purpose.

An Overview

By simplest definition, a balance sheet is a statement of the assets and liabilities of a company *as of* a certain date. The accountant's letter, which will be discussed shortly, states just this.

XYZ CORPORATION
Balance Sheet
December 31, 19X4

One could say a balance sheet is a snapshot of an ongoing entity taken at a certain point. It is analogous to a picture of an airplane in mid-air, showing its position right now, *as of* this moment. One does not know whether the plane is landing or taking off. We do not know where it has been or where it will be. We know where it was at one point.

A balance sheet represents today's assets and liabilities. It is one frame of a constantly changing picture.

The income statement, unlike the balance sheet, is cumulative. It takes yesterday's transactions and adds them to today's and states that these are the totals of the income and expenses for that period. The heading clearly states this.

XYZ CORPORATION
Statement of Income
For the Year Ended December 31, 19X4

Some companies prefer the word earnings to income. The two are interchangeable. If the period under review is less than a year, four months for example, it will state just that.

XYZ CORPORATION
Statement of Income
For the Four Months Ended April 30, 19X4

The balance sheet heading at the end of a four-month period would be the same as at year-end, except for the date change. It would say:

XYZ CORPORATION
Balance Sheet
April 30, 19X4

The balance sheet is still a single snapshot. It just happens on a different date.

Referring back to our airplane analogy, one could say that the income statement will inform you how far the plane has flown and how much gas has been consumed in that period.

The statement of stockholders' equity may either be a separate schedule or it may be merged into the income statement. The manner of presentation will be determined by the number and complexity of transactions. The purpose of this portion of the statement is to report the history of the company's total equity during the period covered by the income statement.

From this schedule, one will learn of dividends that may have been paid, or treasury stock which may have been purchased. The profit earned by the company and reinvested by it is reflected here. If the company received new cash via an investment, then the new stock issued would be easily recognized in this part of the financial report.

The fourth statement, change in financial position, is sometimes referred to as the *source and application* or *cash flow* statement. Its purpose is to summarize the funds available to the company and the way in which the company has elected to use them. If a loan officer seeks to know how repayment is to be made, what could be more important than knowing the amount and source of funds that have been available in past years and, even more important, how management elected to disburse them?

What Do Statements Tell Us?

Confusion about statements and failure to use them effectively arises from a poor understanding of a few basic points. Consider the following.

First of all, who prepares the statement? If you said the accountant or the auditor, you have made a very common mistake. As we will see when reviewing the accountant's letter, he or she clearly states, "we have *examined* the books and records." To examine is not to prepare. His report shows the numbers as they are, and he states his opinion of them.

Who, then, prepares the numbers? Management does. The company keeps its own books and the role of the outsider is to examine them. For a good number of our clients, especially the smaller ones, the place where management's involvement ends and the outside auditor's begins is not clearly marked — and understandably so. Our clients are dependent on their outside advisors for a number of special services, such as tax planning and filing of information with government agencies, in addition to preparing audited statements. The key word which must describe the auditor is independent. Without this, his or her value as an examiner is questionable.

The second thing that must be understood is the period covered by the statement. This period is referred to as the fiscal year and it may be the same as the calendar year or it may end at a different time. This idea is easily grasped, but what is usually forgotten is that management decides when the year-end will be. One of the primary considerations in making this decision is the cost of preparing the statement. The counting and pricing of physical inventory and the confirmation of receivables are expensive but necessary to a complete audit. Because of this, management may choose the *low point* of its business cycle to conclude its year. This is common sense. More than profits would suffer if one were to shut down during the busiest season for an inventory count. And why count all those extra items? Many companies have gigantic inventory sales to remove items from their shelves to avoid the cost of counting them.

Nothing is wrong with a statement of a company at its low point. What is wrong is if this fact is *forgotten* when you are reading the statement. To judge inventory at its low point relative to other assets or to equity may be meaningless.

The third basic point is to understand the major distinction between the two basic methods of accounting. These are the accrual and the cash basis methods. Most individuals file their tax return on a cash basis. That is to say, income is income when received and not when it was originally owed to you. An expense is an expense only when it is paid.

The accrual system seeks to match income and expenditures with the periods in which they were earned or incurred. In other words, it seeks to match income to the point of sales and expenditures to the point of consumption. Most business statements are on the accrual basis, but, since all are not, the difference should be kept in mind.

An example best illustrates the difference. An executive spends $1,000 on various office supplies on December 15. The bill is paid the same day. Under the cash basis, he would show the entire expense in the current year. Under the accrual basis, the portion of supplies remaining would be listed on the year-end balance sheet statement as an inventory asset and the difference, the portion used, would be the current expense.

The final point deals with the question asked by this chapter's heading. What does the statement tell us? We know management prepared it, and it could have been done at the low point of their fiscal year, and that it was done on some basis that makes sense to them. But what does this really tell us? We seem to be describing rather than defining the statement.

The long and short of it is that the statements tell us about a company's *past* record and its relative strength at a previous time so as to allow us to preview what the future may be like.

No, we the readers of the statements are not soothsayers. We do not read statements as if they were tea leaves. What we do is fit them into a pattern by first understanding them and then considering them in the context of the loan request.

There is an old saying which should be passed on at this time as a word of warning. It goes something like this: *"Figures don't lie, but liars do figure."*

The Accountant's Function

Earlier we said that management prepares the financial statement that we seek to analyze. The question to be answered, then, is "What work was done by the accountant?" There are many types of statements; to know exactly what work was done, one must read the letter. This letter or "opinion" by the auditing firm precedes the basic financial statements.

Most letters accompanying audited financial statements consist of two paragraphs. The first is referred to as the scope paragraph and the second as the opinion. The scope paragraph tells us the exact extent of the work that was or was not performed. The opinion paragraph reflects the professional opinion of the auditor on the financial statement. Exhibit 2.1 is a sample letter showing a "clean" opinion. Read it in its entirety and then we will return to discuss certain key phrases contained in it.

"We have examined." The accountant opens with the strong statement that they have not prepared, but have reviewed and have examined the records.

"as of December 31, 19X2 and 19X1." Our pictures are being defined as being at a certain point in time (balance sheet) and for a cumulative period (income statement).

"in accordance with generally accepted auditing standards." This statement implies a great deal. The accountant is saying that his investigation was one that meets the high standards of the profession of which he is a part. There are ten standards which have been formally adopted by the American Institute of Certified Public Accountants. They cover general, fieldwork, and reporting standards. Adherence to these implies that a comprehensive program was laid out and followed.

"such tests . . . as we considered necessary." The same packaged program cannot be used for all audits. Auditors are professionals who exercise discretion in performing their job.

"In our opinion" is the beginning of the opinion paragraph. The auditor is about to deliver his verdict on what he has examined.

"present fairly." This means just what it states. It does not mean exactly or perfectly. It does mean the overall picture is a reasonable portrait of the company.

The Board of Directors
A Company, Inc.:

We have examined the balance sheets of A Company, Inc. as
of December 31, 19X2 and 19X1 and the related statements
of earnings and retained earnings and changes in financial
position for the years then ended. Our examinations
were made in accordance with generally accepted auditing
standards, and accordingly included such tests of the
accounting records and such other auditing procedures as
we considered necessary in the circumstances.

In our opinion, the aforementioned financial statements
present fairly the financial position of A Company, Inc.
at December 31, 19X2 and 19X1 and the results of its
operations and the changes in its financial position for
the years then ended, in conformity with generally accepted
accounting principles applied on a consistent basis.

X, Y, Z, & Co.

February 2, 19X3

Exhibit 2.1   Accountant's Unqualified Opinion Letter ("Clean" Opinion) *"in conformity with generally accepted accounting principles."* Auditing standards are the approach to a statement. Accounting principles are the guidelines of the industry and have been formulated and modified and updated on a continuing basis. An example of such a principle is that capital assets are listed at cost and then depreciated over their useful life. In some European countries, it is accepted practice to list such assets at their fair market value. For purposes of this text it is not necessary to discuss what represents good or bad principles. If the accountant is reputable, the numbers will be likewise.

"on a consistent basis." This phrase allows you to rest assured that if inventory was calculated using a certain method last year, then it was done the same way this year.

The accountant's letter concludes with his signature and the date of his report. This date is not the date of issuance but rather is the date that his actual investigation or work on premise ended. Any major event that takes place between the end of the period under examination and the date of the report should be noted by the auditor.

Financial information of the quality reflected by a clean letter allows us to perform an analysis that is extremely valuable. Very few "small loan bankers" have ever seen such a statement, however. Remember, the back-of-the-envelope variety is what they've been looking at for years. This is why we said earlier that large loans may be easier to make than small ones.

Types of Letters

But the fact that a CPA signed a financial statement does not necessarily mean that the statement has been audited and that it has an unqualified opinion.

CPA's basically perform three different types of examinations. These are the unqualified or clean opinion, which we have just discussed; the limited review; and, finally, the compilation. The accountant's letter will clearly show which he or she has performed. Samples of a review letter and a compilation letter are presented in Exhibits 2.2 and 2.3 respectively.

It is important to note the difference between the first sentence of the unqualified opinion (Exhibit 2.1) and those contained in Exhibits 2.2 and 2.3. The unqualified opinion starts with "We have examined." The others

The Board of Directors
Example Company, Inc.:

We have reviewed the accompanying balance sheets of Example
Company, Inc. as of December 31, 19X2 and 19X1 and the
related statements of earnings and retained earnings and
changes in financial position for the years then ended,
in accordance with standards established by the American
Institute of Certified Public Accountants. All information
included in these financial statements is the representation
of the management of Example Company, Inc.

A review consists principally of inquiries of Company
personnel and analytical procedures applied to financial
data. It is substantially less in scope than an examination
in accordance with generally accepted auditing standards,
the objective of which is the expression of an opinion
regarding the financial statements taken as a whole.
Accordingly, we do not express such an opinion.

Based on our reviews, we are not aware of any material
modifications that should be made to the accompanying
financial statements in order for them to be in conformity
with generally accepted accounting principles.

X, Y, Z, & Co.

February 2, 19X3

Exhibit 2.2 Accountant's Review Letter

The Board of Directors
Example Company, Inc.:

We have compiled the accompanying balance sheets of Example
Company, Inc. as of December 31, 19X2 and 19X1 and the
related statements of earnings and retained earnings
and changes in financial position for the years then ended.

A compilation is limited to presenting in the form of
financial statements information that is the representation
of management. We have not audited or reviewed the
accompanying financial statements and, accordingly, do not
express an opinion or any other form of assurance on them.

X, Y, Z, & Co.

February 2, 19X3

Exhibit 2.3   Accountant's Compilation Letter

start with "We have reviewed" and "We have compiled." They are as different as night and day.

An unqualified opinion includes all of the tests that the CPA deems necessary. For this reason it is often known as a full-scope audit since the purpose is to fully explore each and every aspect of the statement. It includes verification of assets with outside sources.

A review, on the other hand, is much more limited in scope. It usually does not include verification; it involves more limited tests of records, with emphasis placed on interviewing the company personnel. The report concludes with the absolute statement that they are not expressing an opinion on the statement as a whole.

A compilation has even less scope than a review. In essence, the CPA says, "We took your numbers and put them on our stationery." Perhaps this is a slight oversimplification — but only slight.

If the accountant is not stating an opinion or if in fact he has done nothing, why should he even render a report? That's a big question which every loan officer has to come to grips with. Certainly everyone would like a clean opinion statement from a reputable accounting firm for each of its loans. The cost of such a statement can be prohibitive for many small companies, however.

The question remains, though. What advantage does this unaudited statement provide? How good is it?

Insofar as reputable CPAs approach all clients using the same accounting principles, and reputable accountants cannot sign a statement that is in direct conflict with these principles, then the statement has worth. There is no set of rules on how to *not* perform an audit. Reputable CPAs generally will perform a minimum number of auditing procedures before allowing their letter to accompany the report. They should see that cash has been reconciled and that the physical assets register has been properly kept. Although they have not observed the inventory, they have received a listing of it. Likewise, they have received a copy of the receivables and payables. They have in fact done a great deal. At the least, they have given you a starting point.

Statements with unaudited opinions are the most common seen by some bankers. If the firm preparing them is reputable, then the report will be. However, there is *no* substitute for an unqualified opinion, and if a company seeks any substantial credit, it should willingly accept the need for a fully audited statement. But the banker's unique access to the client allows him to delve into the content of any item in a statement and allows him to maximize the value of *all* statements, including unaudited ones.

It should be pointed out that other kinds of letters may, on occasion, be issued. An example of one such occasion would be when a change in accounting principles occurred. The auditor may or may not agree with the change, and this will determine the kind of letter he issues. Exhibit 2.4 is an example of a letter issued when the accountant was in agreement with a change. Exhibit 2.5 is an example of a letter issued when the accountant did not agree. In this case, he could not confirm the value of certain franchising and licensing costs and he did not agree with the company's treatment of certain pension expenses. He clearly tells us this in his letter.

This final report contains another interesting phrase, "going-concern." Whenever one reads a financial statement, he accepts the value applied to certain assets as realistic. This is usually their cost. If the company successfully continues in business and sells them in the normal course of events, they will yield not only this amount but a profit as well. The premise is that the business will continue. Sale of the items in a liquidation would not bring these values. The same is true of capital items. Their effective worth and their value on the statement depend on their continued use.

When a company's overall financial position begins to raise questions as to their future viability, then the accountant must so note in his letter. This is not to say that all "going-concern" statements are a *kiss of death*. What they should be is a warning. What they should not be is a surprise. It's your client and you have followed his progress. If it takes the accountant to tell you there's a problem, it's probably too late.

Before leaving this general area of discussion, there are several additional points to make. Accountants do *not* seek to detect fraud. Their audit programs are not geared to uncover it. In many cases they will; but a company can have funds misallocated or even embezzled without it being detected by the auditors. A clean statement is not an end all. Don't expect too much from it.

A second point is that only CPAs may issue certified statements. Today, a number of public accountants include a letter that at first reading would be confused with the CPA's letter. Unfortunately, this is both legal and ethical in a number of states. However, the same validity can not be attached to such a report as that which is attached to a CPA's. This does not mean that reports done by auditors and public accountants are without

The Board of Directors
A Company, Inc.:

We have examined the balance sheet of A Company, Inc. as
of December 31, 19X1 and the related statements of earnings
and retained earnings and changes in financial position
for the year then ended. Our examination was made in
accordance with generally accepted auditing standards, and
accordingly included such tests of the accounting records
and such other auditing procedures as we considered
necessary in the circumstances.

In our opinion, the aforementioned financial statements
present fairly the financial position of A Company, Inc.
at December 31, 19X1 and the results of its operations
and the changes in its financial position for the year
then ended in conformity with generally accepted accounting
principles which, except for the change, with which we
concur, in the method of computing depreciation as described
in note X to the financial statements, have been applied on
a basis consistent with that of the preceding year.

X, Y, Z, & Co.

February 1, 19X2

Exhibit 2.4 Accountant's Letter Where a Change in Accounting Principles
Occurred — Accountant in Agreement

The Board of Directors
A Company, Inc.:

We have examined the balance sheets of A Company, Inc. as of
December 31, 19X2 and 19X1 and the related statements of earnings
and changes in financial position for the years then ended. Our
examinations were made in accordance with generally accepted
auditing standards, and accordingly included such tests of the
accounting records and such other auditing procedures as we
considered necessary in the circumstances.

As described more fully in note X to the financial statements, the
Company does not provide for pension costs as required by generally
accepted accounting principles.

The accompanying financial statements have been prepared in
conformity with generally accepted accounting principles that
contemplate continuation of the Company as a going concern;
however, the Company has sustained substantial operating losses
during 19X2, 19X1 and prior years, and continuation as a going
concern is dependent upon future profitable operations and
obtaining additional financing.

The balance sheets at December 31, 19X2 and 19X1 include franchise
and licensing costs, less amortization of $900,000 and $750,000,
respectively. The recovery of these costs is dependent upon
future profitable operations of the Company.

In our opinion, except for the effect on the financial statements
of the failure to provide for pension costs as discussed in the
third preceding paragraph and subject to the effects of such
adjustments, if any, as might have been required had the ultimate
resolution of the matter discussed in the two preceding paragraphs been known, the aforementioned financial statements
present fairly the financial position of A Company, Inc. at
December 31, 19X2 and 19X1 and the results of its operations
and the changes in its financial position for the years then
ended, in conformity with generally accepted accounting principles applied on a consistent basis.

February 2, 19X3   X, Y, Z, & Co.

Exhibit 2.5 Accountant's Letter Where a Change in Accounting Principles
Occurred — Accountant Not in Agreement

merit. They can review and examine. What they can *not* do, however, is express an opinion as to conformity with generally accepted principles. They are not certified to do it.

A third point worth noting is that there is currently a major movement in this country to change to what has been incorrectly called "inflation accounting." The name is incorrect in that it assumes an increase in value when a decrease may also be warranted.

The basic thrust of this approach is to reflect for the company's shareholders the current value of the assets and liabilities, as opposed to reflecting their historic or cost value as is now done. Some feel that a current-value statement would provide a truer picture of the company. Many firms whose stocks are listed on the major exchanges must now conform with this approach when filing with the Securities Exchange Commission (SEC). It is not the purpose of this text to argue the validity of "inflation accounting." It is interesting to note, however, that successful bankers have always required this accounting format. They have used the statement as a starting point and then gone beyond the numbers to their true value — sometimes increasing the amounts shown on the statement and sometimes discounting completely the historic valuation as reflected in the statement.

The final and most important point regarding the accountant's letter is to read it. Don't pass it by. *Read it.* You'll understand what it says and then you'll know what work was done and the results of that work.

As discussed earlier, there is a need to have senior commercial lenders available to branches or small-loan officers to answer their questions. This is particularly true in the area of accountant's letters. There will be letters in reports that are not understood and counsel will be needed.

Footnotes — A Critical Part

Many times when reviewing a statement, bankers immediately go to the body and start reading the numbers. Not only do they pass over the letter, but they also fail to look for the background information contained in the footnotes. Everyone's approach to reading a statement differs. An excellent method, used by many, is to read the letter and then go directly to the footnotes and quickly read them, or at least glance at them to find out about any abnormalities before the actual numbers are reviewed.

What are footnotes? They are comments made by the company that explain certain accounting procedures they used and certain background information necessary to evaluate the statements. Footnotes must contain a statement of the significant accounting principles that are used, and they must tell us such things as whether the statement is that of a single company or a consolidation of a number of companies. This, of course, is critical. To whom are you lending? It may not be the same company as implied by the statement.

The footnotes should also spell out lien positions and the breakdown of long-term debt. If the company is contingently liable for debts, this fact should also be reflected in the footnotes. Knowing the background makes the numbers more meaningful.

The Numbers

We said earlier that the banker has the advantage of reviewing a statement in the *context of a request*. He knows the question and starts to look for the answer. If this is his advantage, then the corresponding responsibility is to go past the numbers to their content. For most loans, it is not as important to know the amount of the accounts receivable as it is to know what makes them up. Are they current? Whose are they?

Our guidelines, then, before analysis actually begins are *content and context*. Go beyond the numbers and make sure you know what they say. Read the statement with the client's request in mind.

Summary

To make good loans, lending officers must be well informed, and financial statements provide a large part of their information. If such statements are to be useful to you, you must understand exactly what they say. The letter and footnotes should help you to do this.

Not all statements are prepared by outside independent accountants. That cousin-once-removed may be just what the company needs. His statement might be on the back of an envelope, but if that's all you can get, use it. If the company has statements prepared by a part-time tax accountant, then learn to use them.

Many times, it is not the letter or footnotes that define how good the numbers are. Nor is it the title of the person preparing them that counts. Go past all that and meet the part-time accountant or cousin if you don't already know him. Use that "gut reaction" you developed and determine if he's a "figurer or just a liar." The rule is to know what you have in front of you before you start.

And finally, should you require certified opinions from reputable CPAs in each and every case? There is no doubt that that is your preference. Unfortunately, such audits are expensive. Will you be in business if you require $6,000 of extra work before granting a $25,000 loan? Probably not, but in some cases a certified opinion should be mandatory.

Know what you have and learn to use it.

3 The Balance Sheet

With the preliminaries of the letter and footnotes now behind us, we prepare ourselves for the main course — the position of the company *as of* the date of the review. What follows is a brief discussion, item by item, of what is contained in the balance sheet. A sample balance sheet (Exhibit 3.1) is located at the end of this chapter. You can fold it out and refer to it as we discuss each item. We will not delve too deeply into each one, but will begin to develop a checklist of the questions which should go through your mind when reading the statement.

A balance sheet is composed of three major sections — assets, liabilities, and equity. The asset section comprises those items owned by the company and used by it in its business. The assets are broken out into categories by their nature and their conversion time. Items which usually turn back into cash within the normal business cycle (twelve months) are termed *current assets*. Examples of such assets are inventories and receivables. Because they will be sold and collected within relatively short periods, they are called current.

Items that do not convert during this cycle are called *long-term assets* or *fixed assets*; these consist mainly of physical items such as the building and equipment. They are not expected to convert to cash, but are used to produce the revenue the company earns.

If the difference between the current and fixed assets appears to be obvious, then the need to finance them differently should also be obvious. Most small loans that get in trouble do so because someone failed to make this simple distinction.

A third class of assets is all items which do not qualify as either current or fixed. This section is called, appropriately, *other assets*. Items listed here usually are exceptions to the general rule and should be examined very closely.

The liabilities and equity sections represent the remaining parts of the balance sheet. As in the case of assets, liabilities can be divided into those that are going to be payable within the business cycle and those payable after that period.

The equity portion is sometimes known as the "net" part of the balance sheet. The reason is simple. Net worth of a company is the difference between the assets and liabilities. The company is worth the net difference between what it owns (or is owed) and what it owes to others.

Current Assets

The first part of the asset section is termed current assets. Assets in this category are by their nature liquid and dynamic. They not only change daily, but also during the day.

Current assets are usually composed of four major items. They are:

Cash
Accounts receivable
Inventory
Prepaid expenses

Many other items may be included in this section. Also, each of these items may be listed in greater detail. What follows is a brief summary of what should be known about each item.

Cash

Cash is the first of the current assets and it is the common denominator of all business transactions. In practice, cash is cash, while in fact it may not be cash at all. In the most basic sense, the amount of cash on the statement is the amount of total cash available to be spent by the company at that particular moment. It is a combination of cash on hand and cash in banks.

The bank portion would include any cash in the process of deposit, but it should not include any checks previously written and mailed by the company that have not yet cleared through the bank.

Some companies do other things with their cash than keep it in a bank. Smart corporate treasurers no longer keep funds idle; they invest any surplus. Invested surplus funds are usually given a separate line and described as being certificates of deposit (CD), treasury notes, or short-term marketable securities. If such an item does appear on a statement you are reviewing, then you should be certain you get to the *content* and not just the number. If the company has a CD, what is its term? Is it with your bank? Do the investments in treasury notes represent a potential problem? Can they be liquidated without substantial loss? Is the loan request due in part to cash that is being tied up in these forms of investment?

Most accountants have a tendency to group many cash items together. In cases where they don't, your own credit department might. This could raise serious questions. For example, does the company maintain a *sinking fund* as part of a bond agreement? (A sinking fund is a special cash account in which the company must deposit a certain amount each year to guarantee their ability to meet the bond payments as they become due.) Although such a fund certainly is cash, it is not current and really not available to you. It must be separated from the current assets that would be available to you to meet your debt.

The same applies to a dealer reserve or escrow account. These accounts are highly restricted forms of cash, and if they are not identified they will cause problems.

Most companies will identify such restricted accounts as reserves and sinking funds but fail to point out the various individual balances of a series of general accounts used by the company. For example, assume that a company has four accounts: a general one with your bank, one with your competition, a payroll account with you, and an account with your competition that the company maintains for special reasons such as real estate taxes or insurance premiums. As of the balance sheet date, the balances in the accounts were as follows:

General	— your bank	$ 3,000
General	— competition	(14,000)
Payroll	— your bank	12,000
Special	— competition	4,000

On the balance sheet date, the cash balance is $5,000. If the background were not known, then no one would give that figure a second thought. However, knowing these account balances raises a series of questions. Does the client float checks between the two general accounts? Is the payroll account really a restricted account because it includes deposits for bonuses and for payroll taxes? Or take the cash balance figure and add $25,000 of dealer reserve accounts. Does the company have $30,000 in cash? Not really, and you should be aware of it.

For bankers, the analysis of the *content* of an account is much more critical than its amount — and only a banker has such direct access to the content.

Accounts Receivable

Accounts receivable represents funds due to the company from persons who have bought its goods or services. As with cash, it is necessary to understand what makes up accounts receivable. This is especially important with small loans, since the reason given for borrowing inevitably is that the customer who promised to send a check by today just didn't do it.

Discussing accounts receivable with your client is the fastest way to understand the nature of his or her business. To whom does he sell? On what basis? Cash, credit, or consignment? Are there repurchase agreements? Are returns usual? If there is a continuing service or contract, what are the billing standards? To whom does the competition sell and on what terms? Are your client's sales one-time deals or repeats? Does he sell outright or is he involved in installment sales? If involved in installment sales, does he sell or discount installment notes? If so, is it with recourse? These are but a few of the general questions you should ask.

To really understand the content of the accounts receivable, you must be supplied by the client with an *aging* schedule. Table 3.1 is a sample schedule and its format should be self-explanatory. By reviewing such a schedule, you will learn a number of things.

First, you will know by the fact that an aging exists that management is aware of its delinquent accounts and is following them. Second, a proper aging schedule gives you the names of your customer's clients. This gives you a double advantage: one, you can use your credit department to investigate the creditworthiness of anyone who owes a large part of the overall debt; and two, if you ever needed to pursue the debtors, you would have

Table 3.1 Sample aging schedule

VINCI COMPANY
Accounts Receivable Aging
As of December 31, 19X4
(partial listing)

Name	Total due	Current	30–60	60–90	90 and over
Apex Supply	$ 1,100	$1,100			
Better Homes	357	357			
Cashways, Inc.	(398)				($398)
Joe Cause, Employee	100		$100		
Dozen Village	785	165	400	$220	
Earthen Equipment	400			400	
Fuzzies	515		515		
Goldie's Garage	135			135	
Haskin Supply	1,700	1,700			
.	.	.	.	.	.
.	.	.	.	.	.
.	.	.	.	.	.
Stephenson & Son	437		437		
True Rite	1,500	200	700		600
Ultrasonics	500		500		
Vicar's	92			92	
Joe Vinci, Pres.	2,500				2,500
.	.	.	.	.	.
.	.	.	.	.	.
Total	$14,313	$6,639	$2,719	$943	$4,012

a starting point. If a loan is secured by accounts receivable, or if a loan is made because of an excess accumulation of receivables, then an aging schedule should be submitted monthly and should be insisted upon as part of the loan agreement.

A review of the aging schedule will reveal a number of other things. If management is advancing *funds to employees,* it may be classifying these advances as receivables. If the amounts are small, then it really doesn't matter. However, if a large sum accumulates, it should be noted. Professional standards demand that these advances be listed separately regardless of the amount. Unfortunately, this is not always done. Attention also should be given to *advances to officers,* especially when these advances reach the size of those in the sample aging. These items are not accounts receivable, and they probably are not collectible, at least not when needed. Besides tying up the company's cash, such advances may be indicators of deeper company problems.

The aging also should reveal *sales to affiliates* and list them separately. These sales are not arm's-length transactions and so collectibility becomes harder to judge. In such situations, a bank may find itself financing one company because that company essentially has financed its affiliate by not collecting its bills. Here the question of repayment cannot be judged from the client's statement but only from its affiliate's. Unless accounts receivable is broken down, you cannot make an informed credit decision.

The primary thing we learn from the aging is the isolation of problem accounts. The sample schedule shows that True Rite has not paid in over ninety days, and yet Vinci Company continues to sell to them as the earlier receivables due show. Is the ninety-day billing a disputed bill? How old is it? Why does Vinci continue to sell to True Rite? The aging also shows a large receivable being due from Haskin Supply Company. Haskin is also a client of yours, and you learn in a discussion with him that he really doesn't pay his bill. Instead, once a month, Vinci receives a credit against the Haskin bill for work performed by Haskin. In the accounting world, this is known as a *contra account.* If you were to attempt to collect Haskin's receivable because of default in the loan terms, you would be quickly disappointed. Haskin merely would offset the amount due him.

By knowing the actual nature of the delinquencies, you can judge whether the allowances for bad debts are adequate. Many a charged-off loan has been started by lending against uncollectible accounts receivable.

Companies vary in how they reserve for bad debt. If a reserve is not listed, then you should determine from either the aging schedule or discussions with your client whether one exists and, if it does, whether it is adequate.

If you ask a loan officer why he feels comfortable when lending against marketable securities, he probably will give you a twofold answer. First, the collateral is salable, and second, he knows what it is worth. Why should you lend against accounts receivable, then, without knowing who the accounts are and whether or not they are good?

Inventories

The next item, inventories, is the total of all goods held for use in production or for resale by the company as of the balance sheet date. It may represent goods that are purchased and sold in an "as is" condition, or items in various stages of completion.

More than any other asset, this asset must be reviewed in the context of the loan request as well as the nature of the business. Regarding the latter, it also must be remembered that the balance sheet date may be the low point of the year and a large sale may have preceded the inventory count.

If the nature of the business is manufacturing, how do you value work that is not yet completed? The goods are priced at the total cost expended on each up to that point. The lending officer, however, must look beyond that point. If liquidation were necessary, what value would be assignable? If the bank had to complete production, could the bank do it for the same price as a going-concern could? Obviously not. For these reasons, most loan officers do not attach very much value to work in process and defer loans that use it for collateral.

Raw material inventories are not without their share of problems. Do some of the items represent obsolete or damaged goods? Are some of the items really there on consignment? Is there a market for these products?

Finished goods pose the least problem but they do need review. Will anyone buy this product without a company to service it? Do you really have the ability to sell the product? Do you know the company's clientele so you could sell to them?

This text is not intended to be a guide to what constitutes a good secured loan. All that need be said is that a loan against inventory should be left to the experts in secured lending. The axiom that a company must have enough capital to carry its inventory is given credence by many futile attempts to liquidate "good" inventories.

When reviewing inventory, the loan officer asks two questions: How often do the inventories turn over (replace themselves)? How reasonably are they priced?

In a later chapter we will discuss the ratios that are used to measure turnover. At this point, the thought that should be passed on is this: If a client has inventories beyond his needs, then a backup of his entire cash flow will occur. Your short-term note may become a long-term workout when inventory turns stale. How do you know how much inventory is enough? Common sense will tell you. If your client can buy boxes or barrels of standard items from a host of suppliers with an average delivery of fifteen to twenty days, and you find that he has a six month supply on hand, then you know he has too much inventory. To find out about such matters, you should question him regarding his suppliers, their delivery times, and their terms.

In judging how reasonably inventory is priced, you must look at the value assigned to the items and at the mechanics of pricing. On occasion management may attribute abnormal cost to an item. One such case was the company that performed and sold research and development on a contractual basis. This company accumulated all their cost as inventory and subtracted from it the amount of billings made to the company that had contracted their services. What eventually happened was that the company ended up charging additional research expenses to this inventory account knowing that they would be unable to cover it by the billing. They continued to list this excess as an inventory item on the basis that it represented a pool of knowledge that would be useful in future contracts and would, in effect, be sold in the future. The loan officer was very embarrassed explaining this theory to the loan committee after the company had declared bankruptcy. Examples of what happens when one does not go past the numbers to the content of the assets are frightening.

When pricing inventory, companies use various methods. The most common of these are the first-in, first-out (FIFO) and last-in, first-out (LIFO) methods. These terms do not refer to the physical flow of goods, but only to the value assigned to an item. A brief example demonstrates this. On the dates shown in Table 3.2 a company bought the quantity of widgets listed.

Table 3.2   Inventory pricing example — widgets purchased

Date	Units	Cost	Total
1/ 1/X4	5	$1.00 per unit	$ 5.00
1/10/X4	4	2.00 per unit	8.00
1/17/X4	7	2.50 per unit	17.50
1/25/X4	6	3.00 per unit	18.00
1/31/X4	2	3.24 per unit	6.48
	24		

During the month, they sold seventeen units at various prices above their cost. This left them with seven units. What is their inventory value?

Under the FIFO method, the first ones purchased are the first ones sold. This means that the seven remaining widgets were the last seven purchased and would be valued as shown in Table 3.3.

Under the LIFO method, the last ones purchased are the first ones sold. This means that the seven units remaining are the seven from the beginning of the period and they would be valued as shown in Table 3.4. The units are the same, yet two completely different values are attached to them.

You should not be overly concerned with this phase of accounting for two reasons. First, your valuation of the inventory will be determined not only by the pricing method used but also by a number of things discussed earlier (the stage of completion or the nature of the raw materials). Second, once a method is chosen, it will be used in the following years. Remember the phrase in the accountant's letter: "in conformity with generally accepted accounting principles applied on a consistent basis." As long as the value of both beginning and ending inventories are calculated using the same method, then differences will not be that important. If the method is changed

Table 3.3   Inventory pricing example — FIFO method

Units	Cost	Total
2	$3.24 per unit	$ 6.48
5	3.00 per unit	15.00
7		$21.48

Table 3.4   Inventory pricing example — LIFO method

Units	Cost	Total
5	$1.00 per unit	$5.00
2	2.00 per unit	4.00
7		$9.00

to take advantage of tax savings, then the auditor's opinion must state that this has happened.

The final comment on inventory is really the main point of this section: know your client and know what makes up his inventory. To say it another way, don't stop at the number — get at what is behind it.

Prepaid Expenses

Prepaid expenses usually are payments in advance for items such as real estate taxes and insurance premiums. These expenditures may cover a yearly period that is different from the company's fiscal year, so that at the end of the company year a portion of expenses may not be used up. These then become prepaid expenses. An example best illustrates this point. A company has an August 31 year-end. On April 1, it pays $1,800 of real estate taxes for the upcoming year. By year-end, five months have passed and seven months of taxes are prepaid. At the rate of $150 per month, $1,050 ($150 × 7) would be reflected as prepaid.

The area of prepaid items is one where bank guidelines usually differ from those of the accounting profession. Because of the relative size of prepaid items when compared with total assets, this difference is not pronounced. When bankers review and spread a statement they reclassify prepaid expenses as other assets rather than current assets. This is done for two reasons. First, prepaid expenses really are not current in the sense that they will not convert to cash during the normal business cycle. They will be consumed but not converted. Because the bank's concern is liquidity, this cycle is viewed differently. Second, in the event of liquidation, the chances of collecting on any of these items are almost nil.

From a practical point of view, the loan officer seeks to discover what makes up prepaid items. The size of the item may be so small that time need not be spent on it. What you do need to know is whether any abnormal items may be misclassified as prepaid expense. One example is the company that spent advertising dollars that, they felt, had long-term value. Because of this, they would classify all advertising expenditures as prepaid expense and charge this account for a certain percentage of the expense based on the sales they anticipated. The effect was an enormous amount of prepaid expense on their balance sheet which had no real value. Reading their statement and not knowing the content of the prepaid expense, you would think that the company was in good financial condition. Knowing the make-up of prepaid expenses changes the whole complexion of the statement, turning a handsome profit into a major operating loss.

There are, on occasion, summary items that may be listed under current assets. Many times these items may have a description other than one of the four we have used. Even if they aren't considered cash, receivables, inventory, or a prepaid item per se, they usually are a form of one of these categories. Examples would be income tax refunds receivable or notes receivable. Their relationship to receivables are obvious. Supplies may be listed, but they are not that different from inventory in general. Therefore, whatever the description of an item, the rules remain basically the same. Whatever is listed as current must be an asset which will convert itself into cash within the business cycle.

Fixed Assets

While current assets constantly turn over and replace themselves, fixed assets, as their name states, remain stable. Not only is the physical aspect of the item fixed, but also the cost.

Accounting is an art, not a science, and the art comes under its most serious criticism in the area of fixed-asset pricing. The balance sheet tells us the original cost of these assets as of the balance sheet date. The statement also will tell us what reserve for consumption and attrition has been taken. What the statement does not tell us is the value today of those permanent items that are employed in the business. Current assets generally are listed at today's value because they are new. But with fixed assets, if depreciation has been understated, the assets may be reflected at more than their current value. If the economy is in a rapid inflation cycle, the replacement cost of a fixed asset may be greatly in excess of its net book value.

Valuing Fixed Assets

In valuing fixed assets, the loan officer again has a unique advantage over the general analyst. The content of the numbers and not their amount is the loan officer's goal. If the question boils down to the value of the building, then the simplest answer is to get an outside appraisal and to use that valuation as the initial step in your loan decision.

Analysts other than loan officers usually have no alternative but to use the historic data contained on the statement. This is true for all items on the financial statements, not just fixed assets. Such analysts do not have the immediate access to the company's personnel or records that a loan officer has. In most cases, the client will be sitting opposite your desk as you read the statement.

Although at first glance an appraisal appears to be an easy out, you must consider other facts. Appraisals, like financial statements, are done on a going-concern basis. They assume that the business will continue and that the building will be used for the purpose for which it is currently occupied. Perhaps an example is in order. Let's suppose a building was constructed twenty years ago to fabricate steel components. An appraisal today finds the market value of the building almost double its original cost and four times its net book value (cost less depreciation). You have gotten to the content. On the other hand, should this building *have* to be sold, not in a liquidation or bankruptcy, but because a larger building is needed, what value would it have for someone who would use it in manufacturing boats or skis?

This issue appears paradoxical but it is not. The book value must be updated as part of your decision. This usually means reflecting replacement costs, which may mean an increase or decrease. Once this is done, you must go further and reassign values based on conversion and potential liquidation. The cost to replace a four-year-old back hoe and what you could sell it for are two different things.

The second key to valuing fixed assets is to understand that transportation, installation, taxes, permits, engineering fees, and even the cost of operating for the first few weeks might have been included in the figure on the financial statement. These extras are necessary but without any liquidation value.

Composition

Fixed assets do not convert themselves into current assets, but rather contribute to the utilization of current assets in creating revenues. Most financial statements refer to the fixed-asset section of the balance sheet as Property, Plant, and Equipment. As the heading implies, it includes the land and building, the machinery and equipment, automotive equipment, airline equipment, office furniture and fixtures, leasehold improvements, and any asset whose life exceeds the current business cycle.

Some financial statements will list each individual group of items and then show the individual amounts of depreciation. Other statements reflect the various assets and group the depreciation. Others reflect both items without any breakdown.

A banker rarely needs a breakdown of the fixed assets. Once you know the items that constitute the bulk of value, you can appraise them and set their basis for the loan request you are reviewing. Most bankers value only the major items such as the building and the main pieces of equipment. They ignore the array of smaller items that complement these mainstays. This is a realistic approach for small loan requests.

Depreciation

Depreciation is the reserve for obsolescence and consumption of a fixed asset. In theory depreciation is rather simple. We buy a truck that will last us for four years. Theoretically, then, one-fourth of the truck disappears each year, and at the end of four years, the truck is gone. Of course, at the end of one year the truck may not be worth even 75 percent of its value. We also mentioned that some assets such as buildings really do not consume themselves. In the long run, of course, they do, but in the short run, real value may increase while book value decreases.

If our interest as front-line commercial loan officers is to go beyond the book value that is determined by cost and depreciation, then why should we bother with this part of the statement at all? One reason is to know exactly what is meant by the glib expression, "Depreciation is a repayer of loans." This is crucial to your understanding of a company's true cash flow, and we will discuss this concept in depth when we explore the change in financial position statement. A second reason for knowing about depreciation is to understand the effect it has on reported earnings and taxes due. Let's cover this point by an example.

Depreciation may be calculated in a variety of ways. The most common three are straight-line, double-declining balance, and sum-of-the-years digits. Each method accumulates the same amount of depreciation, but at different velocities. The straight-line method assumes that the asset consumes itself evenly over its useful life. The double-declining balance accelerates the rate of depreciation in the early periods and then eventually tapers it off. In the sum-of-the-years digits method, the rate of depreciation is very intense for the first few years and almost nonexistent at the end.

To calculate straight-line, one merely takes the depreciable portion and divides the number of years of expected life into it. For example, depreciation on a $10,000 back hoe with a five-year life would be $10,000 divided by five years or $2,000 per year.

The double-declining balance assumes that an asset having a life of five years would consume itself at 20 percent per year; it doubles that to get depreciation of 40 percent of the balance per year. The first-year depreciation would be $10,000 times 40 percent, or $4,000. The second year would be $6,000 (the balance of $10,000 less $4,000) times 40 percent, or $2,400. The third-year balance would be $10,000 less $4,000 (first-year depreciation) less $2,400 (second-year depreciation) times 40 percent, and so on until the five years are completed.

The sum-of-the-years digits method works on the same principle as *the rule of 78s* (a method of rebate on installment loans). Under the sum method, a total of each of the years is made. On a five-year asset, the sum would be $5+4+3+2+1$ for a total of 15. The first year depreciation would be $10,000 times 5/15, or $3,334. The second year would be $10,000 times 4/15, or $2,668. The remaining years would continue on the same basis.

Table 3.5 shows the amount of depreciation which would be taken on a $10,000 back hoe for each of five years under each of these three methods.

The double-declining balance does not equal the full amount of the asset since it has built into it an automatic salvage value. We have not included salvage value in our discussion and examples in order to keep confusion to a minimum. Salvage is, of course, any value which remains after the asset

Table 3.5 Three depreciation schedules for a $10,000 back hoe (useful life: 5 years)

Year	Straight-line	Double-declining balance	Sum-of-the years digits
1	$ 2,000	$4,000	$ 3,334
2	2,000	2,400	2,667
3	2,000	1,440	2,000
4	2,000	864	1,335
5	2,000	584	667
Total	$10,000	$9,252*	$10,000

* Salvage value built in.

has been consumed for its intended purpose. In actual practice both of the other methods require that some sort of salvage value be estimated in advance.

Another area that requires quick comment is useful life. Who is to say what the expected life of a given asset is, especially when each company uses the same piece of equipment differently? Most companies and their accountants follow the government guidelines for useful life. These have proven to be realistic appraisals and should cause you no concern.

Let's go back to the example. Using straight-line, the company reported $4,000 of expense after two years. The other two methods produced $6,400 and $6,000 of depreciation respectively. This means the fastest system wrote off 60 percent more than the slowest in just two years. If we were talking about $100,000 of assets, then the difference would be $24,000 in two years. That is a significant difference in anyone's book. In the last two years, the scales are reversed of course.

Making this example more meaningful requires that we go one step further. Let's compare two companies. Both purchased new machinery costing $100,000 in order to enter into the printing business in two different parts of town. Both were successful in their first year and showed identical sales of $200,000 each. Their cost of sales represented 55 percent of sales, and overhead before depreciation was 15 percent. The first company used the straight-line method and the second chose double-declining balance. Both felt that the useful life of the equipment was eight years. Their first-year statements would be as shown in Table 3.6. Overhead for each company was calculated by adding first-year depreciation to the overhead figure of $30,000 (15 percent of $200,000).

Table 3.6 Depreciation comparison — first-year statements of two companies

	Company A	Company B
Sales	$200,000	$200,000
Cost of sales	110,000	110,000
Gross profit	$ 90,000	$ 90,000
Overhead (including depreciation)	42,500	55,000
Profit before taxes	$ 47,500	$ 35,000

Using the straight-line method, Company A arrived at a yearly deprecia-tion of $12,500 ($100,000 ÷ 8 years). Their overhead for the first year, therefore, was $42,500 ($30,000 + $12,500).

To use the double-declining balance method, Company B first established that one year is 12.5 percent of the expected useful life of the asset and then doubled it, which yielded 25 percent. Their first-year depreciation was $25,000 (25 percent of $100,000) and their overhead for the first year was $55,000 ($30,000 + $25,000).

Which company was more profitable, A or B? On paper, and by reading only the numbers, A was. In reality, they were equally profitable. Knowing what the numbers mean is the key to understanding this. Now remember your client has to pay taxes. Company A will pay more taxes than Company B this year. Who is smarter?

If you have just lost all the confidence that you've been slowly building, take heart. Most people do hesitate when the impact of playing with num-bers, especially depreciation numbers, hits them.

And that reluctance to deal with numbers increases even further when the provisions of the new tax laws are introduced. By passing the Economic Recovery Tax Act of 1981, Congress went on record advocating three important changes relating to the nature and treatment of depreciation.

First the Act dropped the word depreciation from the tax vocabulary. In its place they introduced the terminology that hence forth will be reflected on tax returns. It is known as *Accelerated Cost Recovery System* (ACRS). The purpose of the change of philosophy which is inherent in the name change, is to provide an accelerated, fast write-off with the resulting tax savings for those who invest in capital equipment. It is felt such capital expenditures will then in turn aid the recovery of the economy.

Secondly, and more significantly, the new Act simplified all of the pre-vious controversies between the IRS and the taxpayer by removing the need to choose a depreciation method (straight line, declining balance, etc.) and to determine a salvage value. In its place a five-class asset-classification system has been introduced.

To calculate the recovery (depreciation) the taxpayer simply applies a statutory percentage to the unadjusted basis of the property. The percentage is that assigned to the asset class within which the asset falls. ACRS has been designed so that all tangible property will result in the same rate of recovery as 150 percent declining balance in the initial years and then produce the same recovery as a straight line in the latter years. In effect they have combined the two previous methods. A second change occurs after 1984 which speeds up the recovery to effect an equivalent 200 percent declining balance in the initial years.

However, certain options are still available to the taxpayer including a straight-line write-off.

Generally, equipment will fall into a three-year class (autos, light trucks, research related machinery, and equipment) or a five-year class. Buildings primarily fall into a fifteen-year class while a special ten-year and fifteen-year class exist for utilities, certain transportation items, and other separately covered assets.

The final change of the Act is to encourage the use of two different forms of depreciation or recovery of assets. One for financial reporting and one for taxes. The rules of CPAs have not been changed. They will continue to report under a method recognized by the standards of their profession. The Act however does change the classic approach of reporting for taxes on the same basis as the CPA's statement. A second recovery number is generated to pass on tax savings to the client. We'll discuss the reflection of this on the corporate tax return in Chapter 11. For now we only need to remember that two differences do exist and are accented and encouraged by the new legislation.

As a banker in your role of analyst, you have a number of things going for you which tend to minimize the effects of this depreciation variance. Among these is the fact that you will look at financial profits before depreciation and before taxes. (We'll discuss this fully in the section on change in financial position.) Also, whatever method of depreciation is chosen by your client, he or she must follow through with it. Remember, the accountant's letter says that the statement was prepared "on a basis consistent with that of the preceding year." If there is a change, the accountant must make that known to us. As a matter of fact, the first footnote in a good statement will tell us on what basis certain accounting procedures were performed, including depreciation. And finally, it should put your mind at ease to know that, in the long run, all methods will yield the same results.

Later, in Part IV, we will discuss the nature of depreciation more fully and how to interpret profit in relation to depreciation and other noncash expenses. For now, suffice to say that although, in theory, depreciation is a reserve for capital consumption, in practice no such reserve is ever established because assets usually are financed and paid for over the term of their useful lives. Depreciation, then, is simply an allocation of the historic cost of a long-term asset over its useful life and, for our purposes as bankers, an expense that does not require a cash outlay.

Other Assets

As a general rule, this section of the balance sheet represents a small portion of the total assets of a company. Only when the numbers that appear here are substantial is there cause for concern. The two most common items in this section are organization expenses and cash surrender value of life insurance. The nature of these items best explains the nature of this category.

Other assets are assets that are part of the business, but not current in nature; furthermore, they are not used as part of the operation or as part of the production of goods. They may be items with limited life and so are depreciated (usually referred to as amortization). Some have an indefinite life and cannot be depreciated.

Organization expense is an example of the former. It may be assumed that the cost of starting a business (legal fees and so forth) is a cost with a useful life of some limit. That cost may then be amortized over sixty months on a straight-line basis. The length of its useful life may be debated. If you think that it all sounds like an easy tax write-off, then you agree with most analysts. However, because the amount of organization expense is relatively small, we tend to ignore it.

Cash surrender value of life insurance is the accumulation over time of realizable value in certain policies on the lives of the principals. Bankers want companies to properly insure their key personnel. Here again, the nature of the number, its content, is what we seek. Who is the beneficiary? Is the policy corporate or is it really a form of executive bonus? Knowing the answers, one assigns weight to the numbers or dismisses them entirely.

There are other assets which might find their way into this category. They are goodwill, deferred research and development expenses (or any deferred expense for that matter), and patents.

Goodwill is the surplus paid over the cost of an asset. Its value is associated with the intangibles that were purchased with the business. Take for example the man who purchases a drug store for $100,000. For this price he gets the inventories worth $10,000, the building worth $50,000, and some fixtures worth $15,000. The balance of $25,000 is the value of the name of the business or the value generally associated with the fact that he will have a going business complete with customers.

The balance sheet of the new company would show inventory, building, and fixtures at their cost, and the balance as goodwill. The value of goodwill to the loan officer is questionable. Sure, you couldn't have a company without it, but if asked to loan money against it, you would decline. The value of the asset is there only when you don't need it. To collect against goodwill is futile.

Research and development expenses, or any deferred expenses, actually are operating expenses of the company that are not being charged in the present year, but are being deferred until the product is perfected, manufactured, and sold. At that time, the expense will be matched to the income. That all sounds great, but what if the product isn't developed? Even if it is, will it be salable and profitable? Because these matters are so uncertain, most financial people do not attach value to research and development expenses. Some companies do list such costs as an expense each year and it appears as an abnormal item on their income statement. This is probably the best approach. For the banker, only one choice is available. Ignore the asset. Its value doesn't exist. We can be understanding of the client's operation and even show compassion for his problems with completing the research, but gambles of this nature require speculative capital, not lines of credit.

Patents are somewhere between goodwill and research and development. Like goodwill, their importance is obvious. Unlike research, patents may have definable value and they can become valuable collateral if properly assigned to your bank. If the value of patents shown on the statement is low, then probably it won't enter into your decision. If the amount is substantial, then you should consult a commercial loan specialist for advice.

The second major portion of the balance sheet is the liability section. It is separated into two parts — current liabilities and long-term debt. Liabilities are listed under one or the other based on the expected due date of the debt. As one analyst has so aptly said, the liabilities may well be the only certainty on the entire statement. For this reason as well as others, you should learn all you can about its content.

Current Liabilities

Current liabilities are those which are due and payable within twelve months. By their nature, bills owed by the company change daily. They are incurred and repaid. Paid ones are replaced by new ones in a cycle as dynamic as the one that occurs with current assets.

The current liabilities section usually contains five major items. These are as follows:

Notes payable
Accounts payable
Accrued expenses
Accrued taxes
Current portion of long-term debt

There may be additional items, but generally they are subdivisions that are given a separate listing because of their size or nature.

Notes Payable

Notes payable, for the most part, are notes that are due to the bank. If they are not clearly marked as such, they should be discussed. If the notes are not payable to your bank, then use this item as a point of discussion to find out the client's relationship with other banks. Has he been turned down by his bank? How often have we had a potential client come in and, when we ask why he's not taking his request to his present bank, he replies, "My banker doesn't understand me." If his banker knows him and can't understand him, you should look past his comment for a potential problem.

If the note is with your bank, is it in your office? Who is the account officer?

Regardless of location or bank, does the note have a repayment schedule? Is it feasible? Did the client do what he said he would do?

If a note is not payable to the bank, then to whom is it payable? If the answer is a vendor, then you will want to ask why payment wasn't made when due. If the note is payable to an affiliate, then determine the relationship between companies and ask why the company is borrowing. Is it to pay back the affiliate? Is the note payable to an officer? This raises the question of whether working capital was inadequate in the past. Why did the officer loan the company money? Why didn't the bank do it? A final point to question regarding notes payable is whether the notes are secured by some asset. Don't assume that they are not. Investigate.

Again the simple rule applies. Go past the numbers to get at the nature of the item.

Accounts Payable

Accounts payable are the funds that are due to various vendors for products or services they have supplied or performed. This item should trigger a list of questions similar to those raised by accounts receivable. From whom does the company buy? On what terms? Does the company have discounts granted, and if so, do they take advantage of them? It is a good practice to get a listing of accounts payable. This should be an aging similar to an accounts receivable aging. It will show us a number of things, including major concentration of accounts and serious delinquincies that may stop production. The fact that an aging exists is encouraging because it shows that management is aware of its own potential problem areas.

Affiliate relationships may be detected in the aging even if they are not spelled out. Is the big push to pay off a brother-in-law who runs the plant across town? That would influence our review of the loan request. Remember to look for contra accounts and set offs. We will also learn of these through a payables aging.

An accounts payable aging also may be used to check on your client's comments about suppliers. Many a client has said that he has no problems with his suppliers and is allowed to pay them whenever he wants. Upon examination of trade reports and contact with a few of the major suppliers, however, it is found that unless thay are paid in two weeks the account is turned over for collection.

Accrued Expenses

Accrued expenses are accounts payable for nontrade items. An accrued expense is the estimate of the light bill that won't be received until two weeks after the statement date. It is the accountant's fee that won't be billed until the end of the next quarter.

Recalling our example of prepaid items and their unused portion, we can simply say that accruals are the opposite. If the real estate taxes are $150 a month and the company hasn't paid the first five months, then the accrual would be $750 ($150 × 5). It is a bill which the company owes as of the balance sheet date.

Accrued expenses may comprise a series of items. In addition to the normal trade items, items such as salaries and bonuses may be included. If the salaries represent more than just the few days between the balance sheet date and the next pay after it, then this item should be examined carefully. Has there been proper accrual of vacation time and vacation pay? Has management paid bonuses as of the balance sheet date in line with the profits they've generated?

Normally, accrued expenses should be a realtively small portion of current liabilities. If they seem to represent a significant portion, then a breakdown is needed. This is obtained during the interview.

Accrued Taxes

Accrued taxes are the same as accrued expenses in principle, except that the category is limited to taxes. Nothing strikes more fear into the hearts of loan officers than an accumulation in this account. Is management paying taxes as they become due? Are payroll deposits being made as required by the law?

Legal responsibilities are incurred by the banker who advances funds for payroll but does not police payroll tax deposits. Courts and federal agencies have assessed banks for unpaid payroll taxes.

Also, a company's failure to pay payroll taxes will result in an IRS tax lien. This lien will take priority over all unsecured creditors and will, when filed, be an alarm to all trade suppliers, signalling them to be on guard. The house of cards starts to fall shortly after that.

If the unpaid taxes are real estate taxes, they will jeopardize the first position of your mortgage and perhaps lead to an expensive tax sale.

The real importance of excess accrued taxes lies in the fact that it is one of the early warning systems we have. We should recognize and use it.

Current Portion of Long-Term Debt

Current portion of long-term debt (CPLTD) is exactly what its name states. It is the principal amount of a long-term debt that must be paid during the next twelve months. The make-up of this item will be learned from the client when you discuss long-term debt. The key to this number at this point in your analysis is whether or not profits are sufficient to meet the payments. If the CPLTD is $50,000 and this year's cash profit is $25,000, then a warning flag is up. If these numbers are accurate, then the funds you lend your client on his line of credit will be used to pay the term loan. In the long run this practice leads to trouble.

It is not abnormal for other items to be listed under current liabilities. This section does parallel current assets, but it is not as standardized. Special categories will exist because of the size of items. For example, you may see bonuses payable or profit sharing payable if the amounts are large. These items could be grouped and listed under another name, but the management may feel their importance sufficient to justify noting them separately.

Items which are not abnormal that appear with some regularity under current liabilities are *advances* or *deposits*. These funds are paid prior to work being performed. Sometimes the sums are insignificant and we pass over them rather quickly. In other cases, the sums might be significant. Then two questions immediately are raised. First, can the contract be completed, the goods delivered, or the building built? Second, can the job be done with the funds remaining? Identifying the account and discussing it will quickly answer these questions.

Bankers usually do not spend as much time on the current liabilities as they do on the assets. Because the current assets are the items that must be converted to pay off the loan, you must know a great deal about each one in order to judge the feasibility of conversion. Current liabilities do not convert. They take care of themselves. What bankers really should do is understand them before the loan is made so as to avoid problem areas.

The current liabilities which receive the greatest scrutiny are payroll taxes and notes to other banks. Second in importance are management-related or owner-related items.

Long-Term Debt

Long-term debt differs from current liabilities in two principal ways. The obvious difference is in maturity. Long-term debts are not due within the next twelve months. The second difference is that most long-term debt has some type of related contract or agreement tied to it.

The simplest example is a mortgage. The loan has a contract that, at a minimum, spells out the property which secured the indenture as well as the terms of repayment. If the mortgage was part of a general refinancing, then a loan agreement may exist, and that agreement may set out certain conditions covering a wide variety of items.

If the long-term debt is a debenture or bond, then a contract of some sort would exist. The security, if any, would be listed here, as well as covenants covering repayment, future borrowings, future security that may be pledged, and rights of the parties to the contract.

The important thing is first to determine whether the loan or debt is held by an institution other than yours and then to find out what it covers. If in doubt, ask for a copy of the agreement.

A type of long-term debt that causes a great deal of confusion is subordinated debt, sometimes called *friendly debt*. This debt usually comes in the form of advances from people who have an ownership interest in the company. When the company was started or at a point when additional funds were needed, these people agreed to subordinate their debt to the company's debt. In the event of liquidation, their loans would be in back of, or at a lower level of priority than, those of the general creditors. By subordinating their claims they have asked that their loans be considered as part of capital.

Why would someone do this? Why not just put the money in as equity? The reasons are many. First, by making the advance a loan, the lender is entitled to collect interest. The interest collected is a normal expense to the company and tax deductible. If the investment were in the form of stock, then a dividend could be paid. A dividend is not tax deductible to the corporation. Second, when the corporation has earned enough cash profits to retire the debt, it is paid back without tax consequence to the owner. It is merely a loan repayment. If the funds were used to buy back stock instead, then the repayment would be a security sale and taxable. Many times, these subordinated loans may be converted to stock at a predetermined price. This protects the note holder's claim to ownership in a proxy fight and also allows him or her to take advantage of a future stock issue.

You must be careful of subordinations. The fact that a loan is subordinated may not mean the same thing in every case. Some subordinations allow for repayment, others refer only to whatever loan balance is outstanding at the time of a bankruptcy; still others have cancellation clauses should management fail to meet certain standards, which makes them meaningless to the bank officer.

Future references to subordinated debt in this text will relate to friendly debt that has been subordinated to bank debt by an instrument of the bank. In other words, the bank has had the company and the note holder execute the bank's subordination agreement. Thus, the bank knows its rights, and all parties are working under the same rules. Further we assume that such a subordination will not allow for any of this friendly debt to be repaid while the bank holds the agreement and has loans outstanding.

Once a subordination agreement has been executed, the bank can consider subordinated debt and capital as the same item for purposes of review and analysis.

Perhaps an example will illustrate this point. You will recall that we said banks want to *share* in opportunities. This phrase means that some reasonable relationship should exist between what we as a creditor invest and what the ownership invests. Assume a company wants to start a sales outlet in your marketing area and the total funds needed are $100,000. The principals inform you that they will invest $10,000 and will lend their company $40,000 for a total of $50,000.

They seek to borrow $50,000 from you. If this were the entire presentation then your relationship with the company's principals would be unbalanced. You would be investing $5 for their $1 ($50,000 to $10,000 capital). Suppose they agree not to repay any of their $40,000 of advances until you are paid in full and they also agree to accept a secondary position if liquidation occurs. Now the investment is equal ($50,000 to $50,000) and you can begin to consider making the loan.

Other items may be included under long-term debt. Some may be items that we discussed under current liabilities but, because they are not payable for some time in the future, they are classified as long-term debt. It is not uncommon to see deposits in this category, or even unearned or deferred income.

One item that may appear here or be listed as a separate item is *deferred income tax*. This item almost always raises some questions. If a company uses a method to calculate taxes that is different from the method it uses to report earnings, there will be a difference. One example is depreciation. We discussed this concept when exploring the ACRS (accelerated cost recovery system) of the new tax act. It is legal, acceptable, and your client is encouraged to depreciate using one basis for taxes and another for book reporting. Because the tax liability for book purposes is not the same as the actual tax basis for reporting, the difference must be accounted for. The CPA will show the amount due on the tax return as the current portion and the balance not yet due will be accounted for as a deferred item.

A second example will help to clarify this point. A contractor is involved in doing certain highway-related jobs for the state. All jobs are completed during the current year, but only 90 percent of the bill is paid upon completion. The remaining funds are held in the form of a retainage for at least six months and sometimes for as long as eighteen months. The contractor reports on a percentage of completion or accrued basis for his statement, but reports to the IRS on a cash basis. Assuming that the company has a 25 percent profit on each job and that none of the retainages were paid for this year, the comparative statements in Table 3.7 could be drawn.

The income statement of the company would show the full profit and the full taxes. Sometimes these figures are shown in two parts, current and deferred; sometimes they are referenced in the footnotes. However, only $7,500 in taxes is due. The remaining portion is deferred and it will be reflected as such on the balance sheet.

A final note before leaving the liabilities section is on contingent liabilities. These are liabilities that do not exist today but would exist if some other party failed to meet its obligations or if particular future events did or did not happen. The most common contingent liabilities would be guarantees by the company (in the form of an agreement) to take back its product or retire debts related to its product in the event of default by certain third parties. Contingent liabilities can be substantial and should be covered in

Table 3.7 Comparative statements for a contractor
(using accrual and cash basis)

	ABC COMPANY	
	Financial report	*Tax report (cash basis)*
Sales	$100,000	$90,000
Cost of operations	75,000	75,000
Profit before taxes	25,000	15,000
Taxes (50%)	12,500	7,500
Net profit	$ 12,500	$ 7,500

the footnotes. If they are not, you should find out about them in your discussions with the client.

Equity

The third major part of the balance sheet is the equity section. Equity represents the difference between the assets and liabilities. It is the difference between what is owed to (or owned by) the company and what is due others. It is the summary of the investment of the ownership into the venture.

Equity is generally composed of two major items. The first item is that which was invested outright in the company, usually at the time the operation was begun. The second item is the portion of funds earned by the company that it retains in the business. These funds have been reinvested.

The terms for these two types of equity investment depend on the structure of the business. In a corporation, they are called stock and retained earnings. In a proprietorship and a partnership, they simply are combined and called equity.

A corporation may have a series of items in its equity section. A sample corporate equity would appear as follows:

Capital stock	$10,000	
Retained earnings	10,000	
Total equity		$20,000

Capital stock is the phrase used to describe the portion of ownership that is substantiated by a certificate showing which part of the whole is owned. This document is referred to as a stock certificate. There are two types of stock: common and preferred. The major distinction between them is the priority of one over the other. The priority may be in regard to payment of dividends or ownership of the assets of the corporation. In simple terms, the preferred stock could have a fixed dividend regardless of profits and be first to be retired in cases of dissolution. The rights not given with preferred stock usually are those which relate to voting rights.

Common stock usually carried no fixed dividend and in small companies one may not be paid. Common stock does, unless specifically limited, have the right to vote, the right of ownership, and the right to the equity of the company.

Many times stock is referred to as having a certain *par* value. This legal phrase implies certain minimum capital contribution. In most states, par value is no longer meaningful; in some states, however, some liability may be implied. The only effect par value has in our discussion is that it determines the value assigned to stock. For example, if a company has stock with a par value of $1 and it issued 10,000 shares, then the value would be $10,000. If the $1 par value stock sold for $3 a share, then the difference of $20,000 would be classified as *capital in excess of par* or *paid in surplus*. It would appear on the balance sheet as follows:

Capital stock	$10,000	
Capital in excess of par	20,000	
Retained earnings	10,000	
Total equity		$40,000

When reviewing the capital section, many bankers will not look at the various forms of stock, but will consider the entire equity section as one number. This approach makes sense because bankers should be more interested in the total of what was invested than in whether stock is common or preferred.

However, a commitment to pay dividends on a preferred stock issue has an effect on cash flow and thus should be recognized by the banker.

The second part of equity is the reinvested portion. This item is called retained earnings. It is shown at its year-end amount, and then reconciled in the reconciliation of equity statement.

If a company repurchases its own stock, it is called *treasury stock*. It has been placed in the company's treasury and is a deduction from the outstanding stock. It will appear on the equity statement as follows:

Capital stock	$10,000
Capital in excess of par	30,000
Retained earnings	10,000
	$50,000
Less: Treasury stock	5,000
Total equity	$45,000

In a partnership there is no stock. In its place is a partnership agreement which spells out among other things the percentage of ownership of each partner. On the balance sheet, the total amount owned by the partners usually is shown as follows:

Equity

Partners' capital	$20,000

ABC COMPANY
Balance Sheet
December 31, 19X4

ASSETS

Current assets:			
Cash			$ 5,000
Accounts receivable			10,000
Inventories			8,000
Prepaid expenses			2,000
Total current assets			$25,000
Property, plant and equipment:			
Land		$11,000	
Building	$17,000		
Machinery and equipment	9,000		
Office furniture and fixtures	1,000		
Total plant and equipment	$27,000		
Less: accumulated depreciation	3,000	24,000	
Net property, plant and equipment			35,000
Other assets:			
Organization expense (net)		$1,000	
Cash surrender value — officers' life insurance		3,000	
Total other assets			4,000
TOTAL ASSETS			$64,000

LIABILITIES & STOCKHOLDERS' EQUITY

Current liabilities:			
Notes payable — bank			$ 3,000
Accounts payable			8,000
Accrued interest and expenses			2,000
Payroll taxes payable			800
Current portion — long-term debt			1,200
Total current liabilities			$15,000
Long-term debt:			
Mortgage payable	$14,000		
Less: Current portion	1,200	$12,800	
Notes payable		2,000	
Total long-term debt			14,800
Total liabilities			$29,800
Stockholders' equity:			
Capital stock		$ 9,000	
Capital in excess of par		11,000	
Retained earnings		17,200	
Total		$37,200	
Less: Treasury stock		3,000	
Total stockholders' equity			34,200
TOTAL LIABILITIES AND STOCKHOLDERS' EQUITY			$64,000

Exhibit 3.1 Sample Balance Sheet and Income Statement for ABC Company

ABC COMPANY
Statement of Income
For the Year Ended December 31, 19X4

Sales				$210,000
Cost of sales				
Inventory — January 1, 19X4			$ 6,000	
Purchases		$33,000		
Freight		1,000		
Direct salaries		23,000		
Payroll taxes		3,500		
Factory overhead				
Rent	$1,200			
Depreciation	2,000			
Utilities	1,800			
Taxes	700	5,700	66,200	
			$72,200	
Inventory — December 31, 19X4			8,000	
Total cost of sales				64,200
Gross profit				$145,800
Operating expenses				
Selling expense				
Salaries	$51,000			
Office rent	14,000			
Travel expense	9,000			
Phone and utilities	6,000	$80,000		
General and administrative				
Officer salary	$26,000			
Office salary	7,000			
Rent, phone, supplies	18,000	51,000		
Total operating expense				131,000
Net profit before taxes				$ 14,800
Provisions for income taxes				6,200
Net profit				$ 8,600

Exhibit 3.1, continued

Some partnerships will list each partner separately, as follows:

Equity

Partners' capital:	John Jones	$10,000	
	Jim Smith	10,000	
	Total partners' capital		$20,000

On the schedule showing the reconciliation of net worth, you will be given a summary of the earnings and distributions. Individual partners usually are identified on this schedule.

A sole proprietorship is an unincorporated business. As with the partnership, all the balance sheet will reflect is the net equity of the individual. A separate schedule should be included that reconciles his net worth.

Many times the company will present this net worth reconciliation (statement of equity) as part of the balance sheet. Small companies, whether proprietorships, partnerships, or corporations, are especially likely to combine the net worth reconciliation with the balance sheet. Unlike the other sections of the balance sheet, very little needs to be known about the equity section to understand it. Most analysts will look at the total equity and not question it. Questions about equity most often come up when you review the statement of equity.

Summary

With the equity reviewed, discussion of the balance sheet is complete. We can begin now to review the other statements which make up the financial statement. Until now we have concentrated on a picture of the company *as of* a certain date, because this picture is a measure of the company's strength. By understanding the balance sheet items, their underlying meaning as well as their value, we can make informed decisions.

4   Statement of Equity

Before proceeding to the income statement, we must consider the statement of equity. It is one of two statements that ties the balance sheet and the income statement together. In Part IV, the other statement that relates the income statement to the balance sheet — the statement of change in financial position — will be reviewed.

The purpose of the statement of equity is to identify and itemize all of the transactions that affected the net worth of a company during the stated period. This statement may be part of the balance sheet (in the equity section), or part of the income statement (then known as the statement of income and retained earnings), or a separate schedule. The size of the company and the nature of the transactions will determine how the statement of equity is presented.

Net worth can be changed in only a limited number of ways. The most common way is by earning profits, which increases net worth. Increases may also result from new issues of stock. Losses reduce net worth. Decreases usually are the result of distribution of dividends or of a corporation repurchasing its own stock (treasury stock). With the exception of adjustments from prior years, these transactions account for all the possible changes which may affect net worth. A sample statement (Table 4.1) will be self-explanatory.

The equity balance is shown on the balance sheet. If the only change in

Table 4.1 Sample statement

ABC COMPANY
Statement of Equity
For the Year Ended December 31, 19X4

Equity balance, January 1, 19X4		$113,000
Add: Net income for year	$10,000	
Issuance of preferred stock	80,000	90,000
		$203,000
Less: Treasury stock acquired	55,000	
Dividends paid	8,000	63,000
Equity balance, December 31, 19X4		$150,000

equity is a change in retained earnings, then it is very usual to see the statement of equity combined with either the income statement or the balance sheet.

If it is combined with the income statement, it will appear at the bottom.

Net profit after taxes	$ 10,000
Retained earnings, January 1, 19X4	113,000
Retained earnings, December 31, 19X4	$123,000

The retained earnings figure would then appear on the balance sheet under the equity section along with the other capital items.

Stockholders' equity

Capital stock	$ 40,000	
Retained earnings	123,000	
Total stockholders' equity		$163,000

If the statement of equity is combined with the balance sheet, then the equity section will be presented as below.

Stockholders' equity

Capital stock		$ 40,000
Retained earnings	$113,000	
Add: Net profit for year ended		
December 31, 19X4	10,000	
Retained earnings, December 31, 19X4		123,000
Total equity		$163,000

Sometimes companies will take advantage of the statement of equity as a way of presenting ownership information. This practice is especially common in a partnership where the equity is allocated among various partners. Table 4.2 is an example of how such an equity statement is presented.

The equity statement of a proprietorship will appear the same as that of a partnership, except of course that it will cover a single owner.

Whenever you read the statement of a proprietorship or a partnership, remember that the statement is prepared without any reserve for income taxes and that therefore the company appears, at first glance, more profitable than it actually is.

Unless a new investment has been made (or treasury stock purchased), or unless dividends have been paid, the only statement of equity you will see is the earnings figure shown on another statement. The important thing is to know what changes occurred, and why, from the opening equity balance at the beginning of the year to the year-end balance.

As a banker, you are seeking to determine whether there have been any abnormal transactions affecting net worth. Such transactions will be clearly identified in this statement.

Table 4.2 Partners' equity statement

	Total	Smith	Jones	Johnson
Partners' equity 1/1/X4	$15,000	$ 5,000	$ 5,000	$ 5,000
Income per statement	27,000	9,000	9,000	9,000
Partners' drawing	17,000	7,000	6,000	4,000
Partners' equity 12/31/X4	$25,000	$ 7,000	$ 8,000	$10,000

5　Statement of Income

We have now reached the cumulative portion of the financial statement. We use the term cumulative because this statement is a summary of certain financial events for a particular period. The period is clearly evident from the title of the income statement or, as some firms prefer, statement of earnings. Both terms are correct.

ABC COMPANY
Statement of Income
For the Year Ended December 31, 19X4

Of all the statements, the one that is most vital but that receives the least amount of review is the income statement. Its importance derives from the fact that a company without reasonable profits cannot exist for very long. It receives the least review because it is a summary of the past and, with the exception of certain key percentages and expenses that have to be understood, there is not really that much to review. Unlike the balance sheet with its many sections, the income statement has only two parts: revenue and expense. No matter where or how you list them, the calculation has to be the same: revenue less expense equals profit.

Passing the income statement too quickly would be wrong however. Many analysts spend a great deal of their time reviewing its numbers. Others spend very little time on it. How much is enough? You need to know enough to understand the content. (We're sure you expected that line.) You also need to know enough to help you form a judgment about the future.

Refer to the sample income statement located opposite the balance sheet at the end of Chapter 3 (Exhibit 3.1) and keep it folded out as you read this chapter.

The first item is sales. Recalling our discussion of accounts receivable with the client reminds us that we already know a good deal about the company's sources of revenue. We asked to whom he sold, on what terms, which customers were the largest, and so forth. We already should know the content of sales.

The second item is cost of sales. We've talked to our client about materials and inventories. We've discussed his suppliers and the types of items he buys. We've also discussed what the company does with the purchases. It either fabricates, processes, manufactures, or provides services. We learned about his employees — how many there are, what their skills are, and how much they are paid. When we looked at plant, property, and equipment, we learned whether the company rented or owned, and we probably discussed related items such as type and age of machinery. In effect, we know quite a bit about the company's cost of sales.

The difference between sales and cost of sales is the gross profit. This is the markup the company enjoys for manufacturing and/or reselling its product. It is the profit before overhead.

Overhead is the so-called below-the-line expenses that are needed to complete the business cycle. These are selling, administrative, and general expenses. They are called below-the-line because they are listed below the gross profit line.

Bank analysts, especially front-line officers, should not be overly concerned about the classification of an expense. Even if an item that should be above the line is listed below it, the bottom line will not change. You should be concerned with two things when reviewing the income statement. First, do you understand the major expenses listed (either here or on any part of the income statement), and second, are they reasonable?

Bankers will disagree on the next question, and you will have to decide your own position. Should a banker get involved in the make-up of expenses? Should he or she take the role of management by deciding which items are essential and which should be cut? Or, should bankers judge the overall record of management, and, if their operation is successful, conclude that management has reviewed and analyzed expenses and cut them where necessary. Your answer to this question probably will determine just how much time you spend on the profit and loss statement. If the company is performing well, you'll spend a little time analyzing expenses. If the company's profits are down, or if projections and loan payments are in jeopardy, you will have to spend a great deal of time analyzing expenses. This is not to say that you should not ask questions about large items. On the contrary, that's a big part of the interview and statement analysis.

The final item of the income statement is the tax reserve, which should be straightforward unless some unusual procedure was used. Any out-of-the-ordinary practice should be reflected on the balance sheet under deferred taxes or in the footnotes. In any case, you should have already discussed the abnormality before getting this far.

In summary, we can say that the income statement is the travel log of our airplane. The balance sheet tells us where we are on a given date. The income statement shows where we've been and what was consumed or gained in getting there. We still need to know the content of the items, and so we begin the analysis of management by examining their profit record.

It has been argued that the income statement also shows the ability to repay term loans via profitability. Insofar as profit and depreciation are part of the sources of funds available, this contention is correct. But repayment ability should not be judged here; it should be reviewed in the change in financial position statement.

Exercise 1

Rearrange the following list of accounts into a financial statement. Try this exercise without referring to the text. If you cannot do it, then review the sample statement in Exhibit 3.1 and try again. After making a second attempt, compare your statement to the correct one on the next page.

Problem

GROUP V INDUSTRIES
List of Accounts

Goodwill	$ 15,000
Current portion — long-term debt	11,000
Treasury stock	15,000
Accounts receivable — net	97,000
Sales	605,000
Prepaid expense	7,500
Capital in excess of par	65,000
Notes payable — bank	30,000
Finished goods	29,000
Accumulated depreciation	41,000
Accrued taxes payable	17,000
Provision for income tax	12,500
Land	10,000
Cash	13,500
Accounts payable	45,000
Term loan payable	16,000
Retained earnings	57,500
Machinery and equipment	57,000
Cost of sales	345,000
Mortgage payable	100,000
Organization expense — net	23,000
Notes payable — officer	10,000
Building	68,000
Net profit after taxes	12,500
Retained earnings — April 30, 19X4	57,500
Capital stock	20,000
Raw materials	8,000
Operating expenses	235,000
Accrued salaries and expenses	14,500
Goods-in-process	37,000
Certificates of deposit	18,000
Furniture and fixtures	18,000
Retained earnings — May 1, 19X3	45,000

Solution

GROUP V INDUSTRIES
Balance Sheet
April 30, 19X4

ASSETS

Current assets:			
Cash			$ 13,500
Certificate of deposit			18,000
Accounts receivable — net			97,000
Inventories:			
Raw materials		$ 8,000	
Goods in process		37,000	
Finished goods		29,000	74,000
Prepaid expenses			7,500
Total current assets			$210,000
Property, plant and equipment:			
Land		10,000	
Building	$ 68,000		
Machinery and equipment	57,000		
Furniture and fixtures	18,000		
Total plant and equipment	143,000		
Less: accumulated depreciation	41,000	102,000	
Net property, plant and equipment			112,000
Other assets:			
Goodwill		15,000	
Organization expense — net		23,000	
Total other assets			38,000
Total assets			$360,000

LIABILITIES AND EQUITY

Current liabilities:			
Current portion — long-term debt			$ 11,000
Notes payable — bank			30,000
Notes payable — officer			10,000
Accounts payable			45,000
Accrued taxes payable			17,000
Accrued salaries and expenses			14,500
Total current liabilities			$127,500
Long-term liabilities:			
Mortgage payable	$100,000		
Term loan payable	16,000	$116,000	
Less: current portion		11,000	
Total long-term liabilities			105,000
Total liabilities			$232,500
Stockholders' equity:			
Capital stock	$ 20,000		
Capital in excess of par	65,000		
Retained earnings	57,500	$142,500	
Less: treasury stock		15,000	
Total stockholders' equity			127,500
Total liabilities and stockholders' equity			$360,000

Solution — continued

GROUP V INDUSTRIES
Statement of Income and Retained Earnings
For the Year Ended April 30, 19X4

Sales	$605,000
Cost of sales	345,000
Gross profit	$260,000
Operating expenses	235,000
Net profit before taxes	$ 25,000
Provision for income tax	12,500
Net profit after taxes	$ 12,500
Retained earnings — May 1, 19X3	45,000
Retained earnings — April 30, 19X4	$ 57,500

Exercise 2

The next several pages contain the financial statement of a company in the northeastern United States that processes and fabricates metal containers — from standard paint cans to specially designed and custom constructed medical and pharmaceutical canisters. The company sells some of its products itself; other products are manufactured under private labels for national concerns.

The company has been in existence for five years and has gained the respect of the bank's management. It presently enjoys a $500,000 line of credit and is seeking a renewal of it. Management has submitted its annual report. The audit was performed by a nationally known and highly reputable firm.

Read the statement, making notes while you read, and then compare your notes to the comments that follow. This reading is your first, so don't be upset if you don't recognize all the items. We'll discuss them after your review. Your major purpose is to understand what you are reading.

EXAMPLE COMPANY, INC.

Consolidated Financial Statements

December 31, 19X4

(With Accountants' Report Thereon)

The Board of Directors and
    Stockholders
Example Company, Inc.:

We have examined the consolidated balance sheet of Example Company, Inc. and
subsidiaries as of December 31, 19X4 and the related consolidated statements
of earnings, stockholders' equity and changes in financial position for the
years then ended. Our examination was made in accordance with generally
accepted auditing standards, and accordingly included such tests of the
accounting records and such other auditing procedures as we considered necessary in the circumstances.

In our opinion, the aforementioned consolidated financial statements present
fairly the financial position of Example Company, Inc. and subsidiaries at
December 31, 19X4 and the results of their operations and the changes in their
financial position for the years then ended, in conformity with generally
accepted accounting principles applied on a consistent basis.

                         (Signed)

February 9, 19X5

EXAMPLE COMPANY, INC.
AND SUBSIDIARIES

Consolidated Balance Sheet

December 31, 19X4

Assets

Current assets:	
Cash	$ 134,509
Marketable securities, at cost, which approximates market	50,000
Trade accounts and notes receivable, less allowance for doubtful receivables of $22,500 in 19X4	637,205
Inventories:	
Finished goods	265,335
Work in process	192,479
Raw materials and supplies	267,298
Total inventories	725,112
Prepaid expenses	57,843
Total current assets	1,604,669
Investments in affiliated companies (note 2)	161,181
Property, plant and equipment, at cost (notes 3 and 4)	743,756
Less accumulated depreciation and amortization	165,043
Net property, plant and equipment	578,713
Other assets, at cost, less applicable amortization	88,202
	$ 2,432,765

See accompanying notes to consolidated financial statements

EXAMPLE COMPANY, INC.
AND SUBSIDIARIES

Consolidated Balance Sheet

December 31, 19X4

Liabilities and Stockholders' Equity

Current liabilities:	
Notes payable to banks	$ 100,000
Current installments of long-term debt	
(note 4)	21,562
Accounts payable	443,501
Accrued expenses	81,020
Income taxes	181,251
Total current liabilities	827,334
Deferred income taxes (note 5)	91,000
Long-term debt, excluding current	
installments (note 4)	419,794
Stockholders' equity (notes 4 and 6):	
$5 cumulative preferred stock of $100 par	
value, redeemable at $105 plus accrued	
dividends; liquidation value at par.	
Authorized 3,000 shares; issued 2,150	
in 19X4	215,000
Common stock of $1 par value. Authorized	
300,000 shares; issued 143,090 in 19X4	143,090
Additional paid-in capital	177,297
Retained earnings	569,250
	1,104,637
Less cost of common shares in treasury –	
640 in 19X4	10,000
Total stockholders' equity	1,094,637
Commitments and contingent liability	
(notes 8, 10 and 11)	
	$ 2,432,765

See accompanying notes to consolidated financial statements

EXAMPLE COMPANY, INC.
AND SUBSIDIARIES

Consolidated Statement of Earnings

Year ended December 31, 19X4

Net sales	$ 4,022,127
Cost of sales	2,879,719
Gross profit	1,142,408
Selling, general and administrative expenses	400,666
Operating income	741,742
Other income (deductions):	
Equity in earnings of affiliates (note 2)	19,134
Miscellaneous	28,214
Interest expense	(27,690)
	19,658
Earnings before income taxes	761,400
Income taxes (note 5):	
Current	358,000
Deferred	37,000
	395,000
Net earnings	$ 366,400
Earnings per common share and common share equivalent (note 7)	$ 2.42
Earnings per common share - assuming full dilution (note 7)	$ 2.28

See accompanying notes to consolidated financial statements.

EXAMPLE COMPANY, INC.
AND SUBSIDIARIES

Consolidated Statement of Stockholders' Equity

Year ended December 31, 19X4

	$5 cumulative preferred stock	Common stock	Additional paid-in capital	Retained earnings	Treasury stock	Total stockholders' equity (notes 4 and 6)
Balance at December 31, 19X3	$ 215,000	142,580	171,687	502,725	(7,500)	1,024,492
Shares issued in connection with employee stock option plan, 510 shares	-	510	5,610	-	-	6,120
Net earnings	-	-	-	366,400	-	366,400
Dividends declared:						
Preferred, $5 per share	-	-	-	(10,750)	-	(10,750)
Common, $2.03 per share	-	-	-	(289,125)	-	(289,125)
Acquisition of 1,400 common shares	-	-	-	-	(2,500)	(2,500)
Balance at December 31, 19X4	$ 215,000	143,090	177,297	569,250	(10,000)	1,094,637

See accompanying notes to consolidated financial statements.

EXAMPLE COMPANY, INC.
AND SUBSIDIARIES

Consolidated Statement of Changes in Financial Position

Year ended December 31, 19X4

Sources of working capital:
Earnings before extraordinary item	$ 366,400
Items which do not use (provide) working capital:	
Depreciation and amortization of plant and equipment	51,050
Other amortization	6,440
Equity in earnings of affiliates	(19,135)
Provision for deferred income taxes	37,000
Working capital provided by operations, exclusive of extraordinary item	441,755
Proceeds from exercise of employee stock options	6,120
Proceeds from long-term borrowings	110,500
	$ 558,375

Uses of working capital:
Dividends	$ 299,875
Additions to plant and equipment	89,252
Current installments, repayment and conversion of long-term debt	75,062
Purchase of treasury stock	2,500
Increase in working capital	91,686
	$ 558,375

Changes in components of working capital:
Increase in current assets:	
Cash	$ 30,542
Receivables	67,521
Inventories	90,189
Prepaid expenses	2,570
	190,822
Increase in current liabilities:	
Notes payable to banks	20,000
Current installments of long-term debt	12,572
Accounts payable	13,824
Accrued expenses	9,740
Income taxes	43,000
	99,136
Increase in working capital	$ 91,686

See accompanying notes to consolidated financial statements.

EXAMPLE COMPANY, INC.
AND SUBSIDIARIES

Notes to Consolidated Financial Statements

December 31, 19X4

(1) Summary of Significant Accounting Policies

Principles of Consolidation

The consolidated financial statements include the accounts of the Company
and its two wholly owned subsidiaries. All significant intercompany
balances and transactions have been eliminated in consolidation.

Investments in Affiliated Companies

Investments in the common stock of two affiliated companies are stated at
cost plus the Company's share of undistributed earnings since acquisition.

Inventories

Inventories are stated at the lower of cost (first-in, first-out) or
market (net realizable value).

Depreciation

Depreciation of plant and equipment is provided over the estimated useful
lives of the respective assets on the straight-line basis. Leasehold
improvements are amortized on a straight-line basis over the terms of the
respective leases.

Income Taxes

Deferred taxes are provided for all items included in the statement of
earnings regardless of when such items are reported for tax purposes.
Such deferred taxes arise principally from using accelerated depreciation
methods for tax purposes and the straight-line basis for financial statement purposes and from providing, for financial statement purposes, for
income taxes on the Company's share of the undistributed earnings of
affiliated companies as if such earnings were remitted to the Company as
a dividend during the year. Investment credits are recorded as a reduction of the provision for Federal income taxes in the year realized.

Pension Plans

Pension expense includes amortization of prior service costs over periods
of 25 years. The Company's policy is to fund pension costs which are
composed of normal costs and amortization of prior service costs.

EXAMPLE COMPANY, INC.
AND SUBSIDIARIES

Notes to Consolidated Financial Statements, Continued

(2) Investments in Affiliated Companies

Investments in affiliated companies are represented by 34% of the common
stock of ABC Company and 37% of the common stock of XYZ, Inc. Summary
combined information for the investees follows:

Current assets	$ 571,673
Current liabilities	415,359
Working capital	156,314
Property, plant and equipment, net	431,941
Other assets	7,263
Long-term debt	(231,750)
Stockholders' equity	$ 363,768
Represented by:	
Invested capital	$ 303,840
Retained earnings	59,928
	$ 363,768
Sales	$ 1,221,462
Net earnings	$ 56,192

(3) Property, Plant and Equipment

A summary of property, plant and equipment costs at December 31, 19X4
follows:

Land	$ 30,000
Buildings	99,325
Machinery and equipment	522,431
Furniture and fixtures	19,000
Leasehold improvements	73,000
	$ 743,756

EXAMPLE COMPANY, INC.
AND SUBSIDIARIES

Notes to Consolidated Financial Statements, Continued

(4) Long-term Debt

A summary of long-term debt follows:

8% subordinated debentures due December 31, 1984, retired at face value in 19X5	$ 130,000
7% mortgage notes payable, due in monthly installments of $370, including interest, through September 30, 19XX, secured by real property with depreciated cost of $52,800	41,293
Obligation under long-term equipment leases, due in quarterly installments of $1,350, including imputed interest of 11%, through June 30, 19XX, secured by equipment with depreciated cost of $62,600	52,263
5% subordinated debentures due January 1, 19X5	18,000
9-1/2% convertible subordinated debentures dated July 19X9, due 19XX, with annual payments beginning in 19XX	199,800
Total long-term debt	441,356
Less current installments of long-term debt	21,562
Long-term debt, excluding current installments	$ 419,794

The agreement underlying the 7-1/2% notes contains restrictions as to maintenance of working capital and payment of cash dividends. The Company is in compliance with such restrictive covenants. Retained earnings free of restriction approximate $230,000 at December 31, 19X4.

The 9-1/2% convertible subordinated debentures are convertible into 10,000 shares of common stock at $18 per share until July 19X9.

(5) Income Taxes

Income tax expense amounted to $395,000 (an effective rate of 51.9%). The actual tax expense differs from the "expected" tax expense for those years (computed by applying the U.S. Federal corporate tax rate of 48% to earnings before income taxes and extraordinary item) as shown on the following page.

EXAMPLE COMPANY, INC.
AND SUBSIDIARIES

Notes to Consolidated Financial Statements, Continued

(5) Income Taxes, Continued

Computed "expected" tax expense (48% of earnings before income taxes and extraordinary item)	$ 365,472
Equity in earnings of affiliates treated as dividends utilizing dividends received deduction	(7,807)
Investment tax credits	(9,689)
Amortization of excess cost over net assets of subsidiaries acquired	48,001
State and local taxes (net of Federal income tax benefit)	(977)
Other	
	$ 395,000

Depreciation of certain plant and equipment is computed using an accelerated method for tax purposes and the straight-line method for financial reporting purposes. The excess of tax depreciation over financial statement depreciation for 19X4 was $64,994. Deferred income tax expense for 19X4 resulted from timing differences attributable principally to depreciation and the Company's share of undistributed earnings of affiliated companies.

Components of income tax expense are as follows:

	Current	Deferred	Total
Federal	$ 274,201	28,490	302,691
State and local	83,799	8,510	92,309
	$ 358,000	37,000	395,000

(6) Employee Stock Options

Since 1965, stock options have been granted to officers and employees a prices equal to market values at the grant dates. A summary of 19X4 transactions is shown on the following page.

EXAMPLE COMPANY, INC.
AND SUBSIDIARIES

Notes to Consolidated Financial Statements, Continued

(6) Employee Stock Options, Continued

	Number of shares	Exercise price
Outstanding at beginning of year	18,007	$ 12-21
Granted	600	19
	18,607	
Exercised	510	12
Cancelled or expired	462	12
	972	
Outstanding at end of year	17,635	12-21

Options are exercisable upon issuance from the grant dates. At December 31, 1975, 75,000 shares were reserved for granting of additional options.

(7) Earnings per Common Share

Earnings per common share and common share equivalent are based on the weighted average number of shares outstanding and equivalent shares from dilutive stock options; net earnings are reduced for preferred dividend requirements. Earnings per common share, assuming full dilution, are computed by assuming the conversion of all debentures at the beginning of the year.

(8) Pension Plans

The Company and its subsidiaries have noncontributory pension plans covering substantially all employees. Total pension expense was $36,600 in 19X4. The actuarially computed value of vested benefits under the plans exceeded pension fund assets by $230,000 at December 31, 19X4.

(9) Research and Development Costs

Research and development costs are included in expense when incurred. Total research and development expense was $19,588 in 19X4.

(10) Commitments

The Company and its subsidiaries occupy certain manufacturing facilities and sales offices and use certain equipment under operating lease arrangements. Rent expense amounted to approximately $47,500 in 19X4.

EXAMPLE COMPANY, INC.
AND SUBSIDIARIES

Notes to Consolidated Financial Statements, Continued

(10) Commitments, Continued

A summary of lease commitments follows:

Year ending December 31	Total commitment
19X5	$ 43,000
19X6	47,000
19X7	45,000
19X8	40,000
19X9	39,500
19X0	37,500
19X1-19X5	90,000

All leases expire prior to 1986. Real estate taxes, insurance and maintenance expenses are obligations of the Company. It is expected that in the normal course of business, leases that expire will be renewed or replaced by leases on other properties; thus, it is anticipated that future minimum lease commitments will not be less than the amounts shown for 1976.

(11) Contingent Liability

The Company is defendant in a $250,000 suit alleging infringement of patents. Legal counsel for the Company is of the opinion that the plaintiff's claim is without merit and the Company will prevail in defending the suit.

Comments

You've just read what most analysts would agree is an excellent statement. Let's review it. First, what did you read, and second, what did it say?

Starting with the letter, we can make four comments. First and foremost, the work was done by a well-known, reputable firm. Second, the accountants gave the statement a clean opinion. It is certified. The numbers have been examined and found to be in accordance with the standards of the profession. Third, the work was performed quickly. The field audit was concluded by February 5 and was issued shortly thereafter. The fourth and final point to bear in mind is that this is the consolidated statement of several companies.

Your approach to a statement can vary from that of others. The school of analysis that first reads the letter and then goes to the footnotes is one which is growing in popularity — and rightfully so. If certain oddities are mentioned in the footnotes, then you can read the statement fully aware of their existence and impact.

The opening footnote of the statement justifies this approach. We learn that the company has consolidated the results of the parent corporation and two subsidiaries. We also learn that the company is reflecting the ownership of common stock of two affiliated companies *at cost plus the company's share of undistributed earnings since acquisition*. This method is commonly known as the equity basis. You say you don't know what that is? Count yourself in the majority. Many senior analysts would have to stop and perhaps even consult someone.

Nonetheless, you will have to find out what the equity basis of reporting stock ownership is before you can read the statement. A call to your senior analyst or senior commercial officer should provide the answer. There are two different bases for reporting ownership in an affiliate. The first is the cost basis, where the cost of acquired stock is treated just like any other investment. That is, the stock is reflected on the books of the company at its historic cost. The stock value will change only if the stock is sold or if the value drops so substantially that it is written down by the CPAs.

The equity basis is the alternative way of reflecting the value of stock in another company. Basically, the income of the affiliate — pro rata by the shares owned — is shown as income to the parent. Certain key tests must be met in order to be able to report in this manner. Chief among them is that the affiliate be receiving a large degree of control and direction from the company that is seeking to report on an equity basis. Also, this company must have a significant degree of ownership in the affiliate. To say it another way, an individual who owns one share of General Motors could only report the stock at cost on his statement. If he met the ownership and direction criteria, he could report not only the stock but also the earnings from General Motors, as it relates to his stock, as income to him.

You do not have to be an expert in cost versus equity reporting. Your senior officers carry that responsibility and they must be available to direct your efforts. You should understand, however, that certain income contained in the statement is the income of an affiliate, that it is book income only, and that you cannot consider it in your analysis of the statement.

The first footnote continues to summarize the accounting principles. Again, you have got to feel good. The rules are being followed and a reputable firm attests to it.

The second footnote gives details to support the value of the stock the company owns in its affiliates. Although we do not know all about these companies, we at least have seen the main points highlighted. If we have any questions or seek any additional data, we have a place to start.

Footnote three details the contents of the fixed assets. We have consistently stressed the importance of getting behind the numbers. This breakdown gives you the necessary checklist for pursuing that avenue. Because we are seeking to renew a line of credit, the current or real value of the buildings is not as important as it would be if this were a mortgage or trust deed request.

Footnote four provides a critical insight by presenting a detailed schedule of long-term debt. This data includes the actual obligations, their security, if any, the monthly payment terms, and finally, the maturity date. This list gives you information for checking the experience of other creditors as well as a way of knowing the upcoming needs of the company as they relate to debt-service. Finally, the footnote references the terms and conditions of certain notes (of which we should be very aware) and states that those terms and conditions are being met.

The remaining footnotes help expand our knowledge of the company, its operations, taxes, contingent plans for employee stock options and pensions, and any litigation that may exist.

By reading these footnotes, we have learned a good deal about this company and, it is hoped, a few things that we did not know before. With the nature of the numbers understood, we now may commence the main course.

Whenever you have the chance, you should follow the eyes of a senior lending officer while he or she is reading a financial statement. You will be able to learn an awful lot about what the officer thinks is important and how he or she digests the data. The best approach I've seen is to read the heading on the balance sheet and then go to the equity section. Proceed from this point to the long-term debt. Remember the comment made several chapters ago that banks seek to *share* in opportunities. Determine if you are sharing or carrying the whole capital requirement. What is the relationship of capital to long-term debt? We stress long-term debt because it is profit debt. The company must make a profit to have funds available to meet these payments. Short-term debt usually is paid by asset conversion. How many dollars do they have working (equity) to generate income to meet the requirements of your loan?

Once you know the equity, you can see that the sharing is in line. It's actually in our favor. Long-term creditors are contributing a small portion compared with the investors ($420,000 of long-term debt to over $1,000,000 of equity). You, the bank, have present loans of only $100,000 against a $500,000 commitment.

The next step is to locate the equity. In this case, it is favorably spread between working capital (the difference between current assets and current liabilities) and long-term assets. The company has $778,000 ($1,605,000 − $827,000) of net worth invested in working capital and $160,000 of net fixed assets over long-term debt. No particular ratio or measurement is being pointed to here. We are simply getting a feel for the numbers. These figures show that the company does have equity and that it is evenly balanced throughout the statement.

With this overview now fixed in our minds, we begin to read the entire balance sheet in order to examine the individual items. All appear to be normal (except for the investment in affiliates which we have already noted in the footnotes); therefore, no special attention to them is needed. Just start with current assets and read each item.

The income statement also is read first for the overview and then for the composition. In this case, only one item appears to be at all abnormal and that is the earnings from the affiliates. Once again our discussion with the senior lender will allow us to continue with our analysis. We know that these earnings are not ours but that they are of another company. We then discount them from the profit. In this case they total some $19,000, or less than 3 percent of the pretax profit. However, in some cases earnings from affiliates may represent more than half of the company's income and if not properly understood, these earnings will almost certainly cause a loan without any repayment source to be made.

If you are not used to it, you are probably looking for a detailed breakdown of all expenses on the income statement. Look no further. They aren't there. Remember the comment we made earlier. Do we learn anything by having a great deal of detail? Probably not. If we feel we need more, then we must request it from management. Such detail is not a normal part of the financial statement.

Page three of the financial statement contains the statement of the stockholders' equity. A concise schedule of all of the items which changed the company's equity balance is presented to you. Our first reading shows us that the items are normal. That is, there was no major new stock issuance or major conversion of debt or the like. However, the amount of some transactions looks high, in particular the dividends paid to shareholders. Of some $355,000 of after-tax profit, more than 80 percent was paid to shareholders.

Earlier we said that a company needs to show a profit sufficient to meet debt. Actually, a company needs profit for many things, including a return to its investors, debt service, and funds from which to grow. This high dividend policy is a potential problem. If you have not reviewed the restrictive covenants listed in footnote four, now is the time to do it.

That's it. You have read your first statement and, we hope, understood it.

We have not completely analyzed it, but we do understand it. Only by having the client available will we get *past the numbers to their content*. At least we know what the numbers are. To complete the analysis we will measure some of the things we began to feel while reading the statement and then we will try to understand those things that we had passed over quickly.

Reading this statement in the context of the request is fairly easy. The company has good equity, strong profitability, and good internal balance among balance sheet items (this last is really only a feeling which comes from seeing how the equity of the company is invested). Is management capable of having a line and using it properly? Just reading the statements won't answer that. Remember, statement analysis is only part of the decision-making process. At this point however, everything looks positive.

We will return to this statement later. We have avoided intentionally any real discussion of numbers, percentages, ratios, and computer-like phrases. These mechanics of statement analysis are important, and we will discuss them, *but, they are meaningless unless we understand the statement*. Know the real content and *only then* proceed to the mechanics. The subject of the second part of this text will be the mechanics.

What then have we accomplished? At best, you came away with feelings about the company and their financial statement. You have begun to formulate the questions you would ask the client if he were sitting across from you. (Who makes up the receivables? How much steel is now in inventory? Who are the biggest suppliers? Does the company have local competition? Does it have national competition?)

Before proceeding to Part II, return to the statement we just covered and reread it until you begin to feel comfortable with it.

Part II Mechanics

6   The Keys

Ratios

At the end of section one, we began to look at the relationship between certain items on the balance sheet. Many times our instincts give us a feeling for such relationships. However, in some cases it is possible to use quantitative and qualitative measurements called ratios.

Ratios define and rate certain relationships. They do not analyze statements, and they do not make loan decisions. Just as a patient's temperature or blood pressure may help a doctor to identify an illness, so ratios help us to identify financial strengths and weaknesses. There are a seemingly infinite number of ratios. We will be using only a few of the more basic ones.

Most ratios, as used by bankers, are created for the purpose of better understanding repayment sources. Each bank has its own philosophy of commercial lending and thus will emphasize certain aspects of the statement more than others. Regardless of the bank's philosophy however, loans are repayable in only a limited number of ways. The primary ways are asset conversion and profitability. (The other ways are the infusion of new capital and refinancing by a different institution.)

If you lend against an asset that must be sold before you are repaid, then you will want to know how liquid that asset is. How much surplus is there to make your conversion an easier one? Because banks seek to share in opportunities, you will want to know how much equity is being invested and whether it is enough. If profitability is the key to repaying a certain loan, you will want to know whether cash flow is sufficient to meet the current portion of long-term debt.

Answering such questions is the primary purpose of ratios. Ratios measure the liquidity and quality of assets. They measure the adequacy of capital — both working capital and equity capital. They measure the ability of the company to meet debt obligations. Finally, ratios give a preview of the potential of the assets by measuring their past and present return.

The *current ratio* is the most commonly used of all ratios. It expresses the relationship between current assets and current liabilities. It shows us the strength of those things that are owed to the company relative to those things that the company owes.

If a company has $100 of assets that convert to cash within a certain period (one year), and it must make $300 of payments in the same period, you know that there is a problem. On the other hand, if a company has $500 of cash (or its short-term equivalent), and it has $200 of payments due, then you know that your loan can easily be repaid when the cash equivalent converts to cash. Whether the cash equivalent will convert is a qualitative question that will be discussed shortly. The current ratio only quantifies the relationship between current funds due and funds owed.

The current ratio is computed by dividing current assets by current liabilities.

$$\frac{\text{Current assets}}{\text{Current liabilities}} = X$$

The ratio is expressed as X to 1.

The old rule is that a ratio of 2 to 1 (or 2:1) is standard and acceptable. Each company will have a different mix of assets and liabilities, however, and its standard ratio will differ from others. Knowing your customer is once again the key.

The *acid ratio,* or *quick ratio,* is a refined version of the current ratio. Instead of relating all current assets to all current liabilities, this ratio uses only highly liquid cash items for the comparison with liabilities. Thus it excludes all current assets except cash and accounts receivable. Inventory is excluded because it would have to go through two steps to become cash: sale and collection. It is, therefore, not as "cash equivalent" as accounts receivable, which require only one step to convert to cash.

All current liabilities are, by definition, due within the same immediate period and therefore all are included in the computation. (Some texts will differ on this point; your bank's philosophy will be the guideline.)

The acid ratio is computed by dividing cash and accounts receivable by current liabilities.

$$\frac{\text{Cash and accounts receivable}}{\text{Current liabilities}}$$

This ratio is also expressed as X to 1. An acid ratio of 1:1 is considered standard, although it may vary from company to company.

The *total debt/net worth ratio* is the second most common ratio. Its purpose is to help us judge capital adequacy by seeing the relationship between what the borrower has invested and what the bank has lent. It does not tell us how much capital is enough, but does tell us the degree of *leverage*. Leverage is the use of debt to increase the effectiveness of an investment. An example will illustrate this point.

Suppose your client invests $1,000 to purchase 100 shares of stock at $10 per share. Also suppose that the value of the stock increases over time to $15 per share. This $5 gain means a profit of $500, or 50 percent of the investment.

Now let's assume that in addition to the capital investment of $1,000, your client also borrowed $1,000. (The total debt/net worth ratio is now 1:1.) Your client would be able to purchase 200 shares and the gain would be $1,000. The cost of interest aside, your client has leveraged his or her equity and has made a 100 percent profit instead of 50 percent as before.

A schedule summarizing this example is given in Table 6.1.

Leverage may work against the investor, however. Suppose, using the same example, that the stock drops in value to $7 per share. In this case, the schedule in Table 6.2 applies.

Leverage not only can cause a higher rate of loss, it can actually destroy an investment. Suppose you had lent money against the stock (barring any regulations which might apply). You now have a $1,000 loan against a $1,400 collateral package (Future Value column B). You are close to margin.

When speaking about the relationship of debt to equity, we said that banks want to *share* in opportunities. Leverage is an important part of business and a tool which your client should use. A fifty-fifty balance, as in our earlier example, usually is reasonable. The problem comes with extreme swings in the debt to equity relationship. Let's go back to our example and

Table 6.1 Leverage example
(stock value $15 per share)

	A	B
Shares	100	200
Original value	$1,000	$2,000
Future value (after gain)	1,500	3,000
Gain	500	1,000
Interest cost (estimated)	—	100
Profit	$ 500	$ 900
Rate of return	500/1,000	900/1,000
	50%	90%

Table 6.2 Leverage example
(stock value $7 per share)

	A	B
Shares	100	200
Original value	$1,000	$2,000
Future value	700	1,400
Loss on decrease	300	600
Interest cost	—	100
Loss	$ 300	$ 700
Rate of loss	300/1,000	700/1,000
	30%	70%

assume a four to one ratio, meaning that your client borrows $4,000 to his or her $1,000 of investment. Let's see what happens with a $5 increase in stock value and then a $5 drop (Table 6.3).

Look at your collateral in column B. You now have a $4,000 loan against $2,500 of collateral. Why? You didn't share the opportunity. You put up the major portion of the purchase. If you feel this example is too simple to be realistic, think twice about some of the loans on your books. For example, what about that last back hoe you financed? Even though the col-

Table 6.3 Leverage example (stock value increases or decreases by $5)

	A	B
Shares	500	500
Original value	$5,000	$5,000
Price change	(+5/share)	(−5/share)
Future value	$7,500	$2,500
Net gain/loss	$2,500	(2,500)
Interest	400	400
Total gain/loss	$2,100	(2,900)
Rate of gain/loss	2100/1000	2900/1000
	210%	(290%)

lateral is unlikely to disappear, leverage is nevertheless important. Let's compare an 80 percent financing of a back hoe to a 50 percent financing. Assume the unit cost $15,000 and that you finance the loan over six years. The schedule in Table 6.4 shows the difference between the two loans.

In the first case, the profit your client must make to cover the loan payment and income taxes, and still have enough left to make the purchase worthwhile, is much more than in the second case. You have to feel more comfortable with the 50 percent financing. It's more in line.

Capital adequacy is as important in your client's overall operation as is in each individual transaction.

If the bank individually, or all creditors collectively, is carrying an undue

Table 6.4 Leverage example (comparing a 50 percent financing to an 80 percent financing of a backhoe)

	80% financing	50% financing
Unit cost	$15,000	$15,000
Amount financed	12,000	7,500
Interest rate	12%	12%
First year payment	2,815	1,760

portion of the risk, then the company will make more on its investment, but it also must make more to meet your payments. If there is a loss, no cushion will exist to absorb it.

We have to ask, "How much do we have in and how much do they?" Remember, the bank lends funds, not capital.

The total debt/net worth ratio is computed by dividing total debt by net worth.

$$\frac{\text{Total debt}}{\text{Net worth}}$$

Many will express this ratio as X to 1. Others simply state the total debt and net worth figures in ratio form. They say 350 to 190, or 210 to 370. This latter method avoids confusion and makes year-to-year spread sheet comparisons easier. What makes for a reasonable ratio depends upon the overall situation, the nature of the loan, the collateral being offered, and the equity of your client. The client need not be required to match the bank's investment in every case, nor does every loan have to be unleveraged. You should not, however, be expected to grant a loan to someone who has no equity, or only limited equity, in either the collateral or the company.

The next ratio is the *total debt/working capital* ratio.

$$\frac{\text{Total debt}}{\text{Working capital}}$$

Of all the ratios, this one varies most in presentation. It, and its variants, helps to define debt coverage by showing the relationship between what is needed to cover debt and what is available to cover it.

Total debt is the total of all indebtedness of a company. Working capital is the difference between current assets (cash due and its short-term equivalent) and current liabilities (cash requirements in the relatively near future). Working capital is the net cash, or its equivalent, that is available to the company.

In a commercial loan we may use the total debt to working capital ratio to measure how many dollars are available to meet the company's debts. A simple illustration will best explain this. If a company has total debts of $700,000 and working capital of $100,000 (700/100), then it is capable of meeting one-seventh of all its obligations, including current liabilities.

Now let's suppose that another company has $700,000 of total debt and a deficit working capital of $50,000 ($50,000 more current liabilities than current assets). This situation yields a ratio of 700/(50) as compared with the 700/100 of the first example. Which company has a better chance of meeting its obligations, both short-term and long? The answer is the one with a positive working capital of course.

The total debt/working capital ratio is best used for studying changes from year to year rather than for judging one year alone. In this sense there is no one standard ratio that is acceptable; the ratio helps you to define your feelings about a company's ability to meet its obligations.

Total debt/profit is a common variation of the total debt/working capital ratio. The assumption is that, since profit services debt, one should measure the profit available for debt service. Some analysts further refine the measurement by using only long-term debt or profit before taxes for the ratio instead of all debt or all profit. Your bank's philosophy will dictate which version is bested suited for use with your clients.

In mortgage lending, the ratio that helps to define debt coverage is extremely important. It is known as the *debt-service ratio,* and it may be the single most important factor in the real estate loan decision.

The ratio is computed by dividing the profit on an asset by the annual loan payment on that asset.

A number results from this computation which shows the ability to cover debt. If the number is 1, the company or the property just barely is able to cover the outgoing mortgage payments. If the number is less than 1, the building is not capable of generating enough profit to pay the mortgage and an additional infusion of funds will be needed. A ratio of more than 1 is healthy because it shows that the loan can be serviced adequately. Although the acceptable norm for the debt-service ratio varies with circumstances, a 1.25 debt-service ratio is required by most lending institutions.

This ratio is one of the few that are used to determine how large a loan can be. With it, we can figure out how much debt a property is capable of carrying. An example will show how this is done.

Assume a building costs $1,000,000, that it has a gross rental income of $125,000, and that it has operating expenses of $50,000 (not including depreciation). It has a profit before debt payment of $75,000 ($125,000 − $50,000). Assume that we, as lenders, require a 1.25 debt-service ratio. How large a loan can the building support? The calculation we use to answer this question, using the debt-service ratio, is shown in Table 6.5.

Our $1,000,000 building can service a $600,000 loan at the current as-

Table 6.5 Economic loan value using the debt-service ratio

Gross rentals income	$125,000
Operating expense	50,000
Profit	$ 75,000
Debt service required	1.25
Profit to service debt (75,000 ÷ 1.25)	$ 60,000
Serviceable debt (assume 10% constant)* (60,000 ÷ .1)	$600,000

* The constant is the total payment necessary to amortize the debt over its life.

sumed interest. We determined that not by an appraisal but by using the debt-service ratio.

The ratio's use in such calculations does not diminish its value as a tool of measurement and analysis, however. Watching the change in the debt-service ratio from year to year is tremendously valuable for the lender.

The next two ratios which we will discuss are known as qualitative ratios because they are used to measure the quality of individual items. These two are the *accounts receivable turnover* and *inventory turnover* ratios. To really know whether a loan against receivables is good, you must know the make-up of the asset. There is no substitute for this. The best way to find out about the nature of receivables is to use an aging schedule.

The accounts receivable turnover ratio measures the overall quality of the accounts receivable by defining their average age. The aging schedule gives you an exact aging of each item; this ratio averages the ages.

The accounts receivable turnover ratio can be stated either as the number of times accounts receivable turned over during the year, or as the average number of days each account was outstanding. Both ways are acceptable and widely used.

To calculate the turnover, you merely divide sales by accounts receivable (AR). This yields the number of times AR has turned over or been collected on an annual basis. If a company's sales total $100,000 and its AR is $25,000, then the turnover is four times a year (100/25 = 4).

To convert the turnover into an average number of days, divide 360 days by the turnover figure. In the example above, the $25,000 of AR against sales of $100,000 turns over four times a year, or an average of every 90 days (360/4).

The equations for computing accounts receivable turnover and the average age of accounts receivable are as follows.

$$\text{Turnover factor} = \frac{\text{Sales}}{\text{Accounts receivable}}$$

$$\text{Turnover days} = \frac{360 \text{ days}}{\text{Turnover factor}}$$

Combined, the equations are:

$$\text{Turnover days} = 360 \text{ days} \div \frac{\text{Sales}}{\text{Accounts receivable}}$$

or

$$\text{Turnover days} = \frac{360 \text{ days} \times \text{Accounts receivable}}{\text{Sales}}$$

What would the ratios be for a company with sales of $400,000 and accounts receivable of $50,000?

The turnover factor would be eight; expressed as days it would be 45(400/50 = 8; 360 days/8 = 45; or 360 × 50/400 = 45 days).

To understand what we mean by the average age of accounts receivable, consider the company that has accounts receivable which average sixty days. This means that their funds are tied up for sixty days *on the average*. Some accounts are collected immediately and some are probably very old and uncollectible. This company needs more working capital than a company that sells on a net ten-day basis. The turnover of the latter company probably would average ten to fifteen days.

The major shortcoming of the accounts receivable turnover measurement is that it is only true *as of* the balance sheet date. The receivables will change daily and so will the sales. The ratio is subject to a great deal of swing. It only measures one day, and that day is possibly the low point of the year.

The ratio's strength is twofold. First, it is an indicator of management's adherence to its stated collection policy. If you were told when discussing sales with management that the company sells on a net ten-day basis, but the turnover averages thirty days, then you know something is wrong. It may be that a few dead accounts are being carried or that policy in general is not being enforced.

The ratio's second strength is its use in year-to-year comparisons. If a major change of policy regarding collections or sales has occurred, it will be reflected in the turnover rate. The change in the ratio may indicate a serious bad debt problem. It definitely will show the trend of the company.

The real key for the loan officer is the listing of the accounts, the aging. As a tool to diagnose your client's business, AR turnover is most helpful.

The same principles of accounts receivable turnover apply to *inventory turnover*. The equations are the same except that measurement is between inventory and cost of sales.

$$\text{Inventory turnover (in days)} = \frac{360 \text{ days} \times \text{inventory}}{\text{Cost of sales}}$$

A company with a $60,000 inventory and a $360,000 cost of sales has its inventory turn over six times a year, or on an average of every sixty days. A listing of the inventory items is critical because dead inventory could account for most of the turnover drag. Remember that the inventory is almost certainly at its yearly low as of the balance sheet date.

The final two ratios we will discuss are used to measure profitability. A company that lacks profitability eventually will disappear. If profitability does exist, we have to know whether it is adequate for meeting debt payments as well as for funding growth.

The first of these ratios measures *profit to net worth*. The second measures *profit to total assets*. The distinction is that the first measures the company's return on *its* investment, and the second measures return on the *total investment,* the creditors included. (Leverage is once again entering the picture.)

In both cases, the profit referred to is profit before taxes. Why before? First, taxes really are intended to be a distribution of profit. Uncle Sam considers himself a partner, not a parasite. Secondly, taxes are a variable. To be more consistent and to avoid fluctuations because of different tax brackets and so forth, we merely step in front of taxes.

The first ratio is *profit before taxes/net worth*.

$$\frac{\text{Profit before taxes}}{\text{Net worth}}$$

The question we are trying to answer when we look at this ratio is whether or not the company is justifying its effort. If the company's equity is $100,000, then it could earn interest income just by investing in a simple CD. A stock market venture could give income plus growth and perhaps return at a higher rate. If a company cannot earn more than the yield on a conservative investment, that fact is a reflection on company management. Remember that salaries are being paid principals, and this may be the true purpose of being in business. Are salaries profit? Of course. Are they part of our ratio? No. What's out of line? Overreliance on ratios.

The second ratio, *profit before taxes/total assets,* is more informative.

$$\frac{\text{Profit before taxes}}{\text{Total assets}}$$

The question we are trying to answer when we look at this ratio is whether the company is earning a reasonable profit. A company must make a profit sufficient to meet its obligations to you and still make it worthwhile for the principals. The goal in many companies is to earn a 20 percent profit on each new investment before interest, taxes, and depreciation. There is no absolute standard for what constitutes a reasonable profit. You have to develop a feeling for it.

The real value of any of the ratios discussed here is that they are a measureable point for intuitive feelings you have developed when reading the statements. They give you insight into the statement and highlight certain areas.

If the information which you examine is critical enough, you must go past it and get to the content of the numbers.

Statement Spreading

The second area of mechanics which should be explored is statement spreading. This is the process of consolidating, digesting, and re-presenting in shortened form an entire statement. A sample spread form is shown in Exhibit 6.1. All lending officers are quite familiar with spreads, but the preparation of spread sheets usually does not receive enough attention.

The spread sheet allows a great deal of information to be presented in a concise and consistent form. It gives the loan officer an overview and makes comparison of items a simple task.

The overlooked phase of spreading is the mechanics. The person spread-

FIRST EASTERN BANK, N. A.
COMPARISON STATEMENT

000's Omitted

NAME

	ASSETS Date				
1	Cash				
2	Marketable Securities — C/D's				
3	Receivable — Trade (Net)				
4					
5	Inventories				
6					
7					
8	All Other Current				
9	TOTAL CURRENT ASSETS				
10	Fixed Assets — Net				
11					
12					
13	Investments				
14					
15	All Other Noncurrent (Incl. Prepaid)				
16	TOTAL NONCURRENT ASSETS				
17	TOTAL ASSETS				
	LIABILITIES				
18	Notes Payable — Banks				
19	Notes Payable — Other				
20					
21	Current Maturities of L. T. Debt				
22	Accounts Payable — Trade				
23					
24	Interest & Other Accruals				
25	Taxes Payable				
26					
27					
28	All Other Current				
29	TOTAL CURRENT DEBT				
30	Mortgage Payable				
31	Long Term Debt				
32					
33	All Other Noncurrent				
34	TOTAL NONCURRENT DEBT				
35	TOTAL LIABILITIES				
36	Capital				
37	Retained Earnings				
38					
39	NET WORTH				
40	TOTAL LIABILITIES&NET WORTH				
41					
42	NET WORKING CAPITAL (9-29)				
	RATIOS				
43	Quick				
44	Current				
45	Total Debt/Working Capital				
46	Total Debt/Net Worth				
47	Receivable Turnover Days				
48	Inventory Turnover Days				
49	% Profit bef. Taxes/Net Worth				
50	% Profit bef. Taxes/Total Assets				
51					
52	Statement by				
53	Type of Statement				
54	Spread by				
55	Contingent Liabilities				
56					

FORM 18-1

Exhibit 6.1   Sample Spread Sheet

FIRST EASTERN BANK, N. A.

NAME

OPERATIONS	Date		%		%		%		%		%
101 Net Sales											
102 Cost of Sales											
103 Gross Profit											
104 Operating Expenses											
105 Net Profit before Depreciation											
106 Depreciation											
107 Profit from Operations											
108 Extraordinary Items											
109											
110 Profits Before Taxes											
111 Income Taxes											
112											
113 NET PROFIT AFTER TAXES											
RECONCILIATION OF NET WORTH											
114 Net Worth — Beginning											
115 Add: Net Profit After Taxes											
116											
117											
118 Less: Net Loss											
119 Dividend Paid											
120											
121											
122 Net Worth — Ending											
SOURCE & APPLICATION OF FUNDS											
Source of Funds:											
123 Net Profit											
124 Depreciation, Amort., Depletion											
125 Increase Long Term Debt											
126											
127											
128 Other Noncurrent Accounts — Net											
129 TOTAL SOURCES											
Application of Funds:											
130 Net Loss											
131 Dividends Paid											
132 Purchase of Fixed Assets											
133 Reduction Long Term Debt											
134											
135											
136 Other Noncurrent Accounts — Net											
137 TOTAL APPLICATIONS											
138 INC./DEC. OF WORKING CAPITAL											
RECONCIL. OF W/C CHANGES											
139 Cash											
140 Accounts Receivable											
141 Inventory											
142 Other											
143											
144 Notes Payable											
145 Accounts Payable											
146 Current Maturities — L.T. Debt											
147 Other											
148											
149 Inc/Dec W/C (139-143) — (144-148)											

COMMENTS:

Exhibit 6.1, continued

ing the statement is making some rather significant decisions. Because this person usually is not a front line officer, he or she has the advantage of reading the statement at a leisurely pace. He or she can research certain points which may be disputed and choose which items will be combined; this person decides what will be highlighted on the spread. This is a serious responsibility.

Although the loan officer must have a summary of the statement for making comparisons and decisions, he or she cannot base a loan decision on a review of the spreads only. He or she still must read the statement, form an opinion, and then either prepare or review the spread sheet in order to organize his or her thoughts.

Spread sheets do not show the small intangibles which color the statement itself. The goodwill (if small), prepaid expenses, or other assets are generally combined as miscellaneous items. Spreads never show the footnotes which are so critical to understanding any statement.

The rules for good spreading are simply common sense and consistency. Common sense so that potential traps receive adequate disclosure to be a forewarning to the reader. Consistency so that combinations of items are the same year in and year out.

Neither you nor your spreader are accountants; you are bankers. If you don't know what an item means, even a small one, then ask. If an insignificant item has become significant over a number of years, go back and reclassify the item in prior years so as to avoid making it appear that it all happened at once.

Each bank must develop its own philosophy and policy on spreading. A brief summary of one such policy governing statement spreading is given in Exhibit 6.2 as a general guideline.

Credit Files

The final area of mechanics, the credit files, will be reviewed only briefly. These files must contain all the information that you have on your client. Memorandums that summarize prior meetings, inquiries from trade suppliers or other banks, public trade records, and past borrowings by your client all enter into the loan decision and thus into the credit files. A major reason for commercial loans going bad is that Officer B, who took over the account after Officer A was promoted, had no knowledge as to why the loan was made and what the repayment conditions were to be.

GENERAL

1. All figures are rounded to the nearest thousand.
2. Fiscal and interim statements are not spread on the same comparison sheet.
3. Each item is self-explanatory, but our policy in certain areas is different from what the form indicates.

Balance Sheet

Assets
  a. If cash contains any reserve accounts or a special escrow account, then these accounts are to be listed separately.

  b. Notes and accounts receivable are shown net of any reserves.

  c. Prepaid expenses are not listed in the current section but under the miscellaneous section.

  d. Fixed assets are shown at their net figure (cost less depreciation.)

  e. Lines not printed are to be used for other asset breakdowns.

  f. Loans to stockholders, employees, officers, or related companies should never be shown in the current section and should never be grouped with other assets.

Liabilities

  a. Regardless of how long-term obligations are presented, the current portions should be grouped and marked as such.

  b. Other descriptions not printed on the form are to be typed in as needed.

  c. If no breakdown is given of long-term debt, then it should be shown on the line under Real Estate Mortgages.

  d. If a minority interest is shown on the statement it should be put on the line above Net Worth.

  e. Loans due to stockholders, officers, and affiliated companies should always be shown as current and never be grouped with other liabilities, regardless of amount.

  f. Subordinated notes, when subordinated to bank debt by an instrument of the bank, are included as net worth.

Exhibit 6.2   Sample Guidelines for Spreading Statements

Ratios

a. Quick and Current Ratios are calculated to the nearest hundred and are listed as X to 1 (i.e. 1.37 to 1).

b. Total Debt Ratios are shown at their stated amounts (i.e. 123/47).

c. Days are listed as whole numbers.

d. Profit percentages are extended to the nearest hundreds.

Income Statement

a. Sales are shown net of all adjustments.

b. Cost of Sales include all items so listed on the statement less depreciation. Unless depreciation is clearly marked as being part of some other expense category, it should be considered to be part of the cost of sales.

c. Operating Expenses include all expenses that are general as well as expenses that are not listed elsewhere. Any items which are grouped as other income and expenses should be included in this total provided they are not significant. If depreciation can be traced to this area, then it should be subtracted and listed separately.

d. Extraordinary items are exactly that, extraordinary. Examples of such expenses are flood loss, fire loss, major start-up cost, large bad-debt write-offs, etc.

e. Income taxes should be listed even if not current. If no taxes are payable, then a footnote should explain why. If item is paid in lieu of taxes, it should be listed here and so noted and described. If no taxes are paid do not fill in net profit line.

f. Percentages are to be rounded off to the nearest whole number except for net profit which should be taken out to one decimal place.

Source & Application of Funds

a. If a source and application of funds statement is included in the auditor's report, then it should be copied as such. If the statement is prepared by bank personnel, this should be noted in the comment section.

b. Only items which are listed on the form should be extended. Unless a specific figure materially affects the presentation, it should be listed as "Other".

If there are any unusual items on either balance sheet or income statement, explain by a footnote.

Exhibit 6.2, continued

Not every contact with the client needs to be recorded in 500 words. If the time you spent meeting your client was worthwhile, then it's worth the few moments needed to summarize your meeting in a memo. General summaries and updates must be recorded and filed at a central point. There are a number of excellent publications regarding the mechanics of operating a credit department, including the many ways in which files are kept.

Summary

Good statement analysis need not be overburdened with excessive mechanical work. By using the proper mechanical tools, the loan officer should be able to grasp the overall picture and the trend of his or her client. Then the current statement and request may be reviewed. Mechanics such as ratios and spread statements will make the task of digesting the statement easier. Comparisons with previous statements will also be more meaningful because of the highlights provided by ratios and spreads.

7   Reading a Statement

People who are confronted with a financial statement for the first time most often ask, "How do I read it? What do I look for? There appears to be so much, where do I start?"

All of these questions are valid and each analyst must find his own answers. Each will develop a method with which he or she feels comfortable.

One approach has been suggested already — read the letter, then the footnotes, and finally the numbers. We have discussed in detail how to *approach* the numbers. During the next few pages, a step-by-step approach to *reading* the numbers will be illustrated. This procedure can be used for all types of statements.

The example we will use is the ABC Company statement at the end of Chapter 3 (Exhibit 3.1). If you open the foldout and turn back the page, you will be able to read this chapter and follow the statement simultaneously.

After reading the letter and footnotes and seeing that there are no abnormalities what do we do? Here is one suggested method:

The first thing we read after the balance sheet heading is:

Total equity	$34,200

This item tells us what the company's investment is. Looking up a few inches we see:

Total liabilities	$29,800

We immediately note that a balance between equity and debt does exist. There is a reasonable cushion of equity and the leverage is acceptable. The investors and creditors are sharing.

Returning to the top of the statement, we begin to examine the major items to determine *where* the equity is. These items read:

Total current assets	$25,000
Total current liabilities	$15,000

We now know that $10,000 of the equity is in working capital ($25,000 − $15,000).

The difference between fixed assets and long-term debt is approximately $20,000.

Net property	$35,000
Total long-term debt	$14,800

Therefore, we can summarize our first overview as follows:

Working capital	$10,000
Fixed asset equity	20,000
Total equity	$30,000

Although the item called other assets has not been given any specific value, the remaining equity is in this item.

After this preliminary examination, we turn to the income statement. Our first reading of this statement also will be general. We will quickly examine three items: sales — $210,000; gross profit — $146,000; and profit before taxes — $15,000. These figures give us a feel for the company's earning power. The good gross profits are encouraging. The low net profits cause initial concern. We quickly look over the expenses to see if there are any abnormalities in the major concentrations of expense.

We see that cost of sales centers on materials. Overhead expenses really are high selling cost. Are these expenses the owners' salaries, and therefore profit, or are they necessary expenditures?

We now return to the balance sheet and examine each individual item. While reading, we begin to compare balance sheet items with income statement items (turnover rates).

Current assets are without any major concentration. Accounts receivable of $10,000 are well in line with sales of $210,000. The turnover rate is twenty-one times a year. Inventory of $8,000 is low and, although it turns over only eight times a year (cost of sales — $64,000), it is still acceptable.

On the liability side, accounts payable is the largest item. The suppliers are carrying the inventory. In other words, the payables are large when compared with the inventory. When payables are expressed as a proportion of cost of sales, they may be seen as a bit high, yet they may be in line in terms of total dollars.

The fixed assets comprise mainly land and buildings, and these assets are more than reasonable collateral for the mortgage payable. Other assets are normal and do not represent a significant portion of total assets.

Our review is now concluded. We have looked the statement over and seen how it is balanced. We have measured profitability. After a detailed reading of all items, we have gained an understanding of the statement. We should feel comfortable with it at this point.

The next step is to fit the statement into the context of the request. If the request is for renewal of a credit line, then our analysis will bear on the current assets. How good are they, and will they turn over in time to pay off the loan when due?

If the request is for a term loan, either for fixed assets or a permanent increase in a current asset, then the emphasis will be on repayment ability. Will the company's earnings carry its payments? Earnings could be the weakest point of this particular company.

Add the answers to these questions to your knowledge of the company, its management, and past records, and you are ready to conduct a realistic interview and to render an informed decision.

Exercise 3

Here we will review a complete statement and then compare our opinion with a composite of those expressed by other analysts. This statement was prepared by a public accountant. Keep in mind that not all statements prepared by CPAs are good. Likewise, not all non-CPA statements are bad. This particular one was prepared by an accountant whom the bank has known for a number of years. He is considered to be capable and honest and has been used by a number of the bank's old line customers for years.

J. WALTER JONES AND HAROLD D. SMITH

Combined Balance Sheet as of August 31, 19X4

X. JOHN BEANCOUNTER

PUBLIC ACCOUNTANT - TAX ACCOUNTANT

69 Credit Drive

Debittown, Pennsylvania

X. JOHN BEANCOUNTER

PUBLIC ACCOUNTANT - TAX ACCOUNTANT

69 Credit Drive
Debittown, Pennsylvania

September 19, 19X4

Messrs. J. Walter Jones and Harold P. Smith
R. D. #1
Debbittown, Pennsylvania

Gentlemen:

In accordance with your request, I have prepared without
audit from figures supplied by you, Combined Balance Sheet of J.
Walter Jones and Harold P. Smith.

Figures shown in the Balance Sheet reflect combined
individual Assets and Liabilities of J. Walter Jones and Harold
P. Smith, as well as their joint Assets and Liabilities.

Respectfully submitted,

X. John Beancounter

X. John Beancounter

XJB/lg

J. WALTER JONES AND HAROLD D. SMITH

R. D. #1

Debittown, Pennsylvania

Combined Balance Sheet as of August 31, 19X4

ASSETS

Current Assets

Cash on Hand and In Bank	$ 2,800.00	
Accounts Receivable	3,500.00	
Inventory - Materials & Supplies (Estimated)	9,000.00	
Two Homes in Process of Construction		
Debittown, Pa. (Estimated value on completion)	36,000.00	
Surrender Value - Life Insurance ($5,000.00 Paid Up		
Nat'l. Service Life - Estimated Value)	2,500.00	
Total Current Assets		53,800.00

Fixed Assets

*Machinery & Equipment, Tools, Office Equipment	$ 6,400.00	
John Deere 450 Loader	28,000.00	
1969 Dodge 5 Ton Rack Body	3,500.00	
1972 Dodge Van	2,000.00	
1973 Ford Auto	2,800.00	
1973 Dodge Charger	3,000.00	
1968 Buick Auto	750.00	
1966 Buick Auto	200.00	
Pleasure Boat	1,000.00	
Land & Buildings Business Site - Route 781	34,000.00	
Residence - Duplex Dwelling - Debit Lake, Pa.	28,000.00	
Two Family Dwelling - Vacationville, Fla.	45,000.00	
Building Lot - Debittown, Pa.	3,000.00	
Frame Dwelling - Debit Lake, Pa.	25,000.00	
20 Building Lots - Calm Boro, Pa. @ $5,000.00 each	100,000.00	
28 Acres Land @ $6,000.00 per acre	168,000.00	
Total Fixed Assets		450,650.00

TOTAL ASSETS $504,450.00

*All Fixed Assets are listed at Appraised Value

Subject to comment in letter herewith.

<u>LIABILITIES</u>

<u>Current Liabilities</u>

Accounts Payable	$ 3,075.00
Notes Payable - Easy Credit Bank - Vehicles	3,800.00
Notes Payable - Quick Deal Bank - Construction Loan	4,500.00
Mortgage Payable - Quick Deal Bank (Duplex - Debit Lake, Pa.)	2,172.00
Mortgage Payable - First Fed. Bank - Vacationville (Dwell.)	
Far Away County	2,664.00
Mortgage Payable - Business Site - Route 781	1,980.00
Mortgage Payable - Quick Deal Bank (Dwell. Debit Lake, Pa.)	912.00
Notes Payable - John Deere Financing (450 Loader)	6,471.00
Total Current Liabilities	$ 25,574.00

<u>Long Term Liabilities</u>

Mortgage Payable - Quick Deal Bank (Duplex - Debit Lake)	13,636.00
Mortgage Payable - First Fed. Faraway County (Dwelling)	25,336.00
Mortgage Payable - Business Site - Route 781	11,018.22
Mortgage Payable - Quick Deal Bank (Dwelling - Debit Lake)	3,250.65
Notes Payable - Mary Smith	6,000.00
Notes Payable - John Deere Financing	10,529.00
Total Long Term Liabilities	69,769.87

<u>Capital</u>

J. Walter Jones and Harold D. Smith, Capital	409,106.13
TOTAL LIABILITIES AND CAPITAL	$504,450.00

Notes and Mortgages Payable at the following Banks are broken down between
Current and Long Term Portion:
  Quick Deal Bank, First Federal - Far Away County - John Deere - Business Site 781
Current Portions appear as Current Liabilities and Long Term Portions appear under
Long Term Liabilities

Subject to comment in letter herewith.

Comments

Experienced lending officers have seen many statements. In the beginning of their careers, they were taken in by the official look of many reports. The one on Walter Jones and Harold Smith would have fit into this category. The statement is complete, cover and all, and was prepared by a reputable accountant. He is not a CPA, but many of your clients use him, and you find him to be a tough negotiator and a good tax practitioner. You probably assumed that Beancounter was sending Jones and Smith to you indirectly since you know of no relationship between your bank and them at present.

The statement and the names are, of course, fictitious; but statements like these are not rare. At first glance they appear to be genuine and meaningful. In fact, they are pure "junk." Not only is this statement not in conformity with any rules, it is in complete violation of all the rules. It is more an appraiser's report than an accountant's.

A step-by-step review of the statement will prove this point. At the same time we are reviewing the statement, let's begin to raise some questions about the request even though we really don't know what it is yet.

By this time, you should be getting over the fears that are normal for those who are not comfortable with statements — especially statements delivered in person. We know what makes up a statement. We also know that statements are only blueprints that assist us in going about our interview.

On first glance, your suspicions should be raised by the statement's cover. You are looking at the *combined* balance sheet of two individuals. What is combined? Are Smith and Jones a partnership? Are the assets owned jointly? If Smith and Jones are not partners and if the assets are only personal items, then what about the wives' ownership? (We will talk about combined statements a bit later. They are not abnormal. We saw one in the Example Company case. In that one, we knew the relationship of owners and assets. In this one, we do not.)

Passing the official cover, we find a letter. Even if the chapter on accountants' letters seemed superfluous at the time, it is fully justified now because you know just what the letter says. Perhaps you should glance at the letter again. The key is the scope phrase, "without audit from figures supplied by you." As far as we can tell, nothing was done by the accountant — absolutely nothing beyond an official-looking cover and letter. The statement was not only prepared without audit, but the letter states that very little work was done. This statement is not the same as an unaudited review or compilation statement where a minimum of work is done. By virtue of the fact that the letter speaks only of a balance sheet, we begin to wonder if this statement isn't a *special,* a statement prepared especially for your meeting.

The second paragraph seems to confirm some of our earlier apprehensions. Some of the assets are owned individually and some jointly. The same is true of the liabilities. This question of ownership really should raise all the red warning flags. Go slowly. How can you evaluate an item when you don't know who owns it?

Turning to the end of the statement, we find no footnotes. However, the balance sheet has some jotting on the bottom. On the equity statement a note tells us that certain loans are broken down by current and long-term portion. Fine. We expect as much. On the asset side there is a different note. This note is not expected. In fact, it is *the most important* comment on the entire statement. The assets are stated at their appraised value. This practice is against all the rules. Sure, we as lenders have the right and the responsibility to consider an asset's value at other than its historic cost. But even then, is the appraisal we seek sales value, fair market value, or replacement cost? Under what conditions could the value be realized — bankruptcy, forced liquidation, or in a depressed market?

Who supplied the appraisals in the Jones/Smith statement? A realtor? A firm that specializes in such services? We are limited only to the items in front of us. Management supplied the information for the statement. How accurate is it?

The questions building within us should be reaching staggering proportions by now. Where are the other statements? Real statements? Year-end statements? What about profitability?

When we reach the point of reading the numbers, knowing that they have little value, we find a series of oddities. The company purports to have more than $400,000 of equity. Of this, $268,000 is in unencumbered land. The land is valued on a per lot basis at what appear to be reasonable prices for the area. You would, of course, have to know the area. You find out during the interview that these lots have not even been plotted. There are no sewers, roads, or sidewalks; even worse, according to the statement there are no plans for their completion. In fact, you eventually learn that one of the tracts is owned by one of the wives' fathers who said it would be given to his daughter upon his death. Are Smith and Jones stretching the truth? Of course they are. But your job is to get to the truth. How about some other items? The equipment is listed at a value of $40,000, and only two short-term loans and one long-term loan are outstanding. The loans total $20,000. What is the real equity?

More alarming than anything else is the number of banks involved. And we aren't even their bank. Why are they coming to us? (Only by using the statement as a tool can we see how many banks are involved. If the statement didn't break down the loans, then we would have to do it.) Let's go back to the question of why they are coming to us. What has Smith and Jones' bank told them? Their bank has had years of experience with them on which to base a decision. When they say their banker doesn't understand them and they're sure we will because we are better bankers, are we impressed or suspicious? (This point is perhaps best made in a class specializing in interview techniques.)

With the limited information we have been able to garner we say sorry, but we'll have to pass on this one. The interview has taken nearly two hours and, try as we might, we just cannot see that glimmer of light that will allow us to go further. Smith and Jones have been in business together for four months. They want to buy the land from the father-in-law. The value is there, they tell us, and we could get all the accounts from the people who build homes on it. They need $150,000 to buy the land and about four, or at most five, construction mortgages. They propose to put up the land (which we finance); we are to lend the rest. Before we even discuss it, they promise that the line of credit will be cleaned up each year.

You might say this example is ridiculous. But if someone handed you this statement and you saw the cover, letter, and a $400,000 equity, and you wanted some new accounts at your branch, what would you do? Would you consider a $10,000, ninety-day note, or would you read the statement and get to the truth? If not the latter, then maybe the example isn't singularly ridiculous.

Statements that reflect equity at some form of fair market value can be most helpful. However, the equity should be shown along with the cost or net book value (cost less depreciation).

The personal balance sheet of an individual who operated a corporation but personally owned all of the real estate that his company used is contained in a later chapter (Exhibit 8.2). It shows the real estate value both at historic as well as current value. This statement has a great deal of merit. As a banker, you should take your cue from the way it treats current values. Remember the Jones/Smith statement when you read it.

Exercise 4

Using the following information that has been taken from various financial statements, calculate the ratios listed directly below for each company shown. The correct answers appear on the following page.

Current ratio
Acid ratio
Total debt/working capital
Total debt/net worth
Receivable turnover days
Inventory turnover days
Profit before taxes/net worth
Profit before taxes/total assets

Problem

	Company 1	*Company 2*	*Company 3*	*Company 4*
Cash	$ 15	$ 30	$ 40	$ 65
Accounts receivable	50	60	60	54
Inventory	40	80	70	38
Total current assets	120	200	190	171
Total assets	300	400	500	423
Total current liabilities	100	150	180	87
Total liabilities	200	250	325	193
Net worth	100	150	175	230
Sales	1,000	1,350	1,400	938
Cost of sales	600	850	800	647
Net profit before taxes	50	60	75	57

Solution

	Company 1	Company 2	Company 3	Company 4
Current ratio	120/100 1.20 to 1	200/150 1.33 to 1	190/180 1.06 to 1	171/87 1.97 to 1
Acid ratio	65/100 .65 to 1	90/150 .60 to 1	100/180 .56 to 1	119/87 1.37 to 1
Total debt/working capital*	200/20	250/50	325/10	193/84
Total debt/net worth*	200/100	250/150	325/175	193/230
Accounts receivable turnover	1000/50 20/360 18 days	1350/60 22.5/360 16 days	1400/60 23.3/360 15 days	938/54 17.4/360 21 days
Inventory turnover	600/40 15/360 24 days	850/80 10.6/360 34 days	800/70 11.4/360 32 days	647/38 17.0/360 21 days
Profit/net worth	50/100 50%	60/150 40%	75/175 42.8%	57/230 24.8%
Profit/total assets	50/300 16.6%	60/400 15%	75/500 15%	57/423 13.5%

* Based on your bank's policy, these could also be stated as ratios, e.g., 200/20 would be 10:1.

Exercise 5

Problem

Using either your own bank's spread forms or copies of the sample forms from this chapter, prepare a spread for Example Company, Inc. The statement for this company is on page 63 (Exercise 2).

The following two pages contain a spread prepared by a bank analyst. See if your work compares favorably with his and with the comments that follow.

FIRST EASTERN BANK, N. A.
COMPARISON STATEMENT

000's Omitted

NAME EXAMPLE COMPANY, INC.

	ASSETS Date	12/31/x4				
1	Cash	135				
2	Marketable Securities — C/D's	50				
3	Receivable — Trade (Net)	637				
4						
5	Inventories	725				
6						
7						
8	All Other Current					
9	TOTAL CURRENT ASSETS	1,547				
10	Fixed Assets — Net	579				
11						
12						
13	Investments—in Affiliates	161				
14						
15	All Other Noncurrent (Incl. Prepaid)	146				
16	TOTAL NONCURRENT ASSETS	886				
17	TOTAL ASSETS	2,433				
	LIABILITIES					
18	Notes Payable — Banks	100				
19	Notes Payable — Other					
20						
21	Current Maturities of L. T. Debt	22				
22	Accounts Payable — Trade	443				
23						
24	Interest & Other Accruals	81				
25	Taxes Payable	181				
26						
27						
28	All Other Current					
29	TOTAL CURRENT DEBT	827				
30	Mortgage Payable					
31	Long Term Debt ★	420				
32						
33	All Other Noncurrent—DF Inc.Tx.	91				
34	TOTAL NONCURRENT DEBT	511				
35	TOTAL LIABILITIES	1,338				
36	Capital	526				
37	Retained Earnings	569				
38						
39	NET WORTH	1,095				
40	TOTAL LIABILITIES&NET WORTH	2,433				
41						
42	NET WORKING CAPITAL (9-29)	720				
	RATIOS					
43	Quick	.99				
44	Current	1.87				
45	Total Debt/Working Capital	1,338/720				
46	Total Debt/Net Worth	1,338/1,095				
47	Receivable Turnover Days	57 DAYS				
48	Inventory Turnover Days	92 DAYS				
49	% Profit bef. Taxes/Net Worth	70%				
50	% Profit bef. Taxes/Total Assets	31%				
51						
52	Statement by	PMM				
53	Type of Statement	CERTIFIED				
54	Spread by	LG				
55	Contingent Liabilities	NONE				
56						

FORM 18-1 *Includes Subordinated (non-bank) Debt.

FIRST EASTERN BANK, N. A.

NAME EXAMPLE COMPANY, INC.

OPERATIONS Date	12/31/x4	%		%		%		%		%
101 Net Sales	4,022	100								
102 Cost of Sales	2,829	70								
103 Gross Profit	1,193	29								
104 Operating Expenses	401	10								
105 Net Profit before Depreciation	792	19								
106 Depreciation	51	1								
107 Profit from Operations	741	18								
108 Extraordinary Items										
109 Misc. Income-Inc.Aff.Inc.	20									
110 Profits Before Taxes	761	18								
111 Income Taxes	395	9								
112										
113 NET PROFIT AFTER TAXES	366	9.1								
RECONCILIATION OF NET WORTH										
114 Net Worth — Beginning	1,025									
115 Add: Net Profit After Taxes	366									
116 Sale of Stock	6									
117										
118 Less: Net Loss										
119 Dividend Paid	300									
120 Treasury Stock	2									
121										
122 Net Worth — Ending	1,095									
SOURCE & APPLICATION OF FUNDS										
Source of Funds:										
123 Net Profit	366									
124 Depreciation, Amort., Depletion	57									
125 Increase Long Term Debt	111									
126 Misc. Items	18									
127 Sale of Stock	6									
128 Other Noncurrent Accounts — Net										
129 TOTAL SOURCES	558									
Application of Funds:										
130 Net Loss										
131 Dividends Paid	300									
132 Purchase of Fixed Assets	89									
133 Reduction Long Term Debt	75									
134 Purchase-Treas. Stock	3									
135										
136 Other Noncurrent Accounts — Net										
137 TOTAL APPLICATIONS	466									
138 INC./DEC. OF WORKING CAPITAL	92									
RECONCIL. OF W/C CHANGES										
139 Cash	31									
140 Accounts Receivable	68									
141 Inventory	90									
142 Other	3									
143										
144 Notes Payable	20									
145 Accounts Payable	14									
146 Current Maturities — L.T. Debt	13									
147 Other Accruals	10									
148 Income Tax	43									
149 Inc/Dec W/C (139-143) — (144-148)	92									

COMMENTS: Line 126-Misc. Items Include
    Equity Inc.-Affiliates   [19]
    Deferred Income Tax   37
                             ———
                              18

Comments

The balance sheet spread required no major reclassification. The only change was listing prepaid expenses as noncurrent, based on the liquidity of the respective items. The reasoning behind this change is that prepaids usually include prepaid rent, insurance and so forth, and that these would expire by the time the bank sought to use them. Cash surrender value could likewise be reclassified as current on the basis that it would be available in cash.

Many banks have stopped making any adjustments to the statement; the spreads therefore reflect the statement exactly as the CPA originally prepared it. You should follow your bank's policy on this matter.

The fixed assets are listed at net. Because depreciation is listed as one total, there really is no choice. Even in cases where the choice does exist, this particular bank's policy is to consolidate fixed assets and list one net number. Liabilities also are without major change. The consolidation of like items on the spread sheet is the only difference between it and the actual statement.

The spread of the income statement contains a series of combinations and reclassifications. Depreciation (from the footnotes and from the source and application of funds) has been subtracted from the cost of sales and listed separately. The analyst felt that the miscellaneous items were not really extraordinary and all these were combined into one figure.

Finally, the source and application statement contains a number of items that the analyst thought should be listed separately. That was done and details are shown in the comment section.

With the spread now finished it is possible to get an overview of the company in a single glance.

Part III Specialty Items

8   Personal Statements

During the course of a loan review and examination of a company's financial data, it often is necessary to examine the financial strength of a company's key individual. Such examination is especially necessary with small loans to contractors for equipment and small lines of credit to manufacturers. The most common reason is that the principal is going to be required to endorse and guarantee the debt. In other cases, ownership of key assets may be personal and not corporate. To get the overall picture, we have to see the personal statement of the principal.

The rules for analyzing on a personal statement are not at all that different from those for a commercial statement. Your prime objective is still the meaning behind the numbers. That achieved, common sense will take over.

Let's consider a hypothetical situation in order to see how a personal statement is read. We have been asked to consider making available a $35,000 line of credit to a company known as New Jersey Lumber Company. The company has been in existence for three years; it was recommended to us by a prominent local legal firm. The head of the company is John Steele. In the course of the conversation with the applicant, you learn that Steele had a successful management career with a national manufacturer of specialty food items. He functioned as controller-treasurer, and he seemed extremely capable when discussing finances.

He did not bring the company's balance sheet with him for your meeting, but presented you with the statement shown in Exhibit 8.1. The form is

PERSONAL FINANCIAL STATEMENT
(CONFIDENTIAL)

NAME___JOHN STEELE_____   EMPLOYMENT___SELF-EMPLOYED_____

RESIDENCE
ADDRESS____22708 Brace Ave._____   POSITION_____

CITY, STATE, & ZIP____Cypress, CA 90630_____   BUSINESS
                                                 ADDRESS____SAME_____

TO: FIRST MONTGOMERY BANK

OF_____

The following is submitted for the purpose of procuring, establishing and maintaining credit with you in behalf of the undersigned or persons, firms or corporations in whose behalf the undersigned may either severally or jointly with others execute a guaranty in your favor. The undersigned warrants that this financial statement is true and correct and that you may consider this statement as continuing to be true and correct until a written notice of a change is given to you by the undersigned.

Date:___2/5/X3____   Signed:___John Steele___

ASSETS		LIABILITIES & NET WORTH	
1. Cash (on hand and in banks) (see schedule 1)	3,300	13. Notes Payable, Banks, Unsecured (see schedule 1)	
2. U. S. Government and Agency Securities (see schedule 2)		14. Notes Payable, Banks, Secured (see schedule 1)	
3. Marketable Securities (see schedule 2)		15. Notes Payable, Others (see schedule 7)	
4. Non-Marketable Securities (see schedule 3)	65,000	16. Loans Against Life Insurance (see schedule 4)	
5. Notes Receivable—Itemize		17. Accounts and Bills Payable (see schedule 7)	
6. Cash Value—Life Insurance (do not deduct loan) (see schedule 4)	5,000	18. Real Estate Mortgages Payable (see schedule 5)	24,000
7. Real Estate In Own Name (see schedule 5)	55,000	19. Income Taxes Due	
8. Partial Interests in Real Estate—Net Equity Values (see schedule 6)		20. Other Liabilities—Itemize	
9. Automobiles			
10. Furniture and Personal Property	11,500		
11. Other Assets—Itemize			
		21. Total Liabilities	
		22. Net Worth (Line 12 − Line 21)	115,800
12. TOTAL ASSETS	139,800	23. Total Liabilities and Net Worth	139,800

SOURCES OF ANNUAL INCOME			
INCOME FROM ALIMONY, SEPARATE MAINTENANCE OR CHILD SUPPORT NEED NOT BE REVEALED IF YOU DO NOT CHOOSE TO RELY ON IT IN CONNECTION WITH THIS FINANCIAL STATEMENT.		GENERAL INFORMATION	
Salary	30,000	Are you a partner, stockholder, or officer in any other business venture?	NO
Commissions and Bonuses		If so, what	
Dividends			
Real Estate Income			
Other Income—Itemize		Do you have a will?	
TOTAL ANNUAL INCOME		Name of Executor	

CONTINGENT LIABILITIES		CASUALTY INSURANCE COVERAGE	
		Company	Amount
As Endorser, Guarantor or Co-Maker	80,000	Homeowners	
On Leases or Contracts		Automobile	
Legal Claims		Professional Liability	
Income Tax Claims		Are you, or have you ever been defendant in any legal actions, suits, or bankruptcy?	
Other—Itemize		Explain	

(Complete Schedules on Reverse Side)

Exhibit 8.1 Sample Personal Statement

SUPPLEMENTARY SCHEDULES

SCHEDULE 1 — BANKING RELATIONSHIPS

Name of Bank	Location	Checking Balances	Savings Balances	Loan Balance	Terms or Maturity	Collateral	High Credit

SCHEDULE 2 — SECURITIES (GOV'T. AND MARKETABLE)

No. Shares or Face Value	DESCRIPTION	Cost	Market Value	Source of Valuation	Registered in Name of	Is Stock Pledged?

SCHEDULE 3 — NON-MARKETABLE SECURITIES

DESCRIPTION	No. Shares Owned	No. Shares Outstanding	Book Value Per Share	Financial Statement Date	Total Value	Registered in Name of
New Jersey Lumber	1,000	–	–	–	61,000	John Steele
XYZ Corp.	500				4,000	" "

SCHEDULE 4 — LIFE INSURANCE COVERAGE

Face Value	Insurance Co.	Owner of Policy	Name of Beneficiary	Total C.S.V.	Policy Loans	Yearly Premium	Is Policy Assigned?

SCHEDULE 5 — REAL ESTATE IN OWN NAME

Description Including Location or Address	Dimensions or # Acres	Improvements	Cost	Date Acquired	Market Value	Mortgage Balance	Terms or Maturity	Mortgage Holder
Home			–	11/X1	55,000	24,000	19X7	

SCHEDULE 6 — PARTIAL INTERESTS IN REAL ESTATE — NET EQUITY VALUES

Description Including Location or Address	Improvements	% of Ownership	Total Cost	Date Acquired	Market Value	Mortgage Balance	Terms or Maturity	Value of Equity

SCHEDULE 7 — FINANCE COMPANIES, SAVINGS & LOAN ASSOCIATIONS, STORES, AND INDIVIDUALS FROM WHOM CREDIT HAS BEEN OBTAINED.

NAME	ADDRESS	High Credit	Current Balance	Monthly Payments	Collateral

Exhibit 8.1, continued

similar to a standard one used in many banks. Steele suggested that, regardless of the company's numbers, he was sure his personal statement could carry the loan. After reading it, turn to the comments that follow and compare them to your own.

Analysis of the John Steele Statement

As a knowledgeable finance man, Steele should have had his company statements with him. We could be suspicious from the start for this reason alone.

Following our technique for reading statements, we first determined that Steele has $116,000 of net worth, with $31,000 of it in his home and $65,000 in unlisted securities. The other items have little collateral value and we dismiss them. We also note that Steele has $80,000 of contingent liabilities and our first question is, where and why? We must get to the content.

If we are going to place any real value on Steele, we must explore the nature of those items that reflect equity — his home and investments. The second side of the form helps us gain the insight we need.

The majority of Steele's worth comes from his valuation of the stock of his own company. How fair is this value? If you lend to the company, does the stock have any value as a personal asset? Wouldn't that be counting it twice? What value could we attach to the stock in a liquidation? None.

The home has been owned for fourteen months (date acquired to date of statement). $24,000 is a small mortgage for a home valued at $55,000. If the value is real, shouldn't Steele use his equity in the home by increasing his mortgage and making a capital investment in the company? It's a good alternative to taking on a line of credit. In any event, your purpose at this point is to determine what the real equity is. What did Steele pay for the house? His answer is $30,000, and despite a quick follow-up comment about repairs he had made, you feel the equity here has to be limited.

Finally, who owns these assets? The house and miscellaneous furniture belong to Steele and his wife. The stock may be owned by Steele, by his wife, or by both. Shouldn't we see a joint personal statement signed by both husband and wife?

Perhaps the real question which should be raised is whether or not a personal endorsement can ever "carry" a loan. Certainly the endorsement lends moral and even legal support to the loan. But if *repayment* ability is one of our two criteria, we have to ask whether we have it with an endorsement. It's an interesting question.

Exhibit 8.2 is the financial statement of an individual as prepared by a CPA. Although it is unaudited, it contains a wealth of information that can assist you in making your loan decision. Not only is the historic (book) cost shown, but also the current value of assets. As a banker you should delight in the detailed footnotes which both substantiate and define the current values. With this kind of statement to guide you, you can render a valid judgment regarding the worth of the individual.

MR. AND MRS. INDIVIDUAL

DECEMBER 31, 19XX

Exhibit 8.2 **Sample** Financial Statement for an Individual Prepared by a CPA

Exhibit 8.2, continued

Mr. and Mrs. Individual
City, State

The accompanying statement of assets and liabilities of Mr. and Mrs. Individual on the cost basis (Column A) as at December 31, 19   was not audited by us and we do not express an opinion on it, nor do we express an opinion on the amounts shown as estimated values (Column B).

February 18, 19XX

Exhibit 8.2, continued

MR. AND MRS. INDIVIDUAL

STATEMENT OF ASSETS AND LIABILITIES - DECEMBER 31, 19XX
(Unaudited)

	Column A Cost basis	Column B Estimated value basis
Assets:		
Cash	$ 18,485	$ 18,485
Marketable securities (Note 1)	25,444	71,891
Notes receivable	35,033	35,033
Due from ABC Manufacturing Co.	30,000	30,000
Prepaid loan costs	4,374	4,374
Investment properties (Note 2)	261,415	465,000
Partnership interests (Note 3)	50,775	112,000
Investment in Sunshine Paper, Inc. (Note 4)	75,000	127,315
Vested interest in Sunshine Paper, Inc. Pension and Profit Sharing Plans		62,500
Residence	38,500	38,500
Cash value of life insurance less policy loans of $78,914	11,306	11,306
Total assets	550,332	976,404
Liabilities:		
Household bills payable	1,600	1,600
Property taxes payable	12,030	12,030
Mortgage note payable on residence	9,381	9,381
Mortgage notes payable on investment properties	280,846	280,846
Accrued income taxes payable, net of prepayments	6,000	6,000
Accrued income taxes on unrealized asset appreciation (Note 5)		130,000
Contingent liabilities (Note 6)	———	———
Total liabilities	309,857	439,857
Excess of assets over liabilities	$240,475	$536,547

See notes to statement of assets and liabilities

Exhibit 8.2, continued

MR. AND MRS. INDIVIDUAL

NOTES TO STATEMENT OF ASSETS AND LIABILITIES

DECEMBER 31, 19XX
(Unaudited)

1. Marketable securities:

The amounts shown as market value at December 31, 19XX were derived from quoted
closing and/or latest bid prices.

Stock	Shares	Cost	Market value
Main Street Bank of Norfolk	100	$ 2,400	$ 2,650
International Products, Inc.	200	2,000	3,000
American Fabricators Corp.	200	5,360	13,580
United Fashions	500	15,684	52,661
		$25,444	$71,891

2. Investment properties:

	Cost	Accumulated depreciation	Depreciated cost	Estimated value
Warehouse and parking lot:				
Land	$ 15,000		$ 15,000	
Warehouse	90,000	$17,500	72,500	$185,000
Parking lot	9,000	4,475	4,525	
Bank building:				
Land	40,000		40,000	280,000
Building	155,730	26,340	129,390	
	$309,730	$48,315	$261,415	$465,000

Estimated value is based upon independent appraisal made in October 19XX by ABC
Appraisal Co.

3. Partnership interests:

Estimated value is based on an offer by Mr. Individual's partner to purchase his
share of the net assets of the partnerships.

4. Investment in Sunshine Paper, Inc.:

Estimated value of the investment in 25% of the outstanding capital stock of the
corporation is based on unaudited financial statements as at October 31, 19XX.
Management of the Company has reported that no material financial changes have
occurred since that date.

5. Accrued income taxes on unrealized asset appreciation:

Unrealized appreciation in value of assets would, if realized, require payment of
taxes at capital gains rates. Therefore, the accrual has been made on that basis.

6. Contingent liabilities:

Mr. Individual has guaranteed notes payable, bank of Sunshine Paper, Inc. of $20,000.

Exhibit 8.2, continued

9 Special Statements

In the process of making loans, the lending officer is often confronted with odd requests, and also with some rather odd statements. That greasy old bag still appears on a regular basis.

But not all odd statements are odd in the physical sense only. In some industries there are different rules covering statement preparation and format, and this makes for some oddities. An examination of a few types is in order. In unusual situations, special assistance from senior lending officers will be necessary.

Interim Statements

So far we've been talking about year-end statements only — statements that show the position of the company as of the day on which its year closes as well as a statement of its income for the period then ended. Many times we see statements that do not cover a full year. Of what value are they to us? How much credence should be given them?

Like all other statements, they are no more and no less than a tool. In this case, the tool has certain advantages and disadvantages.

Almost all interim statements are unaudited, and so we find ourselves relying more than usual on management and the firm preparing the statements. For example, management will not shut down during the busy season to conduct a full physical inventory; they will estimate their inventory from their perpetual records or by using their historic gross profit margin or standard costs instead. The analyst must then ask, How good is their estimate? It is as good as the estimator. You must judge the statement in this light. We have seen that many of the criteria for a clean statement also must be met in an unaudited statement. Because of our unique position as bankers, we can analyze the numbers regardless of the type of statement. The disadvantage, therefore, is not overwhelming.

What are the advantages of an interim statement? There are many, but primarily an interim statement lets you see the company at other than its low point. If accurate, the interim statement may be a much more realistic portrait of your client than the year-end statement. It shows him at his most vulnerable point, the point at which he is most likely to borrow from you. Another advantage is that it previews his current year. You will see potential weak spots before they fully develop.

An interim statement can be a valuable tool and, in many cases, it should be required. However, interim figures must be compared with previous interim figures for the same time period in order to be meaningful. Even with such comparison they are difficult to evaluate. Many a loan officer has made line increases based on six months of profits and then watched both the profits and his loans disappear in the second half.

Peak-Debt Statements

What about companies that don't supply interim numbers? Are we being less than diligent when we don't find out what they look like at mid-year — especially if mid-year is their most dangerous period? Not really. In our interview we should have discussed the cyclical nature of the company's year, in particular the cycle of the inventory and receivables. We should know what the high and low points are. How can we make an asset conversion loan unless we know the conversion cycles?

Projecting the company's position may be done mechanically or intuitively. Assume your client's year-end statement is the one summarized in Table 9.1. You know from your interview that sometime next summer the inventory and receivables will increase by at least $80,000 and your $50,000 line of credit will be in full use. The suppliers will carry the difference via increased payables as shown in Table 9.1.

The company certainly changed from year-end. The most drastic change

Table 9.1 Sample peak-debt statement

	Year-end	Estimated changes	Peak-debt point
Current assets	$40,000	+$80,000	$120,000
Fixed assets	50,000		50,000
Total assets	$90,000		$170,000
Current liabilities	$20,000	+$50,000	
		+$30,000	$100,000
Long-term liabilities	30,000		30,000
Total liabilities	$50,000		$130,000
Equity	40,000		40,000
Total liabilities & equity	$90,000		$170,000

is the total debt to net worth ratio. What was a reasonable balance of $50,000 to $40,000 at year-end is now $130,000 to $40,000 at the peak point. The current ratio has dropped from 2:1 to 1.2:1.

Does this make your loan a bad one? No. It merely reflects the complexion of the company at a different time, just as interim statements do. Even if you do not perform an elaborate mechanical forecast of peak debt, you should at least weigh the prospects intuitively.

Consolidated and Consolidating Statements

It is quite normal to have a corporate entity made up of a series of separate corporations. The Example Company, whose statements we have reviewed, is one such corporation. The problem the banker faces is making sure that he is lending funds to the company that he thinks he is.

Let's suppose that the XYZ Company has approached you for a short term loan. The highlights of their statement are given in Table 9.2.

The income statement is quite good. It shows sales of $400,000, gross profit of $100,000, and net profit of $15,000 after taxes.

On first review of the balance sheet you find that equity is satisfactory and that it is balanced between current and fixed assets ($80,000 of equity, of which $35,000 is working capital and $45,000 is invested in fixed assets).

Table 9.2 Highlights of XYZ statement

Current assets	$ 80,000
Fixed assets	110,000
Total assets	$190,000
Current liabilities	$ 45,000
Long-term debt	65,000
Total liabilities	$110,000
Equity	80,000
Total liabilities & equity	$190,000

The client stated that on a consolidated basis, this is the best year they have had. Your ears prick up at the word "consolidated." What's been consolidated? You are lending funds to XYZ Company.

After some discussion you find that XYZ Company is a subsidiary of Victory Industries. It's Victory's statement that you have just read. Victory has two subsidiaries: XYZ Company and ABC Sales Company. It seems that the separate sales company and holding company were suggested by the accountant for better cost control and to help the tax situation. That is good business sense.

Do you renew your line (all other things being equal) now that you've seen the statement? Remember, you are lending to XYZ Company, and right now you haven't yet seen their statement. You have seen the *consolidated* statement, and that's for Victory. What you need is a consolidating statement. Table 9.3 gives an example of such a statement.

The income statement must also be seen in its separate parts. As expected, all the profit was in the sales company.

Having both sides of the picture, you determine that the equity you felt your client had in his buildings really is there. Unfortunately, it's not in the company to whom you are lending. Perhaps a simple cross guarantee by ABC Sales would resolve the whole thing, but this is not the place to discuss how to make the loan. What is important is to know what you are reviewing.

The difference between consolidated and consolidating statements lies in the presentation. The consolidated statement lists the total and the consolidating statement shows what was totalled. Even if you are lending to the

Table 9.3   Consolidating statement of Victory Industries (ABC and XYZ subsidiaries)

	XYZ	ABC Sales	Eliminations*	Consolidated
Current assets	$80,000	$ 10,000	$10,000	$ 80,000
Fixed assets	10,000	100,000		110,000
Total assets	$90,000	$110,000	————	$190,000
Current liabilities	$40,000	$ 15,000	$10,000	$ 45,000
Long-term debt	25,000	40,000		65,000
Total liabilities	$65,000	$ 55,000		$110,000
Equity	25,000	55,000		80,000
Total liabilities & equity	$90,000	$110,000		$190,000

* The eliminations are the removal of a bill due from ABC Sales on XYZ Co. and the corresponding liability removed from ABC Sales.

parent, you must isolate and evaluate each individual entity. You need to know where the equity is and where profits are being generated to make a valid decision. You will need to know the legal ownership if for no other reason than to document your loan.

Real Estate Holding Company Statement

The financial statements of a company that invests its funds exclusively in real estate will be different from all others which you will review. Such companies are by their nature highly leveraged; they have no working capital; and they are not profitable except on a cash basis.

When reviewing the statement of such a company, you should know who the tenant is. If the real estate company does not manufacture or sell something, then it is dependent on the successful management and profitability of the operating company, its tenant. This tenant may be an affiliated company. When such is the case, you must review the statement of this related operating company in order to determine its ability to pay the rent necessary for supporting the real estate company.

Profit is measured in many ways. Predepreciation profit usually is referred to as cash profit, depreciation being a noncash expense. You don't make out a check for depreciation as you do for office supplies. You accrue it. It is a book entry. In addition, the book value of fixed assets is critical to all analysts, but as a lending officer you go past this number to its real value. This leads to two things. First, the balance sheet must be considered with your estimate of assets value in mind. Second, if depreciation is not a "real expense" for your analysis, should we look at profit before this item? Should we go even further and look at profit before depreciation and before interest expense? This method would allow us to determine the cash available to meet your mortgage payment. To say it another way, regardless of the paper profit, the company must generate enough cash to meet its payments to the bank.

Real estate firms usually do not find their way to general commercial loan officers, but we are discussing them now for two reasons. First, because they have no other activity, you will see an isolated flow of funds as they pertain to real estate. Remember some of the points outlined above when reviewing a regular statement. Most statements are a combination of a real estate firm and an operating firm. Second, you will see this form of ownership on occasion, and you should be familiar with it. Exercise 6 (page 198) contains a sample statement of a real estate firm. Review it in the context of the keys reviewed here. Go past the numbers and measure cash profitability.

Contractor's Statement

The most difficult kind of loan request that confronts a banker comes from a contractor. All phases of the construction industry have been precarious for lending officers. The Robert Morris Associates' survey on loan losses has shown year after year that loans to contractors constitute one of the major areas of bank charge offs. These are loans to contractors of all sizes. Projections show that this trend will continue.

The cause of this problem cannot be pinpointed. There are many contributing factors, of which poor statement analysis is but one. Not staying within the framework of good financial logic is another.

When a contractor starts a job, he must be certain of his customer's ability to pay. A small contractor would not start a house without verifying the existence of a mortgage. The same holds true for a large contractor starting a new skyscraper. Not only must he confirm the existence of the financing, but the contractor must also establish a payment plan. Such a plan must allow for progress payments to be made based on the degree of completion. For a small remodeling contractor redoing a neighborhood kitchen, such a plan could be half down upon delivery of materials and half upon completion. An office building contract would call for many payments throughout the period of construction. Almost all plans of this nature require an architect's certification of the degree of completion and of the quality of work performed.

Some form of progress payment is standard, regardless of the size of the job. By way of the progress payment, the customer effectively takes responsibility for financing the contractor. In order to do this the customer may require the services of a commercial bank. The bank supplies the funds to the customer (developer), and the developer supplies these funds to the contractor. The relationship between the developer and the bank will be discussed later.

The question now is, *What is the relationship between the banker and the contractor?* Financing the contractor's participation in the project is certainly not the bank's role. That's the developer's job.

What if the contractor cannot manage between construction payments? Should you finance his working capital requirements? The answer has got to be *no,* you cannot honor such a request. A contractor must have sufficient equity to carry through these periods. Unsecured lines of credit in the construction industry are established without basis or logic. It is this type of lending that usually spells disaster.

This is not to say that lending to contractors is wrong. Loans for capital equipment supported by a statement reflecting sound equity and good profitability are reasonable. And although there are circumstances in which short-term financing is required, these cases must be the exceptions and not the rule.

A leading reason for contractor failure, then, is insufficient equity. A man with a trade can become a contractor with very little investment. If he is aggressive, he can grow at a rapid rate. If the equity doesn't increase in proportion to the growth, there is a potential disaster. *Sharing* in opportunities is still the key, especially when a loan is taken in order to acquire capital items on a term basis. Given an adequate down payment, this loan can be profitable for the bank. A loan to a good client who borrows in advance of a job in order to maximize his purchasing power and then retires the loan over the life of the job is workable and profitable.

Another contributing factor to loan failure in the construction industry is the fact that bankers often do not understand contractors' statements. The contractor's statement is different from all others in the way that sales and inventory are recorded.

An illustration should define this difference. Assume a contractor started a job on December 1 and that the job was half completed on December 31 when his year ended. The job is scheduled for full completion by January 31. Is the portion completed a sale during the year just ended and, if so, what is the amount of the sale? Or, is the portion completed really an inventory item which will not become a sale until the time of completion?

Depending on your answer, you have just endorsed either the *percentage-of-completion* or the *completed-contract* basis of accounting for contractors. The difference between them is staggering, and yet it goes completely unnoticed by many analysts.

Let's continue with our example and see how this difference shows up on the income statement. Assume the contractor has a $100,000 contract, and that his cost to complete the job is 80 percent of $100,000. Depending on the method he uses, his income statement will appear as in one of the two columns in Table 9.4.

The completed-contract basis column shows no income because the job has not been completed. The percentage-of-completion basis column shows the estimated sales and corresponding profit.

Where does the contractor's profit come from, sales or performance? Those who advocate the completed-contract basis point to the fact that a contractor cannot give a reasonable estimate of how complete a job is and that, even if he can, he cannot be sure that his profit will be as forecasted. On the other hand, those who favor the percentage-of-completion method will point out that, if a job is profitable, part of the profit was generated in the earlier period.

Table 9.4   Income statement

	Percentage-of-completion basis	Completed-contract basis
Sales (50%)	$50,000	0
Cost of sales (80% × 50,000)	40,000	0
Net profit	$10,000	0

The differences continue to the balance sheet. Based on the completed-contract method the contractor accrued no cost of sales. The expenditures to date become a special type of inventory and they are reflected at their full amount, less any billings made to the client.

If $50,000 is billed for the work completed by December 31, and if the cost to the contractor has been $60,000 to date, has there been a loss? No. More has been spent than has been billed (we are assuming the total cost still will be $80,000) and this means that the contractor has an inventory of $60,000 cost, less billings, or a net inventory of $10,000. This figure appears on the statement not as inventory but simply as itself, and it is listed as a separate item under inventory or under other current assets as:

Cost in excess of billings $10,000

If the billings are $50,000 and the cost expended totals $40,000, then what (assuming that the job will be profitable)? The billings in excess of cost will appear on the statement as a separate, current liability:

Billings in excess of cost $10,000

It is in effect a measurement of unearned income (not profit).

The percentage-of-completion method will yield no such net inventory item. In our example, the company has billed $50,000 by year-end which would be shown as sales. Since the company estimates that the job will cost $80,000 at completion, and the job is 50 percent completed, the company's cost of sales is $40,000 (50 percent of $80,000). The difference, $10,000, is the company's profit as of December 31. The fact that the company actually has expended $60,000 by year-end does not appear on the income statement. Instead, the $20,000 difference between actual cash expended and cost of sales on the income statement usually would be listed as an inventory item (called either work-in-progress or uncompleted work) under current assets on the balance sheet.

What should the practical analyst learn from this discussion? First, remember your role when lending to contractors. Are you taking on the function of the developer? If you are, you have broken the first rule. Second, go past the numbers. Discuss inventory. Does inventory consist of half-finished homes or a half-finished job? If it does, then you must know how much money is available to complete the job (progress payments), and how much it will cost to get the job done. This helps you determine what value the job has at present. You should also find out whether the payments due your client from his customer are being made as they should be. Knowing these facts will allow you to judge how good the assets really are. If the job cannot be completed with the remaining funds, it has got to mean trouble. It also means that the last year's profit was overestimated. This is not a good loan situation.

Finally, remember the context of the request. Working capital advances must come from a source other than the bank, otherwise, you are taking on the role of the developer. If your client is asking for such funds, you should be asking whether his equity is suffering.

You should look into any reasonable request your client makes, of course. If he needs funds because of an undue delay in payments from the developer, for example, then you should find out why there has been a delay. If you make the loan, how and when will you be repaid? Can the contractor repay you when he receives the progress payments, or would repayment come from another source?

Bank As Mortgagee

We have been talking only about commercial loans to contractors. We have not yet discussed the role of the bank as a mortgagee for a construction project.

Here the rules change drastically. The bank is the *source* of the progress payments. The developer will request funds as he needs them, and he will distribute them to the various contractors for work performed. Let's assume that a general home contractor wants to build homes on speculation. He must function as both contractor and developer. There is no ultimate buyer at the moment, but the company seeks to find one either during the construction period or shortly after it. How do we review the contractor's statement? We will focus on two particular points. First, can the contractor support himself on the progress payment schedule he is requesting? Does he have sufficient working capital, or is it going to be a day-to-day struggle to complete the project? Second, does the contractor have sufficient equity to absorb any unforeseen losses? If the home doesn't sell for six months after completion, can the interest payment be met?

For major construction jobs, lending procedures are much more stringent. An outside engineer's appraisal of work done is made prior to each payment. Red tape becomes more abundant. The need for short-term loans also increases. As with the smaller developer, a series of questions must be answered, among them, can the loan, if made, be paid off upon completion of the project? Analysis centers on the estimated cost to completion and on the developer's ability to complete the job with the remaining available funds.

Summary

Loans to contractors are difficult for many reasons: Contractors have a built-in source of funds; their reports vary from others in principles and format used; and their reported profit depends upon an indefinable, or at best uncertain, percentage of completion estimate. Caution is always the byword. Examination of statement contents with an eye to completion of the job is the key.

10   Comparisons

The balance sheet, our isolated picture of a company, has proven to show us a great deal. With it we know the strengths and weaknesses of a particular company *as of* a given date. We have used it as a blueprint, letting it direct our examination to the content of the numbers it lists. The income statement has told us of the gains over the past year, and the extent of the funds being generated and consumed.

However, this picture cannot tell us where the company is going. As with the picture of the airplane, we only know that it is in mid-air. Is it landing? Taking off? How far will it go and when will it get there?

We need a second picture of the company to form a yardstick for the progress being made. In this chapter the means of comparison will be explored.

Internal Comparison

What could be a more appropriate indication of the company's direction than an updated statement? Placing current year-end figures alongside the previous year's year-end figures will tell us the direction the plane is moving. We will know whether it is going higher or faster than before. We will see, in other words, whether the company has made genuine progress or has fallen back.

Exhibit 10.1 is a complete financial statement of Example Company, Inc. for the year ended December 31, 19X5. After reviewing it, turn to the spread sheet in Exhibit 10.2. (If you feel the need for practice, prepare a spread sheet of your own first, and then compare it with the one provided.)

The value of the spread is clearly evident. You can see at one glance all of the data which is contained in many pages of the report.

Upon examination the spread sheet reveals an overall growth in the assets, liabilities and equity of the company. You immediately get the feeling that growth is strong and continuing; however, total equity appears to have grown the least.

Despite the growth, the current ratio has dropped by only .14 (from 1.87 to 1.73). Total debt has increased some $320,000 against a working capital increase of one-third that amount ($100,000). When these figures are expressed as a simple ratio (as they are at many banks) we see that the total debt to net worth has risen from 1.22 to 1.38 — which represents an increase in leverage.

The receivable and inventory turnover days show moderate slowdown of accounts receivable and no change in inventory turnover. Profit remains consistent and high when compared with most companies we see.

The only negative aspect — and one that is only discernible to a very experienced eye — is that although leverage and the company's size, working capital, and equity have all increased, they have not increased to the same degree. The bank loan is higher, and it is financing more of the load than it had in the past. This brings us to the question of whether or not the company is earning and retaining enough profits to sustain growth. Profits were used almost entirely to fund dividends. Problems may be on the horizon.

External Comparison

How does the company you are studying compare with other companies of similar size? Is its net worth adequate? Compared to what? Are profits reasonable? What is the basis for comparing these items and making such judgments?

There are many sources to aid you in making comparisons among companies. Most industries compile certain key ratios and publish them in their trade journals. Some accounting firms publish summaries such as *Laventhol & Horwath on the Lodging and Restaurant Industry*. Some banks do analytical work on a paricular industry and then publish their findings.

EXAMPLE COMPANY, INC.

Consolidated Financial Statements

December 31, 19X5 and 19X4

(With Accountants' Report Thereon)

Exhibit 10.1   Financial Statement of a Corporation (Example Company, Inc.)

Exhibit 10.1, continued

The Board of Directors and
   Stockholders
Example Company, Inc.:

We have examined the consolidated balance sheets of Example Company, Inc. and
subsidiaries as of December 31, 19X5 and 19X4 and the related consolidated
statements of earnings, stockholders' equity and changes in financial position
for the years then ended. Our examinations were made in accordance with
generally accepted auditing standards, and accordingly included such tests of
the accounting records and such other auditing procedures as we considered
necessary in the circumstances.

In our opinion, the aforementioned consolidated financial statements present
fairly the financial position of Example Company, Inc. and subsidiaries at
December 31, 19X5 and 19X4 and the results of their operations and the changes
in their financial position for the years then ended, in conformity with
generally accepted accounting principles applied on a consistent basis.

February 5, 19X6

Exhibit 10.1, continued

```
                    EXAMPLE COMPANY, INC.
                     AND SUBSIDIARIES

                  Consolidated Balance Sheets

                  December 31, 19X5 and 19X4
```

Assets	19X5	19X4
Current assets:		
Cash	$ 207,167	134,509
Marketable securities, at cost, which approximates market	50,000	50,000
Trade accounts and notes receivable, less allowance for doubtful receivables of $25,000 in 19X5 and $22,500 in 19X4	889,967	637,205
Inventories:		
Finished goods	271,785	265,335
Work in process	213,657	192,479
Raw materials and supplies	336,177	267,298
Total inventories	821,619	725,112
Prepaid expenses	47,313	57,843
Total current assets	2,016,066	1,604,669
Investments in affiliated companies (note 2)	185,960	161,181
Property, plant and equipment, at cost (notes 3 and 4)	755,325	743,756
Less accumulated depreciation and amortization	198,449	165,043
Net property, plant and equipment	556,876	578,713
Other assets, at cost, less applicable amortization	81,602	88,202
	$ 2,840,504	2,432,765

See accompanying notes to consolidated financial statements.

Exhibit 10.1, continued

EXAMPLE COMPANY, INC.
AND SUBSIDIARIES

Consolidated Balance Sheets

December 31, 19X5 and 19X4

Liabilities and Stockholders' Equity	19X5	19X4
Current liabilities:		
Notes payable to banks	$ 400,000	100,000
Current installments of long-term debt (note 4)	43,778	21,562
Accounts payable	386,037	443,501
Accrued expenses	91,550	81,020
Income taxes	217,751	181,251
Total current liabilities	1,139,116	827,334
Deferred income taxes (note 5)	125,000	91,000
Long-term debt, excluding current installments (note 4)	386,216	419,794
Stockholders' equity (notes 4 and 6):		
$5 cumulative preferred stock of $100 par value, redeemable at $105 plus accrued dividends; liquidation value at par. Authorized 3,000 shares; issued 2,700 shares in 19X5 and 2,150 in 19X4	270,000	215,000
Common stock of $1 par value. Authorized 300,000 shares; issued 145,000 shares in 19X5 and 143,090 in 19X4	145,000	143,090
Additional paid-in capital	205,717	177,297
Retained earnings	584,455	569,250
	1,205,172	1,104,637
Less cost of common shares in treasury - 860 shares in 19X5 and 640 in 19X4	15,000	10,000
Total stockholders' equity	1,190,172	1,094,637
Commitments and contingent liability (notes 9, 11 and 12)		
	$ 2,840,504	2,432,765

See accompanying notes to consolidated financial statements.

Exhibit 10.1, continued

EXAMPLE COMPANY, INC.
AND SUBSIDIARIES

Consolidated Statements of Earnings

Years ended December 31, 19X5 and 19X4

	19X5	19X4
Net sales	$ 4,561,636	4,022,127
Cost of sales	3,222,285	2,879,719
Gross profit	1,339,351	1,142,408
Selling, general and administrative expenses	497,853	400,666
Operating income	841,498	741,742
Other income (deductions):		
Equity in earnings of affiliates (note 2)	24,773	19,134
Gain on sale of equipment	10,140	-
Miscellaneous	9,342	28,214
Interest expense	(28,348)	(27,690)
	15,907	19,658
Earnings before income taxes and extraordinary item	857,405	761,400
Income taxes (note 5):		
Current	412,000	358,000
Deferred	34,000	37,000
	446,000	395,000
Earnings before extraordinary item	411,405	366,400
Extraordinary item - loss on destruction of plant and equipment, net of income tax benefit of $33,922 (note 7)	36,740	-
Net earnings	$ 374,665	366,400
Earnings per common share and common share equivalent (note 8):		
Earnings before extraordinary item	$ 2.69	2.42
Extraordinary item	(.25)	-
Net earnings	$ 2.44	2.42
Earnings per common share - assuming full dilution (note 8):		
Earnings before extraordinary item	$ 2.54	2.28
Extraordinary item	(.23)	-
Net earnings	$ 2.31	2.28

See accompanying notes to consolidated financial statements.

Exhibit 10.1, continued

EXAMPLE COMPANY, INC.
AND SUBSIDIARIES

Consolidated Statements of Stockholders' Equity

Years ended December 31, 19X5 and 19X4

	$5 cumulative preferred stock	Common stock	Additional paid-in capital	Retained earnings	Treasury stock	Total stockholders' equity (notes 4 and 6)
Balance at December 31, 19X3	$ 215,000	142,580	171,687	502,725	(7,500)	1,024,492
Shares issued in connection with employee stock option plan, 5,100 shares	-	510	5,610	-	-	6,120
Net earnings	-	-	-	366,400	-	366,400
Dividends declared:						
Preferred, $5 per share	-	-	-	(10,750)	-	(10,750)
Common, $2.03 per share	-	-	-	(289,125)	-	(289,125)
Acquisition of 1,400 common shares	-	-	-	-	(2,500)	(2,500)
Balance at December 31, 19X4	215,000	143,090	177,297	569,250	(10,000)	1,094,637
Shares issued in connection with:						
Sale of preferred stock, 550 shares	55,000	-	-	-	-	55,000
Conversion of debentures, 1,100 shares	-	1,100	18,700	-	-	19,800
Employee stock option plan, 810 shares	-	810	9,720	-	-	10,530
Net earnings	-	-	-	374,665	-	374,665
Dividends declared:						
Preferred, $5 per share	-	-	-	(13,500)	-	(13,500)
Common, $2.40 per share	-	-	-	(345,960)	-	(345,960)
Acquisition of 220 common shares	-	-	-	-	(5,000)	(5,000)
Balance at December 31, 19X5	$ 270,000	145,000	205,717	584,455	(15,000)	1,190,172

See accompanying notes to consolidated financial statements.

Exhibit 10.1, continued

EXAMPLE COMPANY, INC.
AND SUBSIDIARIES

Consolidated Statements of Changes in Financial Position

Years ended December 31, 19X5 and 19X4

	19X5	19X4
Sources of working capital:		
Earnings before extraordinary item	$ 411,405	366,400
Items which do not use (provide) working capital:		
Depreciation and amortization of plant and equipment	53,465	51,050
Other amortization	6,600	6,440
Equity in earnings of affiliates	(24,773)	(19,135)
Provision for deferred income taxes	34,000	37,000
Gain on sale of equipment	(10,140)	–
Working capital provided by operations, exclusive of extraordinary item	470,557	441,755
Extraordinary item	(36,740)	–
Item which does not use working capital – cost of plant and equipment destroyed, less accumulated depreciation	70,660	–
Working capital provided by extraordinary item – tax benefit	33,920	–
Proceeds from sale of preferred stock	55,000	–
Conversion of debentures to common stock	19,800	–
Proceeds from exercise of employee stock options	10,530	6,120
Proceeds from sale of equipment	21,035	–
Proceeds from long-term borrowings	160,000	110,500
	$ 770,842	558,375
Uses of working capital:		
Dividends	$ 359,460	299,875
Additions to plant and equipment	113,189	89,252
Current installments, repayment and conversion of long-term debt	193,578	75,062
Purchase of treasury stock	5,000	2,500
Increase in working capital	99,615	91,686
	$ 770,842	558,375

(Continued)

Exhibit 10.1, continued

EXAMPLE COMPANY, INC.
AND SUBSIDIARIES

Consolidated Statements of
Changes in Financial Position, Continued

	19X5	19X4
Changes in components of working capital:		
Increase (decrease) in current assets:		
Cash	$ 72,658	30,542
Receivables	252,762	67,521
Inventories	96,507	90,189
Prepaid expenses	(10,530)	2,570
	411,397	190,822
Increase (decrease) in current liabilities:		
Notes payable to banks	300,000	20,000
Current installments of long-term debt	22,216	12,572
Accounts payable	(57,464)	13,824
Accrued expenses	10,530	9,740
Income taxes	36,500	43,000
	311,782	99,136
Increase in working capital	$ 99,615	91,686

See accompanying notes to consolidated financial statements.

Exhibit 10.1, continued

EXAMPLE COMPANY, INC.
AND SUBSIDIARIES

Notes to Consolidated Financial Statements

December 31, 19X5 and 19X4

(1) Summary of Significant Accounting Policies

Principles of Consolidation

The consolidated financial statements include the accounts of the Company and its two wholly owned subsidiaries. All significant intercompany balances and transactions have been eliminated in consolidation.

Investments in Affiliated Companies

Investments in the common stock of two affiliated companies are stated at cost plus the Company's share of undistributed earnings since acquisition.

Inventories

Inventories are stated at the lower of cost (first-in, first-out) or market (net realizable value).

Depreciation

Depreciation of plant and equipment is provided over the estimated useful lives of the respective assets on the straight-line basis. Leasehold improvements are amortized on a straight-line basis over the terms of the respective leases.

Income Taxes

Deferred taxes are provided for all items included in the statements of earnings regardless of when such items are reported for tax purposes. Such deferred taxes arise principally from using accelerated depreciation methods for tax purposes and the straight-line basis for financial state- ment purposes and from providing, for financial statement purposes, for income taxes on the Company's share of the undistributed earnings of affiliated companies as if such earnings were remitted to the Company as a dividend during the year. Investment credits are recorded as a reduc- tion of the provision for Federal income taxes in the year realized.

Pension Plans

Pension expense includes amortization of prior service costs over periods of 25 years. The Company's policy is to fund pension costs which are composed of normal costs and amortization of prior service costs.

Exhibit 10.1, continued

EXAMPLE COMPANY, INC.
AND SUBSIDIARIES

Notes to Consolidated Financial Statements, Continued

(2) Investments in Affiliated Companies

Investments in affiliated companies are represented by 34% of the common
stock of ABC Company and 37% of the common stock of XYZ, Inc. Summary
combined information for the investees follows:

	Dec.31	
	19X5	19X4
Current assets	$ 649,762	571,673
Current liabilities	436,250	415,359
Working capital	213,512	156,314
Property, plant and equipment, net	411,427	431,941
Other assets	6,741	7,263
Long-term debt	(195,750)	(231,750)
Stockholders' equity	$ 435,930	363,768
Represented by:		
Invested capital	$ 303,840	303,840
Retained earnings	132,090	59,928
	$ 435,930	363,768
Sales	$ 1,346,150	1,221,462
Net earnings	$ 72,162	56,092

(3) Property, Plant and Equipment

A summary of property, plant and equipment follows:

	Cost at Dec. 31	
	19X5	19X4
Land	$ 30,000	30,000
Buildings	111,331	99,325
Machinery and equipment	520,995	522,431
Furniture and fixtures	19,999	19,000
Leasehold improvements	73,000	73,000
	$ 755,325	743,756

Exhibit 10.1, continued

EXAMPLE COMPANY, INC.
AND SUBSIDIARIES

Notes to Consolidated Financial Statements, Continued

(4) Long-term Debt

A summary of long-term debt follows:

	Dec. 31	
	19X5	19X4
8% subordinated debentures due December 31, 1984, retired at face value in 1975	$ –	130,000
7-1/2% unsecured notes payable to bank, due in quarterly installments of $10,000, beginning January 1, 19X6	160,000	–
7% mortgage notes payable, due in monthly installments of $370, including interest, through September 30, 19XX; secured by real property with depreciated cost of $52,800	39,992	41,293
Obligation under long-term equipment leases, due in quarterly installments of $1,350, including imputed interest of 11%, through June 30, 19XX, secured by equipment with depreciated cost of $62,600	50,002	52,263
5% subordinated debentures due January 1, 19X5	–	18,000
9-1/2% convertible subordinated debentures dated July 19X9, due 19XX, with annual payments beginning in 19XX	180,000	199,800
Total long-term debt	429,994	441,356
Less current installments of long-term debt	43,778	21,562
Long-term debt, excluding current installments	$ 386,216	419,794

The agreement underlying the 7-1/2% notes contains restrictions as to maintenance of working capital and payment of cash dividends. The Company is in compliance with such restrictive covenants. Retained earnings free of restriction approximate $250,000 at December 31, 19X5 and $230,000 at December 31, 19X4.

The 9-1/2% convertible subordinated debentures are convertible into 10,000 shares of common stock at $18 per share until July 19X9.

Exhibit 10.1, continued

EXAMPLE COMPANY, INC.
AND SUBSIDIARIES

Notes to Consolidated Financial Statements, Continued

(5) Income Taxes

Income tax expense amounted to $446,000 for 19X5 (an effective rate of 52%) and $395,000 for 19X4 (an effective rate of 51.9%). The actual tax expense for both 19X5 and 19X4 differs from the "expected" tax expense for those years (computed by applying the U.S. Federal corporate tax rate of 48% to earnings before income taxes and extraordinary item) as follows:

	19X5	19X4
Computed "expected" tax expense (48% of earnings before income taxes and extraordinary item)	$ 411,555	365,472
Equity in earnings of affiliates treated as dividends utilizing dividends - received deduction	(10,107)	(7,807)
Investment tax credits	(9,794)	(9,689)
State and local taxes (net of Federal income tax benefit)	55,333	48,001
Other	(987)	(977)
	$ 446,000	395,000

Depreciation of certain plant and equipment is computed using an accelerated method for tax purposes and the straight-line method for financial reporting purposes. The excess of tax depreciation over financial statement depreciation for 19X5 and 19X4 was $58,277 and $64,994, respectively. Deferred income tax expense for 19X5 and 19X4 resulted from timing differences attributable principally to depreciation and the Company's share of undistributed earnings of affiliated companies.

Components of income tax expense are as follows:

	Current	Deferred	Total
19X5:			
Federal	$ 313,751	25,840	339,591
State and local	98,249	8,160	106,409
	$ 412,000	34,000	446,000
19X4:			
Federal	$ 274,201	28,490	302,691
State and local	83,799	8,510	92,309
	$ 358,000	37,000	395,000

Exhibit 10.1, continued

EXAMPLE COMPANY, INC.
AND SUBSIDIARIES

Notes to Consolidated Financial Statements, Continued

(6) Employee Stock Options

Since 1965, stock options have been granted to officers and employees at
prices equal to market values at the grant dates. A summary of 19X5 and
19X4 transactions follows:

	19X5		19X4	
	Number of shares	Exercise prices	Number of shares	Exercise prices
Outstanding at beginning of year	17,635	$ 12-21	18,007	$ 12-12
Granted	720	20	600	19
	18,355		18,607	
Exercised	810	12-16	510	12
Cancelled or expired	565	12	462	12
	1,375		972	
Outstanding at end of year	16,980	12-21	17,635	12-21

Options are exercisable upon issuance from the grant dates. At December 31, 1975, 75,000 shares were reserved for granting of additional
options.

(7) Extraordinary Item

On March 19, 19X5, an earthquake struck the Company's plant in Lawrence,
Massachusetts. Cost of plant and equipment destroyed was $80,694; related
accumulated depreciation was $10,034. The Company recognized the loss
arising from the destruction of this facility as an extraordinary item of
$70,660, less related Federal income tax benefit of $33,920. The loss is
not deductible for state income taxes.

(8) Earnings per Common Share

Earnings per common share and common share equivalent are based on the
weighted average number of shares outstanding and equivalent shares from
dilutive stock options; net earnings are reduced for preferred dividend
requirements. Earnings per common share, assuming full dilution, are
computed by assuming the conversion of all debentures at the beginning of
the year.

Exhibit 10.1, continued

EXAMPLE COMPANY, INC.
AND SUBSIDIARIES

Notes to Consolidated Financial Statements, Continued

(9) Pension Plans

The Company and its subsidiaries have noncontributory pension plans
covering substantially all employees. Total pension expense was $39,800
in 19X5 and $36,600 in 19X4. The actuarially computed value of vested
benefits under the plans exceeded pension fund assets by $220,000 at
December 31, 19X5 and $230,000 at December 31, 19X4.

(10) Research and Development Costs

Research and development costs are included in expense when incurred.
Total research and development expense was $29,544 in 19X5 and $19,588
in 19X4.

(11) Commitments

The Company and its subsidiaries occupy certain manufacturing facilities
and sales offices and use certain equipment under operating lease arrangements. Rent expense amounted to approximately $474,000 in 19X5 and
$475,000 in 19X4.

A summary of lease commitments follows:

Year ending December 31	Total commitment
19X6	$ 47,000
19X7	45,000
19X8	40,000
19X9	39,500
19X0	37,500
19X1–19X5	90,000

All leases expire prior to 19X6. Real estate taxes, insurance and
maintenance expenses are obligations of the Company. It is expected that
in the normal course of business, leases that expire will be renewed or
replaced by leases on other properties; thus, it is anticipated that
future minimum lease commitments will not be less than the amounts shown
for 19X6.

Exhibit 10.1, continued

EXAMPLE COMPANY, INC.
AND SUBSIDIARIES

Notes to Consolidated Financial Statements, Continued

(11) Commitments, Continued

	Interest rate used in present value computation		Present value of lease commitment at Dec.31	
	Range	Weighted average	19X5	19X4
Real property	5-8.5%	6.9%	$ 135,000	125,000
Equipment	7-9	7.8	30,000	28,000
			$ 165,000	153,000

(12) Contingent Liability

The Company is defendant in a $2,500,000 suit alleging infringement of patents. Legal counsel for the Company is of the opinion that the plaintiff's claim is without merit and that the Company will prevail in defending the suit.

Exhibit 10.1, continued

FIRST EASTERN BANK, N. A.
COMPARISON STATEMENT

000's Omitted

NAME EXAMPLE COMPANY, INC.

	ASSETS Date	12/31/x4	12/31/x5			
1	Cash	135	207			
2	Marketable Securities — C/D's	50	50			
3	Receivable — Trade (Net)	637	890			
4						
5	Inventories	725	822			
6						
7						
8	All Other Current					
9	TOTAL CURRENT ASSETS	1,547	1,969			
10	Fixed Assets — Net	579	557			
11						
12						
13	Investments-in Affiliates	161	186			
14						
15	All Other Noncurrent (Incl. Prepaid)	146	129			
16	TOTAL NONCURRENT ASSETS	886	872			
17	TOTAL ASSETS	2,433	2,841			
	LIABILITIES					
18	Notes Payable — Banks	100	400			
19	Notes Payable — Other					
20						
21	Current Maturities of L. T. Debt	22	44			
22	Accounts Payable — Trade	443	386			
23						
24	Interest & Other Accruals	81	92			
25	Taxes Payable	181	218			
26						
27						
28	All Other Current					
29	TOTAL CURRENT DEBT	827	1,140			
30	Mortgage Payable					
31	Long Term Debt *	420	386			
32						
33	All Other Noncurrent —DF Inc.Tx.	91	125			
34	TOTAL NONCURRENT DEBT	511	511			
35	TOTAL LIABILITIES	1,338	1,651			
36	Capital	526	606			
37	Retained Earnings	569	584			
38						
39	NET WORTH	1,095	1,190			
40	TOTAL LIABILITIES&NET WORTH	2,433	2,841			
41						
42	NET WORKING CAPITAL (9-29)	720	829			
	RATIOS					
43	Quick	.99	1.01			
44	Current	1.87	1.73			
45	Total Debt/Working Capital	1,338/720	1,651/829			
46	Total Debt/Net Worth	1,338/1,095	1,651/1,190			
47	Receivable Turnover Days	57 DAYS	65 DAYS			
48	Inventory Turnover Days	92 DAYS	93 DAYS			
49	% Profit bef. Taxes/Net Worth	70%	69%			
50	% Profit bef. Taxes/Total Assets	31%	29%			
51						
52	Statement by	PMM	PMM			
53	Type of Statement	CERTIFIED	CERTIFIED			
54	Spread by	LG	DO			
55	Contingent Liabilities	NONE	NONE			
56						

FORM 18-1 *Includes Subordinated (non-bank) Debt.

Exhibit 10.2 Sample Spread Sheet (Example Company, Inc.)

FIRST EASTERN BANK, N. A.

NAME   EXAMPLE COMPANY, INC.

OPERATIONS Date	12/31/x4	%	12/31/x5	%		%		%		%
101 Net Sales	4,022	100	4,562	100						
102 Cost of Sales	2,829	70	3,169	69						
103 Gross Profit	1,193	29	1,393	30						
104 Operating Expenses	401	10	498	10						
105 Net Profit before Depreciation	792	19	895	20						
106 Depreciation	51	1	53	1						
107 Profit from Operations	741	18	842	19						
108 Extraordinary Items-Net of Tax			[37]	1						
109 Misc. Income-Inc.Aff. Inc.	20		16							
110 Profits Before Taxes	761	18	821	18						
111 Income Taxes	395	9	446	10						
112										
113 NET PROFIT AFTER TAXES	366	9.1	375	8.2						
RECONCILIATION OF NET WORTH										
114 Net Worth — Beginning	1,025		1,095							
115 Add: Net Profit After Taxes	366		375							
116 Sale of Stock	6		85							
117										
118 Less: Net Loss										
119 Dividend Paid	300		360							
120 Treasury Stock	2		5							
121										
122 Net Worth — Ending	1,095		1,190							
SOURCE & APPLICATION OF FUNDS										
Source of Funds:										
123 Net Profit	366		411							
124 Depreciation, Amort., Depletion	57		60							
125 Increase Long Term Debt	111		160							
126 Misc. Items	18		9							
127 Sale of Stock	6		85							
128 Other Noncurrent Accounts — Net			46							
129 TOTAL SOURCES	558		771							
Application of Funds:										
130 Net Loss										
131 Dividends Paid	300		360							
132 Purchase of Fixed Assets	89		113							
133 Reduction Long Term Debt	75		193							
134 Purchase-Treas. Stock	3		5							
135										
136 Other Noncurrent Accounts — Net										
137 TOTAL APPLICATIONS	466		671							
138 INC./DEC. OF WORKING CAPITAL	92		100							
RECONCIL. OF W/C CHANGES										
139 Cash	31		73							
140 Accounts Receivable	68		253							
141 Inventory	90		97							
142 Other	3		[11]							
143										
144 Notes Payable	20		300							
145 Accounts Payable	14		[58]							
146 Current Maturities — L.T. Debt	13		22							
147 Other Accruals	10		11							
148 Income Tax	43		37							
149 Inc/Dec W/C (139-143) — (144-148)										

COMMENTS: Line 126-Misc. Items Include

Equity Inc.-Affiliates	[19]	[25]
Deferred Income Tax	37	34
	18	9

Exhibit 10.2, continued

Today, the best source of external comparison figures comes from the Robert Morris Associates. They publish a guide called *Statement Studies*. The study is the result of a survey in which member banks contribute spread sheets on several of their clients' statements. The results are tabulated and released each year to the RMA members. A copy of this survey should be on the desk of every loan officer, if not for his own good then for his clients'. The survey helps to provide a measurement of your clients' competition.

A sample from this survey is presented in Exhibit 10.3. It is for the industry of which Example Company is a part. In the following section we will discuss how to use the information contained in the RMA study sheet for comparison with our client's statement. For ease of use, we have selected a statement study that does not contain figures for firms in the lowest two asset ranges. However, this does not reflect the usual standard of RMA's statement studies, which generally contain full information on firms of all sizes in each industry.

Common-Base Statement

Comparing statements requires using a common base. Therefore, as can be seen on the RMA study sheet, each line-item is expressed as a percentage of the total for that item's category. This gives us a common-base statement which makes comparison among statements possible.

To transform the Example Company's 19X4 figures (Exhibit 10.2) to common-base figures, start by taking the first item on the spread sheet, cash, and divide it by the total for its category, total assets. This yields 5.5 (135/2,433). Divide each of the other current assets by total assets in order to get a common-base figure for each. When you have completed the operation, the common-base figures for the total assets should equal 100 when added together.

Exhibit 10.4 shows all the common-base figures for Example Company along with the RMA survey figures for their industry. It allows us to compare internal figures with each other as well as with external figures.

Reviewing the spread, we observe two major trends. First, for the most part, the balance sheet composition is in line with the RMA standard. That is, equity of Example is 45.0 and 41.9 for the years shown as compared with 45.1 for the standard. Second, the qualitative ratios are not at all comparable. Receivable turnover for the company is 60 percent slower than

MANUFACTURERS - METAL CANS
SIC# 3411

0-250M (1)	250M-1MM (2)	1-10MM (23)	10-50MM (4)	ALL (30)	ASSET SIZE / NUMBER OF STATEMENTS	%	6/30/76-3/31/77 ALL (37)	6/30/77-3/31/78 ALL (29)	6/30/78-3/31/79 ALL (27)	6/30/79-3/31/80 ALL (30)
%	%	%	%	%	**ASSETS**	%	%	%	%	%
		6.0		5.6	Cash & Equivalents		9.2	7.1	7.8	5.6
		27.3		26.6	Accts. & Notes Rec. - Trade(net)		22.6	25.1	27.4	26.6
		27.5		28.2	Inventory		30.1	30.5	26.0	28.2
		3.3		2.6	All Other Current		1.8	1.9	1.4	2.6
		64.1		63.0	Total Current		63.6	64.5	62.7	63.0
		25.7		28.2	Fixed Assets (net)		31.1	30.2	27.3	28.2
		.1		.2	Intangibles (net)		1.0	.4	.3	.2
		10.0		8.5	All Other Non-Current		4.3	4.9	9.8	8.5
		100.0		100.0	Total		100.0	100.0	100.0	100.0
					LIABILITIES					
		11.4		9.3	Notes Payable-Short Term		8.3	7.5	8.1	9.3
		.9		1.2	Cur. Mat.-L/T/D		2.8	2.7	1.5	1.2
		19.6		18.6	Accts. & Notes Payable - Trade		15.2	15.9	18.0	18.6
		8.7		7.9	Accrued Expenses		4.5	5.8	5.6	7.9
		4.8		4.4	All Other Current		4.1	3.1	2.7	4.4
		45.3		41.4	Total Current		35.0	35.0	35.9	41.4
		8.4		12.4	Long Term Debt		16.1	16.5	13.9	12.4
		1.1		1.5	All Other Non-Current		2.3	1.2	1.0	1.5
		45.1		44.7	Net Worth		46.7	47.3	49.1	44.7
		100.0		100.0	Total Liabilities & Net Worth		100.0	100.0	100.0	100.0
					INCOME DATA					
		100.0		100.0	Net Sales		100.0	100.0	100.0	100.0
		77.8		78.2	Cost Of Sales		82.3	79.9	81.8	78.2
		22.2		21.8	Gross Profit		17.7	20.1	18.2	21.8
		11.9		11.7	Operating Expenses		13.8	13.6	11.9	11.7
		10.3		10.2	Operating Profit		3.9	6.5	6.3	10.2
		4.0		3.3	All Other Expenses (net)		2.2	1.3	1.5	3.3
		6.3		6.9	Profit Before Taxes		1.7	5.2	4.8	6.9
					RATIOS					
		2.4		2.4	Current		4.1	3.2	3.5	2.4
		1.7		1.7			2.1	2.0	1.9	1.7
		1.2		1.2			1.2	1.3	1.3	1.2
		1.4		1.4	Quick		2.0	1.5	2.2	1.4
		.8		.8			1.0	1.0	1.2	.8
		.4		.5			.6	.7	.6	.5
		33 10.9	33	10.9	Sales/Receivables		28 13.2	35 10.4	37 9.8	33 10.9
		43 8.5	43	8.5			37 10.0	41 8.9	43 7.7	43 8.5
		51 7.2	51	7.1			51 7.2	51 7.2	58 6.3	51 7.1
		23 16.1	28	13.0	Cost of Sales/Inventory		47 7.7	42 8.7	38 9.7	28 13.0
		50 7.3	59	6.2			76 4.8	74 4.9	61 6.0	59 6.2
		91 4.0	94	3.9			91 4.0	107 3.4	76 4.8	94 3.9
		6.8		6.2	Sales/Working Capital		3.9	4.2	4.6	6.2
		10.5		9.7			6.3	6.1	8.2	9.7
		24.2		25.5			15.0	15.1	14.9	25.5
		25.1		15.2	EBIT/Interest		19.3	24.0	30.1	15.2
		(17) 9.9	(24)	4.9			(26) 6.6	(24) 7.3	(20) 7.5	(24) 4.9
		3.7		3.1			1.9	2.2	1.9	3.1
		21.6		18.8	Cash Flow/Cur. Mat. L/T/D		12.7	9.6	11.2	18.8
		(13) 9.5	(19)	6.0			(17) 3.4	(19) 2.6	(14) 3.8	(19) 6.0
		4.9		4.8			1.8	1.3	2.3	4.8
		.4		.4	Fixed/Worth		.4	.4	.4	.4
		.6		.7			.7	.6	.6	.7
		1.2		1.2			1.4	1.1	.8	1.2
		.4		.7	Debt/Worth		.4	.3	.3	.7
		1.3		1.3			.9	1.2	.9	1.3
		2.7		2.7			3.7	2.6	2.6	2.7
		44.2		44.2	% Profit Before Taxes/Tangible Net Worth		40.3	33.7	39.8	44.2
		(22) 29.7	(29)	28.6			(34) 23.8	(28) 23.0	(26) 26.9	(29) 28.6
		17.8		17.5			13.2	13.6	15.1	17.5
		18.9		17.7	% Profit Before Taxes/Total Assets		18.5	17.4	19.2	17.7
		12.2		11.5			11.9	10.4	13.3	11.5
		8.2		7.7			5.5	4.6	4.3	7.7
		16.1		15.5	Sales/Net Fixed Assets		16.7	.13.3	15.9	15.5
		12.1		10.6			6.8	5.9	7.6	10.6
		5.4		5.4			4.0	4.5	4.0	5.4
		3.2		2.8	Sales/Total Assets		2.7	2.3	2.5	2.8
		2.3		2.2			2.1	1.9	2.1	2.2
		2.0		1.8			1.6	1.4	1.5	1.8
		1.1		1.1	% Depr., Dep., Amort./Sales		1.0	1.2	1.4	1.1
		(21) 1.3	(27)	1.4			(33) 1.8	(27) 2.3	(23) 1.6	(27) 1.4
		1.6		2.5			3.1	3.0	2.7	2.5
				.5	% Lease & Rental Exp/Sales		.8	.6	1.0	.5
			(12)	.9			(12) 1.6	(15) 1.4	(11) 1.4	(12) .9
				1.1			2.7	1.8	2.2	1.1
					% Officers' Comp/Sales		1.6			
							(10) 3.1			
							7.1			
1577M	1846M	222922M	127932M	354277M	Net Sales ($)		416466M	263902M	325086M	354277M
133M	1247M	93143M	63455M	157978M	Total Assets ($)		251647M	150606M	187101M	157978M

©Robert Morris Associates 1980   M = $thousand   MM = $million

Exhibit 10.3   Sample from RMA *Annual Statement Studies*

FIRST EASTERN BANK, N. A.
COMPARISON STATEMENT

000's Omitted

NAME EXAMPLE COMPANY, INC. - COMMON BASE

	ASSETS Date	12/31/x4	12/31/x5		RMA STUDY	
1	Cash	5.5	7.3		6.0	
2	Marketable Securities — C/D's	2.1	1.8			
3	Receivable — Trade (Net)	26.2	31.3		27.3	
4						
5	Inventories	29.8	28.9		27.6	
6						
7						
8	All Other Current					
9	TOTAL CURRENT ASSETS	63.6	69.3		64.2	
10	Fixed Assets — Net	23.8	19.6		25.7	
11						
12						
13	Investments–In Affiliates	6.6	6.6			
14						
15	All Other Noncurrent (Incl. Prepaid)	6.0	4.5		10.1	
16	TOTAL NONCURRENT ASSETS	36.4	30.7		35.8	
17	TOTAL ASSETS	100.0	100.0		100.0	
	LIABILITIES					
18	Notes Payable — Banks	4.1	14.1		11.4	
19	Notes Payable — Other					
20						
21	Current Maturities of L. T. Debt	.9	1.5		.9	
22	Accounts Payable — Trade	18.2	13.6		19.6	
23						
24	Interest & Other Accruals	3.3	3.2		13.5	
25	Taxes Payable	7.5	7.7			
26						
27						
28	All Other Current					
29	TOTAL CURRENT DEBT	34.0	40.1		45.3	
30	Mortgage Payable					
31	Long Term Debt	17.3	13.6		9.6	
32						
33	All Other Noncurrent –Def.Taxes	3.7	4.4			
34	TOTAL NONCURRENT DEBT	21.0	18.0		9.6	
35	TOTAL LIABILITIES	55.0	58.1		54.9	
36	Capital	21.6	21.3			
37	Retained Earnings	23.4	20.6			
38						
39	NET WORTH	45.0	41.9		45.1	
40	TOTAL LIABILITIES&NET WORTH	100.0	100.0		100.0	
41						
42	NET WORKING CAPITAL (9-29)	29.6	29.2		18.9	
	RATIOS					
43	Quick	.99	1.01		.80	
44	Current	1.87	1.73		1.70	
45	Total Debt/Working Capital	1.86	1.99		2.90	
46	Total Debt/Net Worth	1.22	1.39		1.30	
47	Receivable Turnover Days	57 DAYS	65 DAYS		43 DAYS	
48	Inventory Turnover Days	92 DAYS	93 DAYS		49 DAYS	
49	% Profit bef. Taxes/Net Worth	70%	69%		30%	
50	% Profit bef. Taxes/Total Assets	31%	29%		12%	
51						
52	Statement by					
53	Type of Statement					
54	Spread by					
55	Contingent Liabilities					
56						

FORM 18-1

Exhibit 10.4   Sample Common-Base Spread Sheet

FIRST EASTERN BANK, N. A.

NAME EXAMPLE COMPANY, INC. - COMMON BASE

OPERATIONS Date	12/31/x4	%	12/31/x5	%		%	RMA	%		%
101 Net Sales	100.0		100.0				100.0			
102 Cost of Sales	70.3		69.5				77.8			
103 Gross Profit	29.7		30.5				22.2			
104 Operating Expenses	10.0		10.9				11.9			
105 Net Profit before Depreciation	19.7		19.6				11.9			
106 Depreciation	1.3		1.2							
107 Profit from Operations	18.4		18.4				10.3			
108 Extraordinary Items—Net of Tax			[.8]							
109 Misc. Income-Inc.Aff.	.5		.4							
110 Profits Before Taxes	18.9		18.0				6.3			
111 Income Taxes	9.8		9.8							
112										
113 NET PROFIT AFTER TAXES	9.1		8.2							
RECONCILIATION OF NET WORTH										
114 Net Worth — Beginning										
115 Add: Net Profit After Taxes										
116										
117										
118 Less: Net Loss										
119 Dividend Paid										
120										
121										
122 Net Worth — Ending										
SOURCE & APPLICATION OF FUNDS										
Source of Funds:										
123 Net Profit										
124 Depreciation, Amort., Depletion										
125 Increase Long Term Debt										
126										
127										
128 Other Noncurrent Accounts — Net										
129 TOTAL SOURCES										
Application of Funds:										
130 Net Loss										
131 Dividends Paid										
132 Purchase of Fixed Assets										
133 Reduction Long Term Debt										
134										
135										
136 Other Noncurrent Accounts — Net										
137 TOTAL APPLICATIONS										
138 INC./DEC. OF WORKING CAPITAL										
RECONCIL. OF W/C CHANGES										
139 Cash										
140 Accounts Receivable										
141 Inventory										
142 Other										
143										
144 Notes Payable										
145 Accounts Payable										
146 Current Maturities — L.T. Debt										
147 Other										
148										
149 Inc/Dec W/C (139-143) — (144-148)										

COMMENTS:

Exhibit 10.4, continued

the standard and inventory is almost twice as slow. However, the company's profits are twice as high as the industry standard.

Is Example more profitable than similar companies, or is management overtrading on its equity? Is it profitable because of a large inventory? The job of the analyst is to answer these questions, not merely ask them.

Summary

Comparison is a tool of analysis that you will use to the extent that the size and nature of each loan request requires. The present statement always is compared with the previous statement in order to measure progress from year to year. Comparison of a company with external sources is less frequent, but special industry studies are available and they should be used more often. When making external comparisons, keep in mind that no two companies have the same problems and advantages.

Most of our time in making comparisons is spent examining the changes in a company's statements from year to year. We analyze these changes using the change in financial position statement, also known as the source and application of funds statement. This is the key to financial statement analysis, and we will study it in detail in Part IV.

11   Creating a Statement

Up to this point, we have talked about analyzing statements. We have learned that some types of statements are more valuable than others and we have learned that some have different formats from others. We have emphasized the advantage of reading a statement in the context of a loan request and the necessity of going past the numbers to their content.

All this is fine provided our client has a statement. Not every loan request will come from a client who presents his financial picture by means of a statement. Some reasons for not having a statement will be legitimate. The company is new. A fire destroyed the records and the CPA is trying to reconstruct them. Some reasons given just won't do. The books are kept by the brother-in-law who is working two shifts and can't get to them. Even if the brother-in-law says he has the numbers, he really is referring to the back of an envelope.

What should you do when you are told there is no statement? If you inherited the loan from an officer who had the job before you, is such a state of affairs acceptable? The answer is that it is never acceptable for a company to be without a statement.

Your choices when faced with a company that does not have a statement are many. If it is a new loan application, you can turn it down. You might be passing up some excellent business this way, but you have little choice. There is no question that, in the long run, your client must have some sort of control over his costs. No matter how formal or informal they are, you want access to the records that give him that control. If he doesn't know whether he made or lost money last week or on the last job, then you really don't want him as a client.

The first reply to the client who says he has no statement is to ask how he maintains control. Every client has a statement. You sometimes have to remind him of it, however. He has filed a *tax return*. (If no return has been filed, then a violation of the law has occurred and that is reason enough to defer the request).

You can learn from a tax return almost everything you can learn from a regular statement. At times you may have to use all of your skills, but you will get the picture you seek.

Many a client has complied with the lending officer's request for a tax return and then smiled, winked, and said that those figures were just for Uncle Sam. How do you treat such a comment? Putting legal questions aside for the moment, you can ask if the client did all his cheating this year or a little at a time. Suppose a client told you he had $80,000 of ending inventory but that he only reported $60,000. His cost of sales will appear $20,000 higher and his profit $20,000 lower. Did he do all his cheating this year or did he underestimate his inventory last year as well? The point is simply that, even if he does "hedge," the effect is cumulative. Perhaps only $2,000 of profit is hidden in the current year.

Our response has got to be, however, that we can't accept the client's comment about cheating. If he cheats Uncle Sam, won't he cheat us? As a dear friend of mine says, there are three things you cannot almost be: almost dead, almost pregnant, and almost honest.

We will read the tax return as is or defer the request on character. It's that simple.

The next three parts of this chapter contain tax returns for a corporation, a partnership, and a proprietorship. We will review each in detail. Then we will discuss the final alternative, creating a statement.

Form 1120 — U.S. Corporation Income Tax Return

Review the form presented in Exhibit 11.1. It should look familiar. It is a tax return covering the Example Company. We used this company's statement as the sample in Exercises 2 and 5. The Internal Revenue Service

Form **1120**			**U.S. Corporation Income Tax Return**		OMB No. 1545-0123	
Department of the Treasury Internal Revenue Service			For calendar year 1981 or other tax year beginning ...., 1981, ending ...., 19...... ▶For Paperwork Reduction Act Notice, see page 1 of the instructions		**1981**	

Check if a—			Name	D. Employer identification number
A. Consolidated return	☒	Use IRS label. Other-wise please print or type.	EXAMPLE COMPANY, INC.	24-8254551
B. Personal Holding Co.	☐		Number and street	E. Date incorporated
C. Business Code No. (See page 9 of Instructions) 3410			123 Main Street	1/1/73
			City or town, State, and ZIP code Anywhere, Any State	F. Total assets (see Specific Instructions) $2,840,504

Gross Income

1 (a) Gross receipts or sales $ .... (b) Less returns and allowances $ .... Balance ▶	1(c)	4,561,636
2 Cost of goods sold (Schedule A) and/or operations (attach schedule)	2	3,222,285
3 Gross profit (subtract line 2 from line 1(c))	3	1,339,351
4 Dividends (Schedule C)	4	
5 Interest on obligations of the United States and U.S. instrumentalities	5	
6 Other interest	6	
7 Gross rents	7	
8 Gross royalties	8	
9 (a) Capital gain net income (attach separate Schedule D)	9(a)	
(b) Net gain or (loss) from Form 4797, line 11(a), Part II (attach Form 4797) . . .	9(b)	(60,520)
10 Other income (see instructions—~~attach schedule~~) . MISCELLANEOUS INCOME . . .	10	9,342
11 TOTAL income—Add lines 3 through 10	11	1,288,173

Deductions

12 Compensation of officers (Schedule E)	12	50,500
13 (a) Salaries and wages .... 13(b) Less WIN and jobs credit(s) .... Balance ▶	13(c)	293,233
14 Repairs (see instructions)	14	411
15 Bad debts (Schedule F if reserve method is used)	15	
16 Rents	16	
17 Taxes	17	98,249
18 Interest	18	28,348
19 Contributions (not over 5% of line 30 adjusted per instructions)	19	
20 Amortization (attach schedule)	20	6,600
21 Depreciation from Form 4562 (attach Form 4562) ...., less depreciation claimed in Schedule A and elsewhere on return ...., Balance ▶	21	111,742
22 Depletion	22	
23 Advertising	23	18,500
24 Pension, profit-sharing, etc. plans (see instructions)	24	44,600
25 Employee benefit programs (see instructions)	25	
26 Other deductions (attach schedule) . . RESEARCH & DEVELOPMENT.	26	29,544
27 TOTAL deductions—Add lines 12 through 26	27	682,727
28 Taxable income before net operating loss deduction and special deductions (subtract line 27 from line 11) .	28	605,446
29 Less: (a) Net operating loss deduction (see instructions—attach schedule) . 29(a)		
(b) Special deductions (Schedule C) . . . . 29(b)	29	
30 Taxable income (subtract line 29 from line 28)	30	605,446

Tax

31 TOTAL TAX (Schedule J)	31	249,461
32 Credits: (a) Overpayment from 1980 allowed as a credit		
(b) 1981 estimated tax payments 250,000		
(c) Less refund of 1981 estimated tax applied for on Form 4466 . ( ) 250,000		
(d) Tax deposited: Form 7004............ Form 7005 (attach)............... Total ▶		
(e) Credit from regulated investment companies (attach Form 2439)		
(f) Federal tax on special fuels and oils (attach Form 4136 or 4136–T)	32	250,000
33 TAX DUE (subtract line 32 from line 31). See instruction C3 for depositary method of payment . (Check ▶ ☐ if Form 2220 is attached. See instruction D.) ▶ $	33	
34 OVERPAYMENT (subtract line 31 from line 32)	34	
35 Enter amount of line 34 you want: Credited to 1982 estimated tax ▶ .... Refunded ▶	35	539

Please Sign Here

Under penalties of perjury, I declare that I have examined this return, including accompanying schedules and statements, and to the best of my knowledge and belief, it is true, correct, and complete. Declaration of preparer (other than taxpayer) is based on all information of which preparer has any knowledge.

▶ *John Smith*	3/1/82	▶ President
Signature of officer	Date	Title

Paid Preparer's Use Only

Preparer's signature ▶ *B. J. Able*	Date 2/24/82	Check if self-employed ☐	Preparer's social security no.
Firm's name (or yours, if self-employed) and address	Willing & Able Anywhere, Any State	E.I. No. ▶ ZIP code ▶ 11111	23 : 9783434

Exhibit 11.1 Sample U.S. Corporation Income Tax Return (Example Company, Inc.)

Form 1120 (1981) **Schedule A** **Cost of Goods Sold** (See Instructions for Schedule A)   Page **2**

1 Inventory at beginning of year	725,112
2 Merchandise bought for manufacture or sale	1,789,563
3 Salaries and wages	1,529,229
4 Other costs (attach schedule)	
5 Total—Add lines 1 through 4	4,043,904
6 Inventory at end of year	821,619
7 Cost of goods sold—Subtract line 6 from line 5. Enter here and on line 2, page 1	3,222,285

8 (a) Check all methods used for valuing closing inventory: (*i*) ☐ Cost (*ii*) ☒ Lower of cost or market as described in Regulations section 1.471–4 (see instructions) (*iii*) ☐ Writedown of "subnormal" goods as described in Regulations section 1.471–2(c) (see instructions)

(b) Did you use any other method of inventory valuation not described above? . . . . ☐ Yes ☒ No

If "Yes," specify method used and attach explanation ▶ --

(c) Check if the LIFO inventory method was adopted this tax year for any goods (If checked, attach Form 970.) . . . . . ☐

(d) If the LIFO inventory method was used for this tax year, enter percentage (or amounts) of closing inventory computed under LIFO . . . . N/A

(e) If you are engaged in manufacturing, did you value your inventory using the full absorption method (Regulations section 1.471–11)? . . . . ☒ Yes ☐ No

(f) Was there any substantial change in determining quantities, cost, or valuations between opening and closing inventory? . . . ☐ Yes ☒ No
If "Yes," attach explanation.

Schedule C **Dividends and Special Deductions** (See instructions for Schedule C)

	(A) Dividends received	(B) %	(C) Special deductions: multiply (A) × (B)
1 Domestic corporations subject to 85% deduction		85	
2 Certain preferred stock of public utilities		59.13	
3 Foreign corporations subject to 85% deduction		85	
4 Wholly-owned foreign subsidiaries subject to 100% deduction (section 245(b)) . .		100	
5 Total—Add lines 1 through 4. See instructions for limitation			
6 Affiliated groups subject to the 100% deduction (section 243(a)(3))		100	
7 Other dividends from foreign corporations not included in lines 3 and 4 . . .			
8 Income from controlled foreign corporations under subpart F (attach Forms 3646) .			
9 Foreign dividend gross-up (section 78)			
10 DISC or former DISC not included in line 1 (section 246(d))			
11 Other dividends			
12 Deduction for dividends paid on certain preferred stock of public utilities (see instructions)			
13 Total dividends—Add lines 1 through 11. Enter here and on line 4, page 1 ▶			
14 Total deductions—Add lines 5 through 12. Enter here and on line 29(b), page 1 ▶			

Schedule E **Compensation of Officers** (See instruction for line 12)

1. Name of officer	2. Social security number	3. Time devoted to business	Percent of corporation stock owned 4. Common	5. Preferred	6. Amount of compensation	7. Expense account allowances
John Smith	123-45-6789	100%	5		28,000	
John Doe	234-56-7891	100%	3		22,500	

Total compensation of officers—Enter here and on line 12, page 1 . . . .

Schedule F **Bad Debts—Reserve Method** (See instruction for line 15)

1. Year	2. Trade notes and accounts receivable outstanding at end of year	3. Sales on account	Amount added to reserve 4. Current year's provision	5. Recoveries	6. Amount charged against reserve	7. Reserve for bad debts at end of year
1976						
1977						
1978						
1979						
1980						
1981						

Exhibit 11.1, continued

Form 1120 (1981)   Page **3**

Schedule J   Tax Computation (See instructions for Schedule J on pages 7 and 8)

Note: *Fiscal year corporations, see instructions on pages 10 and 11. Omit line 1, complete line 2(a) and, if applicable, line 2(b), and enter on line 3, the amount from line 44, Part III, of the fiscal year worksheet provided on page 11 of the instructions.*

1 Taxable income (line 30, page 1)   605,446

2 (a) Are you a member of a controlled group? . . . . ☐ Yes ☒ No

  (b) If "Yes," see instructions and enter your portion of the $25,000 amount in each taxable income bracket:

    (i) $............................ *(ii)* $............................ *(iii)* $............................ *(iv)* $............................

3 Income tax (see instructions to figure the tax; enter this tax or alternative tax from Schedule D, whichever is less). Check if from Schedule D ▶ ☐   259,255

4 (a) Foreign tax credit (attach Form 1118) . . . .

  (b) Investment credit (attach Form 3468)   9,794

  (c) Work incentive (WIN) credit (attach Form 4874) . . . .

  (d) Jobs credit (attach Form 5884) . . . .

  (e) Other credits (see instructions—attach forms and schedule) . . . . . .

5 Total—Add lines 4(a) through 4(e)   9,794

6 Subtract line 5 from line 3   249,461

7 Personal holding company tax (attach Schedule PH (Form 1120)) . . . .

8 Tax from recomputing prior-year investment credit (attach Form 4255) . . . .

9 Minimum tax on tax preference items (see instructions—attach Form 4626) . . . .

10 Total tax—Add lines 6 through 9. Enter here and on line 31, page 1   249,461

Additional Information (See page 8 of instructions)

	Yes	No
G Did you claim a deduction for expenses connected with:		
(1) Entertainment facility (boat, resort, ranch, etc.)?		X
(2) Living accommodations (except employees on business)? . .		X
(3) Employees attending conventions or meetings outside the North American area? (See section 274(h))		X
(4) Employees' families at conventions or meetings?		X
If "Yes," were any of these conventions or meetings outside the North American area? (See section 274(h)) . . .		
(5) Employee or family vacations not reported on Form W–2? . .		X

H (1) Did you at the end of the tax year own, directly or indirectly, 50% or more of the voting stock of a domestic corporation? (For rules of attribution, see section 267(c).) . . . . .   ☐ X

If "Yes," attach a schedule showing: (a) name, address, and identifying number; (b) percentage owned; (c) taxable income or (loss) (e.g., if a Form 1120: from Form 1120, line 28, page 1) of such corporation for the tax year ending with or within your tax year; (d) highest amount owed by you to such corporation during the year; and (e) highest amount owed to you by such corporation during the year.

(2) Did any individual, partnership, corporation, estate or trust at the end of the tax year own, directly or indirectly, 50% or more of your voting stock? (For rules of attribution, see section 267(c).) If "Yes," complete (a) through (e).   ☐ X

  (a) Attach a schedule showing name, address, and identifying number.

  (b) Enter percentage owned ▶ N/A

  (c) Was the owner of such voting stock a person other than a U.S. person? (See instructions) . . . .

     If "Yes," enter owner's country ▶ N/A

  (d) Enter highest amount owed by you to such owner during the year ▶ N/A

(e) Enter highest amount owed to you by such owner during the year ▶ N/A

(Note: For purposes of H(1) and H(2), "highest amount owed" includes loans and accounts receivable/payable.)

I If you were a member of a controlled group subject to the provisions of section 1561, check the type of relationship:
(1) ☐ parent-subsidiary   (2) ☐ brother-sister
(3) ☐ combination of (1) and (2) (See section 1563.)

J Refer to page 9 of instructions and state the principal:
Business activity   METAL FABRICATION
Product or service   STEEL CONTAINERS

K Were you a U.S. shareholder of any controlled foreign corporation? (See sections 951 and 957.) If "Yes," attach Form 3646 for each such corporation   X

L At any time during the tax year, did you have an interest in or a signature or other authority over a bank account, securities account, or other financial account in a foreign country (see instructions)?   X

M Were you the grantor of, or transferor to, a foreign trust which existed during the current tax year, whether or not you have any beneficial interest in it?   X
If "Yes," you may have to file Forms 3520, 3520-A or 926.

N During this tax year, did you pay dividends (other than stock dividends and distributions in exchange for stock) in excess of your current and accumulated earnings and profits? (See sections 301 and 316)   X
If "Yes," file Form 5452. If this is a consolidated return, answer here for parent corporation and on Form 851, Affiliations Schedule, for each subsidiary.

O During this tax year was any part of your tax accounting records maintained on a computerized system?   X

Exhibit 11.1, continued

Form 1120 (1981)

Page **4**

Schedule L Balance Sheets	Beginning of tax year		End of tax year	
ASSETS	(A)	(B)	(C)	(D)
1 Cash		134,509		207,167
2 Trade notes and accounts receivable	659,705		914,967	
(a) Less allowance for bad debts	22,500	637,205	25,000	889,967
3 Inventories		725,112		821,619
4 Gov't obligations: (a) U.S. and instrumentalities .				
(b) State, subdivisions thereof, etc.				
5 Other current assets (attach schedule) Sched 1 .		107,843		97,313
6 Loans to stockholders				
7 Mortgage and real estate loans				
8 Other investments (attach schedule) . Sched.1 .		161,181		185,960
9 Buildings and other depreciable assets	713,756		725,325	
(a) Less accumulated depreciation	165,043	548,713	198,449	526,876
10 Depletable assets				
(a) Less accumulated depletion				
11 Land (net of any amortization)		30,000		30,000
12 Intangible assets (amortizable only)				
(a) Less accumulated amortization				
13 Other assets (attach schedule)		88,202		81,602
14 Total assets		2,432,765		2,840,504
LIABILITIES AND STOCKHOLDERS' EQUITY				
15 Accounts payable		443,501		386,037
16 Mtges, notes, bonds payable in less than 1 year . .		121,562		443,778
17 Other current liabilities (attach schedule) Sched 1		262,271		309,301
18 Loans from stockholders				
19 Mtges, notes, bonds payable in 1 year or more . .		419,794		386,216
20 Other liabilities (attach schedule) Sched 1 .		91,000		125,000
21 Captial stock: (a) Preferred stock	215,000		270,000	
(b) Common stock	143,090	358,090	145,000	415,000
22 Paid-in or capital surplus		177,297		205,717
23 Retained earnings—Appropriated (attach sch.) . .				
24 Retained earnings—Unappropriated		569,250		584,455
25 Less cost of treasury stock		(10,000)		(15,000)
26 Total liabilities and stockholders' equity . . .		2,432,765		2,840,504

Schedule M-1 Reconciliation of Income Per Books With Income Per Return				
1 Net income per books	374,665		7 Income recorded on books this year not included in this return (itemize)	
2 Federal income tax	279,831			
3 Excess of capital losses over capital gains . . .			(a) Tax-exempt interest $	
4 Income subject to tax not recorded on books this year (itemize)			Equity in earnings of unconsolidated affiliates	24,773
5 Expenses recorded on books this year not deducted in this return (itemize)			8 Deductions in this tax return not charged against book income this year (itemize)	
(a) Depreciation . . . . $			(a) Depreciation . . . $ 58,277	
(b) Contributions carryover . . $			(b) Contributions carryover . $	
Deferred Income Taxes	34,000			58,277
			9 Total of lines 7 and 8	83,050
6 Total of lines 1 through 5	688,496		10 Income (line 28, page 1)—line 6 less 9 . .	605,446

Schedule M-2 Analysis of Unappropriated Retained Earnings Per Books (line 24 above)				
1 Balance at beginning of year	569,250		5 Distributions: (a) Cash	359,460
2 Net income per books	374,665		(b) Stock	
3 Other increases (itemize)			(c) Property	
			6 Other decreases (itemize)	
				0
			7 Total of lines 5 and 6	359,915
4 Total of lines 1, 2, and 3	943,915	0	8 Balance at end of year (line 4 less 7) . . .	584,455

U.S. GOVERNMENT PRINTING OFFICE : 1981—0—343-447   13-134-8150

Exhibit 11.1, continued

Form **3468**	**Computation of Investment Credit**	OMB. No. 1545-0155
Department of the Treasury Internal Revenue Service (0)	▶ Attach to your tax return. ▶ Use separate Schedule B (Form 3468) to figure your tentative business energy investment credit.	**1981** 27

Name	Identifying number as shown on page 1 of your tax return
EXAMPLE COMPANY, INC.	24-8254551

Part I   Elections (Check the box(es) below that apply to you (see Instruction D).)

A The corporation elects the basic or basic and matching employee plan percentage under section 48(n)(1) . . . . ☐

B I elect to increase my qualified investment to 100% for certain commuter highway vehicles under section 46(c)(6) . . . . . ☐

C I elect to increase my qualified investment by all qualified progress expenditures made this tax year and all later years . . . . ☐

Enter total qualified progress expenditures included in column (4), Part II ▶...

D I claim full credit on certain ships under section 46(g)(3). (See Instruction B for details.) . . . . ☐

Part II   Qualified Investment

Figure your qualified investment in new or used investment credit property acquired or constructed and placed in service during the tax year. The qualified investment for qualified progress expenditures and qualified rehabilitation expenditures is allowed in the tax year the expenditure is incurred or in the case of self-constructed property the year the expenditure is chargeable to a capital account for the property.

For certain taxpayers, the basis or cost of property placed in service after February 18, 1981, is limited to the amount the taxpayer is at risk for the property at year end. See Instruction E.

Note: Include your share of investment in property made by a partnership, estate, trust, small business corporation, or lessor.

1 Recovery Property	Line	(1) Recovery Period	(2) Unadjusted Basis	(3) Applicable percentage	(4) Qualified investment (Column 2 × column 3)
New	(a)	3-Year		60	
New	(b)	Other		100	
Used	(c)	3-Year		60	
Used	(d)	Other		100	

2 Total—Add lines 1(a) through 1(d) **2**

3 Nonrecovery Property	Line	(1) Life years	(2) Basis or cost	(3) Applicable percentage	(4) Qualified investment (Column 2 × column 3)
New	(a)	3 or more but less than 5		33⅓	
New	(b)	5 or more but less than 7		66⅔	
New	(c)	7 or more		100	
Used	(d)	3 or more but less than 5		33⅓	
Used	(e)	5 or more but less than 7		66⅔	
Used	(f)	7 or more		100	

4 Total—Add lines 3(a) through 3(f) . . . . **4** | 0

5 New commuter highway vehicle—Enter total qualified investment. (See Instruction D) . . . **5**

6 Used commuter highway vehicle—Enter total qualified investment. (See Instruction D) . . . **6**

7 Qualified rehabilitation expenditures incurred before January 1, 1982, for: (see specific instructions)

    (a) Improvements with 5 or more but less than 7 years—Enter 66⅔% of expenditures . . . **7(a)**

    (b) Improvements with 7 or more life years—Enter 100% of expenditures . . . . **7(b)**

8 Total qualified investment in 10% property—Add lines 2, 4, 5, 6, 7(a) and 7(b). (See instructions for special limits) . **8** | 0

9 Enter 100% of qualified rehabilitation expenditures incurred after December 31, 1981, for:

    (a) 30-year old buildings **9a**

    (b) 40-year old buildings **9b**

    (c) Certified historic structures (Enter the Dept. of Interior assigned project number ....) **9c**

10 Total qualified investment—Add lines 8, 9(a), 9(b), and 9(c) . . . . **10** | 0

Part III   Tentative Regular Investment Credit

11 10% of line 8 . . . . **11**

12 15% of line 9(a) **12**

13 20% of line 9(b) **13**

14 25% of line 9(c) **14**

15 Corporations electing the basic or basic and matching employee plan percentage for contributions to tax credit employee stock ownership plans—Check box A above (see Instruction D)

    (a) Basic 1% credit—Enter 1% of line 10 . . . . **15a**

    (b) Matching credit (not more than 0.5%)—Enter allowable percentage times adjusted line 10 (attach schedule) . **15b**

16 Credit from Cooperative—Enter regular investment credit from cooperatives **16**

17 Current year regular investment credit—Add lines 11 through 16 . . . . **17** | 0

18 Carryover of unused credits . . . . **18** | 9,794

19 Carryback of unused credits **19**

20 Tentative regular investment credit—Add lines 17, 18, and 19, enter here and in Part IV, line 21 . **20** | 9,794

For Paperwork Reduction Act Notice, see page 2.

Form **3468** (1981)

Exhibit 11.1, continued

Form 3468 (1981)   Page **2**

Part IV Tax Liability Limitations

21 Tentative credit from Part III, line 20	**21**	9,794
22 (a) Individuals—Enter amount from Form 1040, line 37, page 2		
(b) Estates and trusts—Enter amount from Form 1041, line 26, page 1	**22**	259,255
(c) Corporations—Enter amount from Schedule J (Form 1120), line 3, page 3		
(d) Others—Enter tax before credits from your return		
23 (a) Credit for the elderly (individuals only) . . . . [23(a)]		
(b) Foreign tax credit . . . . [23(b)]		
(c) Tax on lump-sum distribution from Form 4972 or Form 5544 . [23(c)]		
(d) Possessions corporation tax credit (corporations only) . . . [23(d)]		
(e) Section 72(m)(5) penalty tax (individuals only) . . . . . [23(e)]		
24 Total—Add lines 23(a) through 23(e)	**24**	0
25 Subtract line 24 from line 22	**25**	259,255
26 (a) Enter smaller of line 25 or $25,000. See instruction for line 26	**26(a)**	25,000
(b) If line 25 is more than line 26(a), and your tax year ends in 1981, enter 80% of the excess (if your tax year ends in 1982, enter 90% of the excess)	**26(b)**	
27 Regular investment credit limitation—Add lines 26(a) and 26(b)	**27**	25,000
28 Allowed regular investment credit—Enter the smaller of line 21 or line 27	**28**	9,794
29 Business energy investment credit limitation—Subtract line 28 from line 25	**29**	249,461
30 Business energy investment credit—Enter amount from line 14 of Schedule B (Form 3468) .	**30**	0
31 Allowed business energy investment credit—Enter smaller of line 29 or line 30	**31**	0
32 Total allowed regular and business energy investment credit—Add lines 28 and 31. Enter here and on Form 1040, line 41; Schedule J (Form 1120), line 4(b), page 3; or the proper line on other returns	**32**	9,794

Paperwork Reduction Act Notice.—The Paperwork Reduction Act of 1980 says we must tell you why we are collecting this information, how we will use it, and whether you have to give it to us. We ask for the information to carryout the Internal Revenue laws of the United States. We need it to ensure that you are complying with these laws and so that we can figure and collect the correct amount of tax. You are required to give us this information.

☆ U.S. GOVERNMENT PRINTING OFFICE: 1981—O-343-453 58-040-1110

Exhibit 11.1, continued

| Form **4684**
Department of the Treasury
Internal Revenue Service | **Casualties and Thefts**
▶ See instructions on back.
▶ To be filed with Form 1040, 1041, 1065, 1120, etc. | OMB No. 1545-0177
1981 |

Name(s) as shown on tax return	Identifying Number
EXAMPLE COMPANY, INC.	24-8254551

Part I Casualty or Theft Gain or Loss (Use a separate Part I for each different casualty or theft.)

	Item or article	Item or article	Item or article	Item or article
1 (a) Kind of property and description	PLANT	EQUIPMENT		
(b) Date of purchase or acquisition	11/12/79	11/26/79		
2 Cost or basis of each item	60,660	10,000		
3 Insurance or other reimbursement you received or expect to receive	0	0		
4 Gain from casualty or theft. If line 3 is more than line 2, enter difference here and on line 15 or 20, column C. However, see instructions for line 19. Also, skip lines 5 through 14 . . . . *If line 2 is more than line 3, enter zero on line 4 and complete lines 5 through 14.*	0	0		
5 Fair market value before casualty or theft . . .	110,500	13,000		
6 Fair market value after casualty or theft . . .	0	0		
7 Subtract line 6 from line 5	110,500	13,000		
8 Enter smaller of line 2 or line 7	60,660	10,000		
Note: *If the loss was to property used in a trade or business or for income-producing purposes, and totally destroyed by a casualty or lost from theft, enter on line 8, in each column, the amount from line 2.*				
9 Subtract line 3 from line 8	60,660	10,000		

10 Casualty or theft loss. Add amounts on line 9	70,660
11 Enter the part of line 9 that is from trade, business, or income-producing property here and on line 15 or 20 .	70,660
12 Subtract line 11 from line 10	0
13 Enter the amount from line 12 or $100, whichever is smaller	0
14 Subtract line 13 from line 12. Enter here and on line 15 or 20, column B(ii)	0

Part II Summary of Gains and Losses (From separate Parts I)

(A) Identify casualty or theft	(B) Losses from casualties or thefts		(C) Gains from casualties or thefts includible in income
	(i) Trade, business, rental or royalty property	(ii) Other property	
Casualty or Theft of Property Held One Year or Less			
15			
16 Totals. Add amounts on line 15 for each column			
17 Combine line 16, columns (B)(i) and (C). Enter the net gain or (loss) here and on Form 4797, Part II, line 8(a) . (If Form 4797 is not otherwise required, see instructions.) .			
18 Enter line 16, column (B)(ii) here and on line 29 of Schedule A (Form 1040)—identify as "4684"			
Casualty or Theft of Property Held More Than One Year			
19 Any casualty or theft gains from Form 4797, Part III, line 26			
20 PLANT	60,660	0	
EQUIPMENT	10,000	0	
21 Total losses. Add amounts on line 20, columns (B)(i) and (B)(ii) . .	70,660	0	//////
22 Total gains. Add lines 19 and 20, column (C)			0
23 Add line 21, columns (B)(i) and (B)(ii)			70,660
If this form is filed by a partnership, enter line 24 or line 25 on Schedule K (Form 1065), line 7.			
24 If the loss on line 23 is more than the gain on line 22			
a. Combine line 21, column (B)(i) and line 22. Enter the net gain or (loss) here and on Form 4797, Part II, line 8(a). (If Form 4797 is not otherwise required, see instructions.)			70,660
b. Enter line 21, column (B)(ii) here and on line 29 of Schedule A (Form 1040)—identify as "4684" . . .			0
25 If the loss on line 23 is equal to or smaller than the gain on line 22, enter the net gain here and on Form 4797, Part I, line 2(a). (If Form 4797 is not otherwise required, see instructions.)			

For Paperwork Reduction Act Notice, see back of form.   Form **4684** (1981)

Exhibit 11.1, continued

Form **4797**	**Supplemental Schedule of Gains and Losses**	OMB No. 1545-0184
Department of the Treasury Internal Revenue Service (O)	(Includes Gains and Losses From Sales or Exchanges of Assets Used in a Trade or Business and Involuntary Conversions) To be filed with Form 1040, 1041, 1065, 1120, etc.—See Separate Instructions	19**81** 31

Name(s) as shown on return	Identifying number
EXAMPLE COMPANY, INC.	24-8254551

Part I Sales or Exchanges of Property Used in a Trade or Business, and Involuntary Conversions From Other Than Casualty and Theft—Property Held More Than 1 Year (Except for Certain Livestock)

Note: Use Form 4684 to report involuntary conversions from casualty and theft.
Caution: If you sold property on which you claimed the investment credit, you may be liable for recapture of that credit. See Form 4255 for additional information.

a. Kind of property and description	b. Date acquired (mo., day, yr.)	c. Date sold (mo., day, yr.)	d. Gross sales price minus expense of sale	e. Depreciation allowed (or allowable) since acquisition	f. Cost or other basis, plus improvements	g. LOSS (f minus the sum of d and e)	h. GAIN (d plus e minus f)
1							

2 (a) Gain, if any, from Form 4684, Part II, line 25 . . . .

(b) Section 1231 gain from installment sales from Form 6252, line 19 or 27 . . . . .

3 Gain, if any, from line 26, Part III, on back of this form from other than casualty and theft . .

4 Add lines 1 through 3 in column g and column h . . . . ( )

5 Combine line 4, column g and line 4, column h. Enter gain or (loss) here, and on the appropriate line as follows:
(a) For all except partnership returns:
(1) If line 5 is a gain, enter the gain as a long-term capital gain on Schedule D (Form 1040, 1120, etc.) that is being filed. See instruction E.
(2) If line 5 is zero or a loss, enter that amount on line 6.
(b) For partnership returns: Enter the amount shown on line 5 above, on Schedule K (Form 1065), line 8.

Part II Ordinary Gains and Losses

a. Kind of property and description	b. Date acquired (mo., day, yr.)	c. Date sold (mo., day, yr.)	d. Gross sales price minus expense of sale	e. Depreciation allowed (or allowable) since acquisition	f. Cost or other basis, plus improvements	g. LOSS (f minus the sum of d and e)	h. GAIN (d plus e minus f)
6 Loss, if any, from line 5(a)(2)							
7 Gain, if any, from line 25, Part III on back of this form							
8 (a) Net gain or (loss) from Form 4684, lines 17 and 24a						70,660	0
(b) Ordinary gain from installment sales from Form 6252, line 18 or 26							
9 Other ordinary gains and losses (include property held 1 year or less):							
EQUIPMENT	8/5/80	2/5/81	18,000	2,250	10,110		10,140

10 Add lines 6 through 9 in column g and column h . . . . (70,660) 10,140

11 Combine line 10, column g and line 10, column h. Enter gain or (loss) here, and on the appropriate line as follows: (60,520)
(a) For all except individual returns: Enter the gain or (loss) shown on line 11, on the line provided on the return (Form 1120, etc.) being filed. See instruction F for specific line reference.
(b) For individual returns:
(1) If the loss on line 6 includes a loss from Form 4684, Part II, column B(ii), enter that part of the loss here and on line 29 of Schedule A (Form 1040). Identify as from "Form 4797, line 11(b)(1)" . . . . .
(2) Redetermine the gain or (loss) on line 11, excluding the loss (if any) entered on line 11(b)(1). Enter here and on Form 1040, line 14 . . . .

Part III Gain From Disposition of Property Under Sections 1245, 1250, 1251, 1252, 1254, 1255

Skip lines 20 and 21 if there are no dispositions of farm property or farmland, or if this form is filed by a partnership.

12 Description of sections 1245, 1250, 1251, 1252, 1254, and 1255 property:	Date acquired (mo., day, yr.)	Date sold (mo., day, yr.)
(A)		
(B)		
(C)		
(D)		

Part III is continued on page 2.

For Paperwork Reduction Act Notice, see page 1 of separate instructions.   Form **4797** (1981)

Exhibit 11.1, continued

Form **4562**	**Depreciation**	OMB No. 1545-0172
(Rev. September 1981) Department of the Treasury Internal Revenue Service (0)	▶ See separate instructions. ▶ Attach this form to your return.	Expires 12/31/82

Name(s) as shown on return	Identifying number
EXAMPLE COMPANY, INC.	24-8254551

▶ Generally, you must use the Accelerated Cost Recovery System of depreciation (ACRS) for all assets you placed in service after December 31, 1980. Report these assets in Part I, lines 1(a) through 1(f).

▶ You may elect to exclude certain property. Report this property in Part I, line 2.

▶ Use Part II for assets you placed in service before January 1, 1981, and certain other assets for which you cannot use ACRS.

▶ Filers of Schedule C (Form 1040), Schedule E (Form 1040) and Form 4835 should see the instructions for those forms before completing Form 4562.

Part I   Assets placed in service after December 31, 1980

A. Class of property	B. Date placed in service	C. Cost or other basis	D. Recovery period	E. Method of figuring depreciation	F. Percentage	G. Deduction for this year
1 Accelerated Cost Recovery System (ACRS) (See instructions for grouping assets):						
(a) 3-year property						
(b) 5-year property						
(c) 10-year property						
(d) 15-year public utility property						
(e) 15-year real property—low-income housing						
(f) 15-year real property other than low-income housing						
2 Property subject to section 168(e) (2) election (see instructions):						
3 Totals (add amounts in columns C and G) . . .						0

4 Depreciation from Part II, line 3	111,742
5 Total (add column G, lines 3 and 4). Enter this amount on the depreciation expense line (where it applies) of your return	111,742

See Paperwork Reduction Act Notice on page 1 of the separate instructions.   Form **4562** (Rev. 9-81)

Exhibit 11.1, continued

Form 4562 (Rev. 9–81)   Page **2**

Part II   Assets placed in service before January 1, 1981 and other assets not qualifying for ACRS

A. Description of property	B. Date acquired	C. Cost or other basis	D. Depreciation allowed or allowable in earlier years	E. Method of figuring depreciation	F. Life or rate	G. Depreciation for this year
1 Class Life Asset Depreciation Range (CLADR) System Depreciation . . . . ▶						NONE
2 Other depreciation (for grouping assets, see instructions for Part II):						
Buildings	VARIOUS	111,331		150db	VAR.	18,450
Furniture and fixtures . .	VARIOUS	19,999		200db	VAR.	5,021
Transportation equipment						
Machinery and other equipment	VARIOUS	520,995		200db	VAR.	86,140
Other (specify)						
LEASEHOLD IMPROVE-MENTS	VARIOUS	73,000		S/L	VAR.	2,131
						111,742

3 Total (add amounts in column G). Enter here and in Part I, line 4 . . . .

Exhibit 11.1, continued

EXAMPLE COMPANY, INC.   IDENT. NO. 24-8254551

SCHEDULE 1 - BALANCE SHEET

December 31, 1981

						1980		1981	
OTHER CURRENT ASSETS									
MARKETABLE SECURITIES						50	000	50	000
PREPAID EXPENSES						57	843	47	313
TOTAL OTHER CURRENT ASSETS						107	843	97	313
OTHER INVESTMENTS									
INVESTMENT IN AFFILIATED COMPANIES						161	181	185	960
OTHER CURRENT LIABILITIES									
ACCRUED EXPENSES						81	020	91	550
INCOME TAXES						181	251	217	751
TOTAL OTHER CURRENT LIABILITIES						262	271	309	301
OTHER LIABILITIES									
DEFERRED INCOME TAXES						91	000	125	000

Exhibit 11.1, continued

form presents the income statement first, supplemental schedules next, and a balance sheet at the end.

While reviewing the numbers do not forget that our purpose is to gain enough insight into the company to allow us to render a decision. The return will act only as a blueprint; many questions will have to be asked of your client.

The heading of the first page tells us several things. It shows the correct name of the company and its date of incorporation, something often missed on statements. It also tells us the company's fiscal year if it is different from the calendar year. We learn whether the statement is consolidated and what the total assets of the company are.

The first page is broken down into three major sections: Gross Income, Deductions, and Tax. Gross Income gives us a breakdown of sales and miscellaneous income items. The cost of sales is on a supplementary schedule which we will review when we examine page two. Deductions break out certain key expenses. Line 12 for example, lists officers' compensation. The questions to ask here are: Is it too much? Are the profits needed to retire your debt suffering because the company is "milking" profits with excessive salaries? Are the salaries too low? Can the company hire competent management at this price? Employee salaries are either listed as indirect salaries (line 13) or they are reported by the accountant as cost of sales. Interest expense, bad debts, and depreciation are given individual status on lines 18, 15, 21 respectively. These are items analysts usually have to track down. Taxable income, as listed on line 30, is profit before taxes. The final section of this page is the tax which is due and payable.

Page two of the corporate tax return gives further information on certain items that were listed on page one. The first schedule is the cost of sales; it explains the type of inventory procedure used and discloses any changes in method as well. Schedule E further analyzes officers' salaries; it is self-explanatory. If a company is requesting a loan against receivables and its bad debt is substantial, Schedule F will prove invaluable as it provides a record of the past year's experience. Form 4562 on depreciation is critical. Not only will it show you the depreciation expense, but it also lets you know the life of the assets and which method of calculating depreciation was used. If you are making a loan against assets, it is extremely important to know the cost and date acquired of each item, and this form will give you this information. In addition to the historical date, Form 4562 gives you a point of departure for discussing the present value of items. Sometimes you will find a separate schedule listing all of the equipment in detail, and the totals transposed to the categories listed on Form 4562. This is all the more information for you to use. Sometimes the assets will be grouped. You can request a breakdown of the schedule from the accountant if you need it. Finally, recall our earlier discussions of the new tax law with its accelerated write-offs. Starting with the 1981 return, two separate schedules will be used for depreciation — one for assets placed in service before January 1, 1981 and one for those acquired after that date.

Schedule J is the actual computation of taxes. Most of the information in Schedule K is general data and may be passed over quickly.

Summaries of other deductions, or explanations of any large group of expenses or assets not covered by one of the schedules, will be listed on a separate schedule and included either at this point in the return or at the end.

It seems that the IRS saves the best for last. Page four covers three areas of great importance. First, Schedule L is a balance sheet for the past two years. Imagine, the client who said he didn't have a statement actually has a comparative balance sheet. Second, Schedule M-1 reconciles the income as shown on the company's books with that shown on the returns. This section is not for confessions of inventory hedges. Rather, it is to show the differences that result when accounting for income and resultant profit is done one way on a company's books and another way for taxes. Remember our friend who reported sales on a cash basis for taxes and on an accrual basis for his statement. These differences would be recorded here. The use of more than one method of calculating depreciation or the effect of reporting under the new tax law would appear here as well. Note line 8 of Schedule M-1.

The final schedule, M-2, is a reconciliation of net worth. It has all the information you need in order to follow the change in a company's equity, regardless of the nature of the transaction. It is a complete statement in itself.

As we already have reviewed the Example Company's statement twice, our purpose is not to analyze their tax return now, but only to demonstrate, as we have, that a tax return provides us with a complete and detailed financial statement, including comparative and detailed balance sheets. Since every corporate client must have such a return, every loan decision can and must include a review of a statement in order to be valid.

Form 1065 — U.S. Partnership Return

The partnership return is very similar to the corporate return, except that it has no tax calculation section. The tax is paid by the partners individually and only taxable income is calculated.

Exhibit 11.2 is a sample of the Form 1065. The heading of the return tells us the period covered, the date the partnership started, the principal product, and the total assets as well as the correct name of the company. The remainder of page one is an income statement. Cost of sales is shown on the bottom of this page.

Page two contains support schedules for certain income and expenses that are listed on page one. Once again, the key schedules appear here as they do on the corporate return.

Page three is a schedule of distribution of earnings to the partners. This schedule will determine what each partner will report as income on his personal return. At this point, you do not know yet what the partners drew from the business.

Page four contains the comparative balance sheet which is similar to the one given in the corporate statement. It also contains a reconciliation of the partnership account. This reconciliation does tell you the combined draw of the partners.

Schedule C (Form 1040) — Profit or (Loss) From Business (Proprietorship)

Unlike the two tax returns previously discussed, this return, which is filed as an addendum to one's personal income tax form, does not contain a balance sheet. It does give a great deal of income statement information, and it does provide certain keys which, properly used, may generate a balance sheet. Exhibit 11.3 is a sample of Schedule C.

The top section of the form gives general information. Line E, however, provides a bonus. It tells us the nature of the accounting method used. This is quite important in individual cases — more so than in corporate.

The body of the return is divided into two sections: income and deductions. The income portion is limited to business revenue. If there is other income, it will be reflected on a separate personal schedule.

The expense section lists certain key items and has room at the bottom

Form **1065**	**U.S. Partnership Return of Income**	OMB No. 1545-0099
Department of the Treasury Internal Revenue Service	For calendar year 1981, or fiscal year beginning ...., 1981, and ending ...., 19	**1981**

A Principal business activity (see page 12 of Instructions) Advertising	Use IRS label. Other-wise, please print or type.	Name PROFESSIONAL ASSOCIATES	**D** Employer identification no. 24-6752786
B Principal product or service (see page 12 of Instructions) Consulting		Number and street 1300 Main Street	**E** Date business started 1957
C Business code number (see page 12 of Instructions) 7310		City or town, State, and ZIP code Smithville, Pennsylvania 18612	**F** Enter total assets from Schedule L, line 13, column (D). $ 21,500

G Check method of accounting: (1) ☒ Cash   (2) ☐ Accrual   (3) ☐ Other (attach explanation)

H Check applicable boxes: (1) ☐ Final return (2) ☐ Change in address.

IMPORTANT—Fill in all applicable lines and schedules. If you need more space, see page 2 of the Instructions. Enter any items specially allocated to the partners on Schedule K, line 17, and not on the numbered lines on this page or in Schedules A through I.

Income

1a	Gross receipts or sales $.135,000....... 1b Minus returns and allowances $.......0........... Balance ▶	1c	135,000
2	Cost of goods sold and/or operations (Schedule A, line 34)	2	23,000
3	Gross profit (subtract line 2 from line 1c)	3	112,000
4	Ordinary income (loss) from other partnerships and fiduciaries (attach statement)	4	
5	Nonqualifying dividends	5	
6	Nonqualifying interest	6	
7	Net income (loss) from rents (Schedule H, line 2)	7	
8	Net income (loss) from royalties (attach schedule)	8	
9	Net farm profit (loss) (attach Schedule F (Form 1040))	9	
10	Net gain (loss) (Form 4797, line 11)	10	
11	Other income (attach schedule)	11	
12	**TOTAL** income (loss) (combine lines 3 through 11)	12	112,000

Deductions

13a	Salaries and wages (other than to partners) $.63,000.... 13b Minus jobs credit $.....0............ Balance ▶	13c	63,000
14	Guaranteed payments to partners (see page 4 of Instructions)	14	
15	Rent	15	12,000
16	Interest (**Caution—see page 4 of Instructions**)	16	
17	Taxes	17	
18	Bad debts (see page 5 of Instructions)	18	
19	Repairs	19	250
20	Depreciation from Form 4562 (attach Form 4562) $...1,300........................, less depreciation claimed in Schedules A and H and elsewhere on return $......0............, Balance ▶	20	1,300
21	Amortization (attach schedule)	21	
22	Depletion (other than oil and gas, attach schedule—see page 5 of Instructions)	22	
23a	Retirement plans, etc. (see page 5 of Instructions)	23a	
23b	Employee benefit programs (see page 5 of Instructions)	23b	
24	Other deductions (attach schedule)	24	
25	**TOTAL** deductions (add lines 13c through 24)	25	76,550
26	Ordinary income (loss) (subtract line 25 from line 12)	26	35,450

Schedule A—COST OF GOODS SOLD AND/OR OPERATIONS (See Page 6 of Instructions)

27	Inventory at beginning of year (if different from last year's closing inventory, attach explanation) .	27	
28a	Purchases $...20,000...... 28b Minus cost of items withdrawn for personal use $.......................0... Balance ▶	28c	20,000
29	Cost of labor	29	
30	Materials and supplies	30	3,000
31	Other costs (attach schedule)	31	
32	Total (add lines 27 through 31)	32	23,000
33	Inventory at end of year	33	
34	Cost of goods sold (subtract line 33 from line 32). Enter here and on line 2, above	34	23,000

Please Sign Here	Under penalties of perjury, I declare that I have examined this return, including accompanying schedules and statements, and to the best of my knowledge and belief it is true, correct, and complete. Declaration of preparer (other than taxpayer) is based on all information of which preparer has any knowledge.		
	▶ *Albert George* Signature of general partner	▶ 3/12/82 Date	

Paid Preparer's Use Only	Preparer's signature ▶	Date	Check if self-employed ▶ ☐	Preparer's social security no.
	Firm's name (or yours, if self-employed) and address ▶		E.I. No. ▶	
			ZIP code ▶	

For Paperwork Reduction Act Notice, see page 1 of Form 1065 Instructions

Exhibit 11.2 Sample U.S. Partnership Return

Form 1065 (1981)   **Schedule A** *(Continued)*   Page **2**

35 a Check all methods used for valuing closing inventory: *(i)* ☐ Cost

(ii) ☐ Lower of cost or market as described in regulations section 1.471–4 (see page 6 of Instructions) *(iii)* ☐ Writedown of "subnormal" goods as described in regulations section 1.471–2(c) (see page 6 of Instructions).   Not Applicable

b Did you use any other method of inventory valuation not described in line 35a? . . . .

If "Yes," specify methods used and attach explanation . .

	Yes	No
b		X

c Check if the LIFO method was adopted this tax year for any goods. (If checked, attach Form 970) . . . . ☐

d If you are engaged in manufacturing, did you value your inventory using the full absorption method (regulations section 1.471–11)? . . . .

e Was there any substantial change in determining quantities, cost, or valuations between opening and closing inventory? If "Yes," attach explanation.

	Yes	No
c		
e		X

Schedule D—CAPITAL GAINS AND LOSSES (See Page 6 of Instructions)

Part I Short-term Capital Gains and Losses—Assets Held One Year or Less

a. Kind of property and description (Example, 100 shares of "Z" Co.)	b. Date acquired (mo., day, yr.)	c. Date sold (mo., day, yr.)	d. Gross sales price minus expenses of sale	e. Cost or other basis	f. Gain (loss) for the year (d minus e)	g. Gain (loss) after 6/9/81
1a						

1b Short-term capital gain from installment sales from Form 6252, line 19 or 27 . . . . .

2 Partnership's share of net short-term gain (loss), including specially allocated items, from other partnerships and from fiduciaries . . . .

3 Net short-term gain (loss) from lines 1a, 1b, and 2. Enter here and on Schedule K (Form 1065), line 5 . . . .

Part II Long-term Capital Gains and Losses—Assets Held More Than One Year

4a						

4b Long-term capital gain from installment sales from Form 6252, line 19 or 27 . . . . . .

5 Partnership's share of net long-term gain (loss), including specially allocated items, from other partnerships and from fiduciaries . . . .

6 Capital gain distributions . . . .

7 Net long-term gain (loss) from lines 4a, 4b, 5, and 6. Enter here and on Schedule K (Form 1065), line 7 . . . .

Schedule H—INCOME FROM RENTS (See Page 4 of Instructions) If you need more space, attach schedule.

a. Kind and location of property	b. Amount of rent	c. Depreciation (explain on Form 4562)	d. Repairs (attach schedule)	e. Other expenses (attach schedule)

1 Totals . . . .

2 Net income (loss) (subtract total of columns c, d, and e from column b). Enter here and on page 1, line 7 . . .

Schedule I—BAD DEBTS (See Page 5 of Instructions)

a. Year	b. Trade notes and accounts receivable outstanding at end of year	c. Sales on account	Amount added to reserve — d. Current year's provision	e. Recoveries	f. Amount charged against reserve	g. Reserve for bad debts at end of year
1976						
1977						
1978						
1979						
1980						
1981						

Exhibit 11.2, continued

Form 1065 (1981)   Page **3**

Schedule K—PARTNERS' SHARES OF INCOME, CREDITS, DEDUCTIONS, ETC. (See Pages 7–11 of Instructions)

	a. Distributive share items		b. Total amount
Income (loss)	1 Ordinary income (loss) (page 1, line 26)	1	35,450
	2 Guaranteed payments	2	
	3a Interest qualifying for exclusion under section 116	3a	
	b Qualifying interest from All-Savers Certificates	3b	
	4 Dividends qualifying for exclusion	4	
	5 Net short-term capital gain (loss) (Schedule D, line 3): a Total for year . . . . . ▶	5a	
	b From sales or exchanges after 6/9/81	5b	
	6 Net long-term capital gain (loss) (Schedule D, line 7): a Total for year . . . . . ▶	6a	
	b From sales or exchanges after 6/9/81	6b	
	7 Net gain (loss) from involuntary conversions due to casualty or theft (Form 4684):		
	a Total for year . . . . ▶	7a	
	b From casualties or thefts after 6/9/81	7b	
	8 Other net gain (loss) under section 1231: a Total for year . . . . ▶	8a	
	b From sales or exchanges after 6/9/81	8b	
	9 Other (attach schedule)	9	
Deductions	10 Charitable contributions (attach list): 50% ...., 30% ...., 20%	10	
	11a Payments for partners to an IRA	11a	
	b Payments for partners to a Keogh Plan (Type of plan ▶............................)	11b	
	c Payments for partners to Simplified Employee Pension (SEP)	11c	
	12 Other (attach schedule)	12	
Credits	13 Jobs credit	13	
	14 Credit for alcohol used as fuel	14	
	15 Other (attach schedule)	15	
Other	16a Gross farming or fishing income	16a	
	b Net earnings (loss) from self-employment	16b	
	c Other (attach schedule)	16c	
Specially Allocated Items	17a Short-term capital gain (loss) (attach schedule): (1) Total for year . . . . . . ▶	17a(1)	
	(2) From sales or exchanges after 6/9/81	17a(2)	
	b Long-term capital gain (loss) (attach schedule): (1) Total for year . . . . . . ▶	17b(1)	
	(2) From sales or exchanges after 6/9/81	17b(2)	
	c Ordinary gain (loss) (attach schedule)	17c	
	d Other (attach schedule)	17d	
Tax Preference Items	18a Accelerated depreciation on real property:		
	(1) Low-income rental housing (167(k))	18a(1)	
	(2) Other nonrecovery real property and 15-year real property	18a(2)	
	b Accelerated depreciation on leased property that is personal property or recovery property other than 15-year real property	18b	
	Amortization: c ...., d ...., e ...., f	18c-f	
	g Reserves for losses on bad debts of financial institutions	18g	
	h Depletion (other than oil and gas)	18h	
	i (1) Excess intangible drilling costs from oil, gas, or geothermal wells	18i(1)	
	(2) Net income from oil, gas, or geothermal wells	18i(2)	
Investment Interest	19a Investment interest expense:		
	(1) Indebtedness incurred before 12/17/69	19a(1)	
	(2) Indebtedness incurred before 9/11/75, but after 12/16/69	19a(2)	
	(3) Indebtedness incurred after 9/10/75	19a(3)	
	b Net investment income (loss)	19b	
	c Excess expenses from "net lease property"	19c	
	d Excess of net long-term capital gain over net short-term capital loss from investment property	19d	
Foreign Taxes	20a Type of income		
	b Foreign country or U.S. possession		
	c Total gross income from sources outside the U.S. (attach schedule)	20c	
	d Total applicable deductions and losses (attach schedule)	20d	
	e Total foreign taxes (check one): ☐ Paid ☐ Accrued	20e	
	f Reduction in taxes available for credit (attach schedule)	20f	
	g Other (attach schedule)	20g	

Exhibit 11.2, continued

Form 1065 (1981)   Page **4**

Note: Family farm partnerships, family-owned wholesale or retail store partnerships, and co-owners of investment property, see "Filing a Complete Return" on page 11 of the Instructions before completing Schedules L and M.

If the partnership meets **ALL** the requirements shown on page 11 of the Instructions under "Filing a Complete Return," check here . . . . ▶ ☐

Schedule L—BALANCE SHEETS (See Page 11 of Instructions)

ASSETS	Beginning of tax year (A)	Beginning of tax year (B)	End of tax year (C)	End of tax year (D)
1 Cash		3,000		4,000
2 Trade notes and accounts receivable	11,000		15,000	
a Minus allowance for bad debts	0	11,000	0	15,000
3 Inventories				
4 Government obligations: a U.S. and instrumentalities . .				
b State, subdivisions of State, etc.				
5 Other current assets (attach schedule)				
6 Mortgage and real estate loans				
7 Other investments (attach schedule)				
8 Buildings and other depreciable assets	13,000		13,000	
a Minus accumulated depreciation	9,200	3,800	10,500	2,500
9 Depletable assets				
a Minus accumulated depletion				
10 Land (net of any amortization)				
11 Intangible assets (amortizable only)				
a Minus accumulated amortization				
12 Other assets (attach schedule)				
13 Total assets		17,800		21,500
LIABILITIES AND CAPITAL				
14 Accounts payable		1,500		2,000
15 Mortgages, notes, and bonds payable in less than 1 year .				
16 Other current liabilities (attach schedule) . . .		2,500		3,000
17 All nonrecourse loans (attach schedule) . . .				
18 Mortgages, notes, and bonds payable in 1 year or more . .				
19 Other liabilities (attach schedule)				
20 Partners' capital accounts		13,800		16,500
21 Total liabilities and capital		17,800		21,500

Schedule M—RECONCILIATION OF PARTNERS' CAPITAL ACCOUNTS (See Page 11 of Instructions)
(Show reconciliation of each partner's capital account on Schedule K–1, item E)

a. Capital account at beginning of year	b. Capital contributed during year	c. Ordinary income (loss) from page 1, line 26	d. Income not included in column c, plus non-taxable income	e. Losses not included in column c, plus unallowable deductions	f. Withdrawals and distributions	g. Capital account at end of year
13,800		35,450			32,750	16,500

Schedule N—ADDITIONAL INFORMATION REQUIRED

	Yes	No
1 Is this partnership a limited partnership (see page 2 of Instructions)?		X
2 Number of partners in this partnership ....2........		
3 Is this partnership a partner in another partnership?		X
4 Are any partners in this partnership also partnerships?		X
5 At any time during the tax year, did the partnership have an interest in or a signature or other authority over a bank account, securities account, or other financial account in a foreign country (see page 11 of Instructions)?		X
6 Was the partnership the grantor of, or transferor to, a foreign trust which existed during the current tax year, whether or not the partnership or any partner has any beneficial interest in it? If "Yes," you may have to file Forms 3520, 3520–A, or 926. (See page 11 of Instructions.)		X

★ U.S. GOVERNMENT PRINTING OFFICE: 1981—O-343-446   52-0237640

Exhibit 11.2, continued

Form 4562
(Rev. September 1981)
Department of the Treasury
Internal Revenue Service (O)

Depreciation

▶ See separate instructions.
▶ Attach this form to your return.

OMB No. 1545-0172
Expires 12/31/82

Name(s) as shown on return	Identifying number
PROFESSIONAL ASSOCIATES	24-6752786

▶ Generally, you must use the Accelerated Cost Recovery System of depreciation (ACRS) for all assets you placed in service after December 31, 1980. Report these assets in Part I, lines 1(a) through 1(f).

▶ You may elect to exclude certain property. Report this property in Part I, line 2.

▶ Use Part II for assets you placed in service before January 1, 1981, and certain other assets for which you cannot use ACRS.

▶ Filers of Schedule C (Form 1040), Schedule E (Form 1040) and Form 4835 should see the instructions for those forms before completing Form 4562.

Part I Assets placed in service after December 31, 1980

A. Class of property	B. Date placed in service	C. Cost or other basis	D. Recovery period	E. Method of figuring depreciation	F. Percentage	G. Deduction for this year
1 Accelerated Cost Recovery System (ACRS) (See instructions for grouping assets):						
(a) 3-year property						
(b) 5-year property						
(c) 10-year property						
(d) 15-year public utility property						
(e) 15-year real property—low-income housing						
(f) 15-year real property other than low-income housing						
2 Property subject to section 168(e) (2) election (see instructions):						
3 Totals (add amounts in columns C and G) . . .						0
4 Depreciation from Part II, line 3						1,300
5 Total (add column G, lines 3 and 4). Enter this amount on the depreciation expense line (where it applies) of your return						1,300

See Paperwork Reduction Act Notice on page 1 of the separate Instructions.

Form **4562** (Rev. 9–81)

Exhibit 11.2, continued

Form 4562 (Rev. 9–81)   Page **2**

| **Part II** | Assets placed in service before January 1, 1981 and other assets not qualifying for ACRS |

A. Description of property	B. Date acquired	C. Cost or other basis	D. Depreciation allowed or allowable in earlier years	E. Method of figuring depreciation	F. Life or rate	G. Depreciation for this year
1 Class Life Asset Depreciation Range (CLADR) System Depreciation ▶						
2 Other depreciation (for grouping assets, see instructions for Part II):						
Buildings						
Furniture and fixtures . .	VARIOUS	13,000	9,200	SL	10	1,300
Transportation equipment						
Machinery and other equipment						
Other (specify)						
3 Total (add amounts in column G). Enter here and in Part I, line 4						1,300

☆ U.S. GOVERNMENT PRINTING OFFICE: 1981—O-343-455 58-040-1110

Exhibit 11.2, continued

SCHEDULE C (Form 1040) Department of the Treasury Internal Revenue Service (0)	**Profit or (Loss) From Business or Profession** (Sole Proprietorship) Partnerships, Joint Ventures, etc., Must File Form 1065. ▶ Attach to Form 1040 or Form 1041. ▶ See Instructions for Schedule C (Form 1040).	OMB. No. 1545–0074 **1981** 08

Name of proprietor JOHN J. JONES	Social security number of proprietor 211 : 32 : 9113

A Main business activity (see Instructions) ▶ CONTRACTOR   ; product ▶ HOMES

B Business name ▶

C Employer identification number

D Business address (number and street) ▶ 130 Main Street
City, State and ZIP Code ▶ Pleasantville, Pennsylvania   2 , 3 : 1 , 2 , 4 , 5 , 7 , 9 , 6

E Accounting method: (1) ☒ Cash   (2) ☐ Accrual   (3) ☐ Other (specify) ▶

F Method(s) used to value closing inventory:
(1) ☐ Cost   (2) ☐ Lower of cost or market   (3) ☐ Other (if other, attach explanation) Not Applic.

	Yes	No
G Was there any major change in determining quantities, costs, or valuations between opening and closing inventory? . . If "Yes," attach explanation.		X
H Did you deduct expenses for an office in your home?		X

Part I   Income

1 a Gross receipts or sales	**1a**	121,700	
b Returns and allowances	**1b**	0	
c Balance (subtract line 1b from line 1a)	**1c**		121,700
2 Cost of goods sold and/or operations (Schedule C–1, line 8)	**2**		81,000
3 Gross profit (subtract line 2 from line 1c)	**3**		40,700
4 a Windfall Profit Tax Credit or Refund received in 1981 (see Instructions)	**4a**		
b Other income (attach schedule)	**4b**		
5 Total income (add lines 3, 4a, and 4b) . . . . ▶	**5**		40,700

Part II   Deductions

6 Advertising	1,100		29 a Wages . .		
7 Amortization			b Jobs credit		
8 Bad debts from sales or services .			c WIN credit		
9 Bank service charges			d Total credits		
10 Car and truck expenses			e Subtract line 29d from 29a .		
11 Commissions	1,500		30 Windfall Profit Tax withheld in		
12 Depletion			1981		
13 Depreciation (see Instructions) .	4,100		31 Other expenses (specify):		
14 Dues and publications . . .			a Salaries not part of		
15 Employee benefit programs . .			b cost of goods sold	4,800	
16 Freight (not included on Schedule C–1) .			c		
17 Insurance	1,400		d Small tool expense	300	
18 Interest on business indebtedness	1,500		e		
19 Laundry and cleaning			f		
20 Legal and professional services .	600		g		
21 Office supplies and postage . . .			h		
22 Pension and profit-sharing plans .			i		
23 Rent on business property . . .	4,800		j		
24 Repairs	1,200		k		
25 Supplies (not included on Schedule C–1) .			l		
26 Taxes (do not include Windfall Profit Tax, see line 30)			m		
			n		
27 Travel and entertainment . . .	750		o		
28 Utilities and telephone	450		p		

32 Total deductions (add amounts in columns for lines 6 through 31p) . . . . ▶	**32**		22,500
33 Net profit or (loss) (subtract line 32 from line 5). If a profit, enter on Form 1040, line 11, and on Schedule SE, Part II, line 5a (or Form 1041, line 6). If a loss, go on to line 34	**33**		18,200

34 If you have a loss, do you have amounts for which you are not "at risk" in this business (see Instructions)? . . ☐ Yes ☒ No
If you checked "No," enter the loss on Form 1040, line 11, and on Schedule SE, Part II, line 5a (or Form 1041, line 6).

For Paperwork Reduction Act Notice, see Form 1040 Instructions.

Exhibit 11.3   Sample Schedule C (Form 1040) — Profit or (Loss) from Business (Proprietorship)

Schedule C (Form 1040) 1981   Page **2**

SCHEDULE C–1.—Cost of Goods Sold and/or Operations (See Schedule C Instructions for Part I, line 2)

1 Inventory at beginning of year (if different from last year's closing inventory, attach explanation) .	**1**		0
2 a Purchases **2a** 33,000			
b Cost of items withdrawn for personal use **2b** 0			
c Balance (subtract line 2b from line 2a)	**2c**		33,000
3 Cost of labor (do not include salary paid to yourself)	**3**		41,000
4 Materials and supplies	**4**		7,000
5 Other costs (attach schedule)	**5**		
6 Add lines 1, 2c, and 3 through 5	**6**		81,000
7 Inventory at end of year	**7**		0
8 Cost of goods sold and/or operations (subtract line 7 from line 6). Enter here and on Part I, line 2 . ▶	**8**		81,000

SCHEDULE C–2.—Depreciation (See Schedule C Instructions for line 13)

Complete Schedule C–2 if you claim depreciation ONLY for assets placed in service before January 1, 1981. If you need more space, use Form 4562. If you claim a deduction for any assets placed in service after December 31, 1980, use Form 4562 to figure your total deduction for all assets; do NOT complete Schedule C–2.

Description of property (a)	Date acquired (b)	Cost or other basis (c)	Depreciation allowed or allowable in prior years (d)	Method of computing depreciation (e)	Life or rate (f)	Depreciation for this year (g)
1 Depreciation (see Instructions):						
Furniture & Fixtures	Various	3,800	1,530	SL	10 yrs	380
Transportation Equipment	1980	6,100	450	SL	3 yrs	2,033
Machinery & Equipment	Various	15,000	11,500	DB	10 yrs	887
Scaffolds	6/1/80	4,000	0	DDB	5 yrs	800
2 Totals		28,900			**2**	4,100
3 Depreciation claimed in Schedule C–1					**3**	
4 Balance (subtract line 3 from line 2). Enter here and on Part II, line 13 . . . . ▶					**4**	4,100

SCHEDULE C–3.—Expense Account Information (See Schedule C Instructions for Schedule C–3)

Enter information for yourself and your five highest paid employees. In determining the five highest paid employees, add expense account allowances to the salaries and wages. However, you don't have to provide the information for any employee for whom the combined amount is less than $50,000, or for yourself if your expense account allowance plus line 33, page 1, is less than $50,000.

Name (a)	Expense account (b)	Salaries and wages (c)
Owner		
1		
2		
3		
4		
5		

Did you claim a deduction for expenses connected with:	Yes	No
A Entertainment facility (boat, resort, ranch, etc.)?		X
B Living accommodations (except employees on business)?		X
C Conventions or meetings you or your employees attended outside the North American area? (see Instructions) . . .		X
D Employees' families at conventions or meetings?		X
If "Yes," were any of these conventions or meetings outside the North American area?		
E Vacations for employees or their families not reported on Form W–2?		X

☆ U.S. GOVERNMENT PRINTING OFFICE : 1981—O–343-409 13-5606244

Exhibit 11.3, continued

for listing general expenses. A number of items are listed individually, and this makes analysis simpler.

Net profit appears on line 33. You must remember that this is a taxable, personal income. The salary of the proprietor is not shown. The bottom line is both salary and profit. Also, there is no tax reserve. What may look like reasonable profit could be a loss after a reasonable salary and appropriate taxes are deducted.

On page two, Schedule C-1 (cost of sales) is very much the same as in other tax returns we have reviewed. It provides a breakdown of sales expense and it lists the ending inventory. Because there is no balance sheet this inventory figure becomes quite important.

Also on page two is the depreciation section, Schedule C-2, which tells us the date acquired, original cost, method of computation used, expected life, and net book value of all fixed assets. This section functions as a checklist of all the equipment a company owns. It is of extra value when there is no balance sheet.

In the past few pages we have summarized the information available to a lending officer merely by requesting a tax return. Analysis becomes more creative and, yes, even more difficult; as long as there is a tax return, however, no one can ever claim he has no statement. Now let us take a look at how we can "create" a balance sheet for the client who is without a financial statement.

The Interview

During the interview is when we really discover the nature of our client. Those "gut decision" juices start to flow. We are beginning to make judgments of the character and capability of the officer representing the company and of the company itself. We are seeking to determine the fiber of the company. There are many topics to be covered during these precious moments of direct contact. Financial matters are sometimes pushed to the background. This is a mistake. Even if you don't have the client's statement in front of you, you should at this point know enough about statements to make sure you spend a moment or two covering each of the major categories. Follow the statement in your mind: cash, receivables, inventories, and so forth.

In getting past the numbers to the content, you need the insight provided by your client — especially when dealing with smaller companies where abnormalities are common. A statement really cannot be analyzed by someone not directly associated with the loan, unless an academic approach is taken.

Putting It Together

We have come to the final point of this chapter. As we have said before, the statement is really a blueprint to guide us as we delve into the facts. Where a statement does not exist we must prepare one. It may not meet all accounting standards, but should give us a preliminary overview of the company.

There is no question that we are "reaching." Loans of any real size require statements. But if you have a client who has been with you for some time, you may not be able to get a good statement and still keep him as a client.

Let us illustrate how to approach such a situation. Suppose your client is John Doe of Doe's T.V. You have a personal tax return which was prepared by an accountant and you are presently halfway through the interview. (Without the tax return as a minimum, you should not even begin to discuss seriously this or any loan request.)

John is sitting across from you. During the conversation, as certain topics are covered, you slowly begin to prepare a personal and business balance sheet on a scratch pad.

John is your client and you have reviewed the status of his accounts prior to the meeting. The personal accounts average $500, and the company account is about $4,000. "John, how were sales last year? What about collections? How much is outstanding now?"

With answers to these questions, your makeshift balance sheet begins to take shape.

	COMPANY	PERSONAL
CASH	$ 4,000	$ 500
ACCOUNTS RECEIVABLE	9,000	

"Do you have any really bad accounts? Are there any accounts over 90 days? Who are the bigger ones?

"John, I see you had a sale last week. Was your inventory reduced a lot?"

You now add the amount of his present inventory. If present inventory is abnormally low, then you should use his normal inventory.

INVENTORY	$15,000

Because you place little value on prepaid expenses, you pass over them.

The depreciation schedule on the tax return tells you about the fixed assets. The original cost of the fixtures, as well as of trucks and equipment, is reviewed. "John, how's that truck of yours? What about your tools? A value is determined. Granted, it's somewhat arbitrary, but it's also realistic. Our next line then becomes:

MACHINERY & EQUIPMENT	$27,000

John's mortgage is with your bank. His house is in a nice section of town. It has good value, and John is a stickler for repairs. You know the values in the area and the next line is written:

HOME	$41,000

John buys his product from a number of people. A discussion of suppliers, terms, and delivery will yield an accounts payable balance. Is this normal or seasonally low? Remember the inventory and adjust it so that inventory and accounts payable are shown at a similar point in the business cycle. You know the balance of his car loan, the family's mortgage, and the equipment term loan. There is no need to separate short- from long-term. You know what the payments will be and you keep it in mind. You now write:

	COMPANY	PERSONAL
ACCOUNTS PAYABLE	$10,000	
NOTES PAYABLE	5000	$2,000
MORTGAGE		17,000
TERM LOAN	16,000	

You ask, "John, not counting what you owe these suppliers and my notes, how much is outstanding now?" Your makeshift balance sheet is completed with this last entry:

BILLS-GENERAL $2,000 $ 1,000

Putting together all the items covered in the interview, you get a statement which looks something like the one in Table 11.1.

This crude statement along with the income statement on his tax return will give a fairly realistic picture of your client's personal as well as business worth.

You have thus increased your ability to render an informed loan decision. You have "created" a financial statement.

Table 11.1 Sample statement created by banker

	Company	Personal
JOHN DOE		
Cash	$ 4,000	$ 500
Accounts receivable	9,000	
Inventory	15,000	
Total current assets	$28,000	$ 500
Machinery and equipment	27,000	
Home		63,000
Total assets	$55,000	$63,500
Accounts payable	$10,000	
Notes payable	5,000	$ 2,000
Miscellaneous payables	2,000	1,000
Total current liabilities	$17,000	$ 3,000
Mortgage		$36,000
Term loan	16,000	
Total liabilities	$33,000	$39,000
Equity	$22,000	$24,500

Exercise 6

What follows is a statement of Main Realty, Inc. This real estate company is owned by the same individuals who own the Main Restaurant Company, an affiliated company. The companies are not consolidated.

The audit was performed by a well known and highly respected firm. You are familiar with the local managing partners and feel the firm to be of the highest quality.

Review the statement and compare your conclusions with those of the other analyst which directly follow the statement.

```
                    MAIN REALTY, INC.

                    JUNE 30, 19XX
```

Board of Directors
Main Realty, Inc.
Wilkes-Barre, Pennsylvania

   The accompanying balance sheet of Main Realty, Inc. as at June 30, 19

and the related statements of income and retained earnings and of changes in

financial position for the year then ended were not audited by us and accordingly

we do not express an opinion on them.

August 16, 19XX

MAIN REALTY, INC.

BALANCE SHEET - JUNE 30, 19XX
(Unaudited)

ASSETS

Real estate (Note 2):	
Land	$ 117,346
Building	2,142,044
	2,259,390
Less accumulated depreciation	304,718
	1,954,672
Cash	19,426
Due from Main Restaurant Company, affiliate	31,434
Loans receivable, shareholders	8,374
Organization costs, net	750
	$2,014,656

LIABILITIES AND SHAREHOLDERS' EQUITY

Liabilities:	
Mortgage payable (Note 2)	$1,684,035
Term notes payable (Note 3)	53,692
Due to contractor and architect	29,314
Accrued expenses	19,107
Payroll taxes	417
Income taxes	4,470
Total liabilities	1,791,035
Deferred income taxes	11,912
Commitments (Note 4)	
Shareholders' equity:	
Common stock, $1 par; authorized 100,000 shares; issued and outstanding 88,000 shares	88,000
Capital in excess of par	72,000
Retained earnings	51,709
	211,709
	$2,014,656

See notes to financial statements

MAIN REALTY, INC.

STATEMENT OF INCOME AND RETAINED EARNINGS

YEAR ENDED JUNE 30, 19XX
(Unaudited)

Rental income	$273,000
Operating expenses:	
Salaries, officer	4,500
Payroll taxes	213
Amortization, organization cost	100
Interest	123,614
Pennsylvania capital stock tax	1,500
Professional services	1,750
Repairs and maintenance	1,413
	133,090
Income from operations before depreciation	139,910
Depreciation	125,710
Income before income taxes	14,200
Income taxes:	
Current	4,312
Deferred	3,715
	8,027
Net income	6,173
Retained earnings, beginning of year	45,536
Retained earnings, end of year	$ 51,709
Earnings per common share	$.59

See notes to financial statements

MAIN REALTY, INC.

STATEMENT OF CHANGES IN FINANCIAL POSITION

YEAR ENDED JUNE 30, 19XX
(Unaudited)

Source of funds:	
Net income	$ 6,173
Add items not affecting cash:	
Depreciation	125,710
Amortization, organization costs	100
Increase in deferred taxes	3,715
Cash provided from operations	135,698
Increase in:	
Mortgage payable	158,631
Term note payable	35,000
Other	5,127
	334,456
Application of funds:	
Purchase of building	238,404
Decrease in:	
Mortgage payable	10,000
Term notes payable	34,318
Due to contractor and architect	17,417
Increase in due from Main Restaurant Company, affiliate	30,000
	330,139
Increase in cash	$ 4,317

See notes to financial statements

MAIN REALTY, INC.

NOTES TO FINANCIAL STATEMENTS

YEAR ENDED JUNE 30, 19XX
(Unaudited)

1. Summary of significant accounting policies:

Real estate, deferred taxes and depreciation:
Real estate is stated at cost. Depreciation is being provided on assets acquired prior to June 30, 19XX by the straight-line method for both financial reporting and income tax reporting purposes. Depreciation on assets acquired subsequent to June 30, 19XX is provided by the straight-line method for financial reporting and accelerated methods for income tax reporting purposes. Deferred income taxes result from this difference in treatment.

Organization costs:
Organization costs are being amortized by the straight-line method over 60 months.

2. Mortgage payable:

Current portion	$ 71,610
Long-term portion	1,612,425
Total	$1,684,035

All real estate is pledged as collateral for the 8% mortgage which is payable $12,750 per month, including interest, through 1990.

3. Term notes payable:

Description	Interest rate	Due in one year	Due after one year	Maturity	Monthly payment including interest
Unsecured note	8 1/2%	$ 2,178	$13,417	19	$311
Unsecured note	8 1/2%	8,338	29,759	19	317
		$10,516	$43,176		

4. Commitments:

The Company leases its facilities to Main Restaurant Company, an affiliated company. The lease provides for rental of $22,750 per month on a net basis and expires May 31, 19XX.

Comments

A statement by a reputable firm, even though it is unaudited, is a most useful tool. The information we need to render a decision should be contained in it.

The notes to the financial statements contain two important pieces of information. The first is that management is reporting depreciation on certain assets one way for income tax purposes and another way for financial statements. The net result, as the note tells us is deferred income taxes. Because the statement is issued by a reputable firm, you know this matter is being handled properly. If you were told of a similar difference in reporting by a client whose statement was prepared by a brother-in-law, your reaction certainly would be less favorable.

The fourth note tells us that the lease between the two affiliated companies requires payments of $22,750 to Main Realty per month. This amount must be sufficient to cover necessary expenses plus allow for payments to us. The amounts of our payments are covered by the other footnotes.

The balance sheet is quite interesting. Looking first at the equity, we see that the original investment was $160,000; with retained earnings, equity totals only $212,000. The total liabilities are $1.8 million. The leverage is extremely high, almost 9 to 1. This is not unusual for a real estate company. The permanent nature of the collateral is what justifies this abnormal extension of credit.

The presentation of the assets is different from what we have been seeing in other statements. The fixed assets are listed first. This is because they represent a major portion of all the assets. The current assets are listed below fixed assets. They are not classified as current, however, but merely are described as individual items.

The same is true of liabilities. They are not listed as current and long-term. We have this classification in the footnotes and are not alarmed by the presentation of liabilities on the balance sheet.

Our first reading then shows more than $200,000 of equity which is highly leveraged by mortgage and term loans against a large concentration of fixed assets.

We now turn our attention to the top of the balance sheet and read each item. The fixed assets have depreciated about 15 percent. The net value shown appears to be fairly realistic. Your credit file has the amount of the last appraisal. You should check it if you are not familiar with it. Cash appears to be in line. The next two items are of concern however.

First, we see that funds are due from the operating company. This could mean that the operating company is not generating enough cash to meet its rental payments, and therefore funds are due to the real estate company. It could mean that additional funds were needed by the operating company and borrowed from the real estate company, but because we have not yet seen the income statement, it is too soon to judge inter-company loans. If a strong cash flow exists, then perhaps excess funds have been accumulated by the real estate company and these funds are being shuffled back and forth. If it develops that the real estate company is carrying the operating company, instead of the other way around, then the long-term prospects of your client are questionable. We will have to see the affiliate's statement in order to find out about the funds due to the real estate company, and to make a judgment concerning these funds.

The next item is loans receivable from shareholders. This item should be cause for great concern to any loan officer. You are a banker and in the business of lending money. You have invested a great deal of money in your client's venture. You dictate both the interest and the repayment. In this case, your loans are secured. Now your client has taken some of these funds and has entered the lending business by making loans to its owners. On what basis were these funds loaned? Is the loan secured? Is there a repayment schedule?

It is unfair to say that if these funds were not lent, the amount you would lend would be decreased. It is fair to say that if the owners want or need funds they should see you, and not look to their own company. Loans to key officers or employees, for whatever reason, are potentially dangerous; in many cases, they leave a company with scars that will not heal. Therefore, this item must be explored in great detail. Close scrutiny by all parties is warranted.

Moving to the liability section we see no listing of liabilities by due dates. The liabilities will have to be reviewed in terms of current and long-term payments. The notes show that the mortgage payments plus the two term notes have a principal payment due next year of $82,000 ($72,000 + $10,000). The other liabilities appear to be current, and discussions with the client should bear this out. Of the $1.8 million in liabilities, then, approximately $150,000 is due in cash within the next twelve months, not counting interest on loans due within the same period. The $150,000 represents $65,000 in ordinary payables listed on the balance sheet plus $82,000 which is the current portion of long-term debt. There is only one current asset to offset this, and that is the $20,000 in cash. This is the minimum amount that should be on hand. (An old financial rule of thumb is to have one month's sales on hand in cash.) Therefore, all payments must be generated from profit. With this in mind, we proceed to the income statement.

Rental income consists primarily of the payments from the affiliate ($22,750 per month under the existing contract according to the notes). Gross profit is not reflected as we are used to seeing it. All expenses have been grouped together and called operating expenses. Most of this expense is interest. Income from operations before depreciation is clearly marked. Even if it weren't, we should be thinking in these terms. Profit appears to be minimal, and, as expected from the footnotes, we see taxes stated on both a current and deferred basis.

As the key to any real estate loan is an asset's ability to service debt, we should determine the amount available for repayment of debt and calculate the debt service ratio (see page 91).

The first step is to determine the true profit from ownership of the asset, that is the profit before any interest or depreciation expense. The best way to do this is to take the net profit and add to it interest and depreciation expense.

Net income	$ 6,173
Depreciation	125,710
Interest expense	123,614
Total amount available to service debt	$255,497

Next we determine the amount currently needed to service existing long-term debt. The annual payment on the mortgage is $153,000 ($12,750 monthly) and the annual payment on the two term loans combined is $7,536 ($311 and $317 monthly). Altogether, the amount needed is $160,536.

$$\frac{\$255,000}{\$160,500} = 1.59$$

Our client's profit is better than one-and-a-half times the loan payment requirement. We can feel comfortable with this debt service ratio.

What should be most evident now is that the key to the situation continues to be the ability of the tenant to make payments. As the tenant is an affiliated company, you can request and review its statement. If it were an independent third party, then you would have to explore with your client the financial strength of his tenant. The question is: Why have loans been made to the tenant?

The final page is the statement of changes in financial position. Even though we have not yet covered such statements, we have examined Main Realty's balance sheet and income statement with emphasis on cash profits and their use in making necessary payments and so we are in a position to review in a general way its statement of changes in financial position.

The statement's purpose is to summarize cash flow. It tells us where cash has come from during the last year and how it was used. We see that cash from operations was $135,000 and that this amount plus what was probably the final mortgage draw ($158,000) was used to pay for and finish the buildings. We also see under the use of funds that reductions were started on the term loans. Finally, we know that $30,000 of the $31,400 in advances to the affiliated company were made during the past year.

Although we have said that all financial statements should be reviewed in the context of a loan request, this statement was not presented with a request. The loan already has been made. The focus of the review, therefore, is the former request for this loan; the emphasis shifts from the making of the loan to the repayment of the loan. In this case, Main Realty's cash flow and the affiliates ability to make payments are the keys to repayment.

Problem

Company X *(in thousands of dollars)*		Company Y *(in thousands of dollars)*	
ASSETS		ASSETS	
Cash	$ 27	Cash	$ 18
Accounts receivable	340	Accounts receivable	157
Inventory	138	Inventory	93
Prepaid expenses	10	Prepaid expenses	4
Total current assets	$ 515	Total current assets	$ 272
Land and buildings	241	Furniture and fixtures	54
Total assets	$ 756	Total assets	$ 326
LIABILITIES AND NET WORTH		LIABILITIES AND NET WORTH	
Notes payable	$ 135	Notes payable	$ 50
Accounts payable	157	Accounts payable	106
Accruals	71	Accruals	19
Total current liabilities	$ 363	Total current liabilities	$ 175
Long-term debt payable	100	Long-term debt payable	50
Total liabilities	$ 463	Total liabilities	$ 225
Common stock $100		Common stock $ 50	
Surplus 193		Surplus 51	
Total equity	293	Total equity	101
Total liabilities & net worth	$ 756	Total liabilities & net worth	$ 326
OPERATIONS		OPERATIONS	
Net sales	$1,769	Net sales	$ 624
Cost of sales	1,026	Cost of sales	412
Net profit before taxes	$ 29	Net profit before taxes	$ 18

Solution

FIRST EASTERN BANK, N. A.
COMPARISON STATEMENT

000's Omitted

NAME	COMPANY X	COMPANY Y		COMPANY X	COMPANY Y
ASSETS Date					
1 Cash	27	18		3.6	5.5
2 Marketable Securities — C/D's					
3 Receivable — Trade (Net)	340	157		45.0	48.2
4					
5 Inventories	138	93		18.2	28.5
6					
7					
8 All Other Current					
9 TOTAL CURRENT ASSETS	505	268		66.8	82.2
10 Fixed Assets — Net	241	54		31.9	16.6
11					
12					
13 Investments					
14					
15 All Other Noncurrent (Incl. Prepaid)	10	4		1.3	1.2
16 TOTAL NONCURRENT ASSETS	251	58		33.2	17.8
17 TOTAL ASSETS	756	326		100.0	100.0
LIABILITIES					
18 Notes Payable — Banks	135	50		17.8	15.4
19 Notes Payable — Other					
20					
21 Current Maturities of L. T. Debt					
22 Accounts Payable — Trade	157	106		20.8	32.5
23					
24 Interest & Other Accruals	71	19		9.4	5.8
25 Taxes Payable					
26					
27					
28 All Other Current					
29 TOTAL CURRENT DEBT	363	175		48.0	53.7
30 Mortgage Payable					
31 Long Term Debt	100	50		13.2	15.3
32					
33 All Other Noncurrent					
34 TOTAL NONCURRENT DEBT	100	50		13.2	15.3
35 TOTAL LIABILITIES	463	225		61.2	69.0
36 Capital					
37 Retained Earnings					
38					
39 NET WORTH	293	101		38.8	31.0
40 TOTAL LIABILITIES&NET WORTH	756	326		100.0	100.0
41					
42 NET WORKING CAPITAL (9-29)	142	93		18.8	28.5
RATIOS					
43 Quick	1.01 to 1	1.00 to 1			
44 Current	1.39 to 1	1.53 to 1			
45 Total Debt/Working Capital	463/142	225/93			
46 Total Debt/Net Worth	463/293	225/101			
47 Receivable Turnover Days	64 days	91 days			
48 Inventory Turnover Days	48 days	81 days			
49 % Profit bef. Taxes/Net Worth	9.8%	17.8%			
50 % Profit bef. Taxes/Total Assets	3.8%	5.5%			
51					
52 Statement by					
53 Type of Statement					
54 Spread by					
55 Contingent Liabilities					
56					

FORM 18-1

FIRST EASTERN BANK, N. A.

NAME

OPERATIONS	Date	COMPANY X	%	COMPANY Y	%		%	COMPANY X	%	COMPANY Y	%
101 Net Sales		1,769		624				100.0		100.0	
102 Cost of Sales		1,026		412				58.0		66.0	
103 Gross Profit		743		212				42.0		34.0	
104 Operating Expenses		714		194				40.4		31.1	
105 Net Profit before Depreciation		29		18				1.6		2.9	
106 Depreciation											
107 Profit from Operations		29		18				1.6		2.9	
108 Extraordinary Items											
109											
110 Profits Before Taxes		29		18				1.6		2.9	
111 Income Taxes											
112											
113 NET PROFIT AFTER TAXES		29		18				1.6		2.9	
RECONCILIATION OF NET WORTH											
114 Net Worth — Beginning											
115 Add: Net Profit After Taxes											
116											
117											
118 Less: Net Loss											
119 Dividend Paid											
120											
121											
122 Net Worth — Ending											
SOURCE & APPLICATION OF FUNDS											
Source of Funds:											
123 Net Profit											
124 Depreciation, Amort., Depletion											
125 Increase Long Term Debt											
126											
127											
128 Other Noncurrent Accounts — Net											
129 TOTAL SOURCES											
Application of Funds:											
130 Net Loss											
131 Dividends Paid											
132 Purchase of Fixed Assets											
133 Reduction Long Term Debt											
134											
135											
136 Other Noncurrent Accounts — Net											
137 TOTAL APPLICATIONS											
138 INC./DEC. OF WORKING CAPITAL											
RECONCIL. OF W/C CHANGES											
139 Cash											
140 Accounts Receivable											
141 Inventory											
142 Other											
143											
144 Notes Payable											
145 Accounts Payable											
146 Current Maturities — L.T. Debt											
147 Other											
148											
149 Inc/Dec W/C (139-143) — (144-148)											

COMMENTS:

Exercise 8

The following pages contain the tax return of Custom Home Builders, Inc. This three-year-old company has both speculative construction mortgages and a line of credit with your bank. You are in charge of the bank's problem loan department and have just finished a review of this company. The line has been renewed a number of times; at present, it is past due.

Your client said he kept no "real" books; he knew by his checkbook how things were going. You then asked for and received the tax return.

Review it and compare your comments to those of other analysts which follow. If you have not been jotting down key points before reading the comments section, then you are missing the purpose of the exercise.

Form **1120**	**U.S. Corporation Income Tax Return**		OMB No. 1545–0123

Department of the Treasury
Internal Revenue Service

For calendar year 1981 or other tax year beginning ..April..1.., 1981, ending March..31.,19.82

▶For Paperwork Reduction Act Notice, see page 1 of the instructions

1981

Check if a—

A. Consolidated return ☐
B. Personal Holding Co. ☐
C. Business Code No. (See page 9 of Instructions)
     1510

Use IRS label. Otherwise please print or type.

Name
Custom Home Builders. Inc.

Number and street
147 New Development Drive

City or town, State, and ZIP code
Top of the Mountain. California 93522

D. Employer identification number
24–5671234

E. Date incorporated
7/1/78

F. Total assets (see Specific Instructions)
$ 462,625

Gross Income

1	(a) Gross receipts or sales $ _____ (b) Less returns and allowances $ _____ Balance ▶	1(c)	1,163,739
2	Cost of goods sold (Schedule A) and/or operations (attach schedule)	2	1,046,322
3	Gross profit (subtract line 2 from line 1(c))	3	117,417
4	Dividends (Schedule C)	4	
5	Interest on obligations of the United States and U.S. instrumentalities	5	
6	Other interest	6	
7	Gross rents	7	
8	Gross royalties	8	
9	(a) Capital gain net income (attach separate Schedule D)	9(a)	
	(b) Net gain or (loss) from Form 4797, line 11(a), Part II (attach Form 4797)	9(b)	
10	Other income (see instructions—attach schedule)	10	
11	TOTAL income—Add lines 3 through 10	11	117,417

Deductions

12	Compensation of officers (Schedule E)	12	25,600
13	(a) Salaries and wages _____ 13(b) Less WIN and jobs credit(s) _____ Balance ▶	13(c)	12,500
14	Repairs (see instructions)	14	1,427
15	Bad debts (Schedule F if reserve method is used)	15	
16	Rents	16	
17	Taxes . Real. estate	17	412
18	Interest	18	22,427
19	Contributions (not over 5% of line 30 adjusted per instructions)	19	100
20	Amortization (attach schedule)	20	
21	Depreciation from Form 4562 (attach Form 4562) _____, less depreciation claimed in Schedule A and elsewhere on return _____, Balance ▶	21	10,106
22	Depletion	22	
23	Advertising	23	4,546
24	Pension, profit-sharing, etc. plans (see instructions)	24	
25	Employee benefit programs (see instructions)	25	
26	Other deductions (attach schedule)	26	36,103
27	TOTAL deductions—Add lines 12 through 26	27	113,221
28	Taxable income before net operating loss deduction and special deductions (subtract line 27 from line 11)	28	4,196
29	Less: (a) Net operating loss deduction (see instructions—attach schedule) . 29(a) _____		
	(b) Special deductions (Schedule C) . . . . 29(b) _____	29	
30	Taxable income (subtract line 29 from line 28)	30	4,196

Tax

31	TOTAL TAX (Schedule J)	31	702
32	Credits: (a) Overpayment from 1980 allowed as a credit . . _____		
	(b) 1981 estimated tax payments . . . . . _____		
	(c) Less refund of 1981 estimated tax applied for on Form 4466 . (_____)		
	(d) Tax deposited: Form 7004 _____ Form 7005 (attach) _____ Total ▶ _____		
	(e) Credit from regulated investment companies (attach Form 2439) . . . . . _____		
	(f) Federal tax on special fuels and oils (attach Form 4136 or 4136–T)	32	
33	TAX DUE (subtract line 32 from line 31). See instruction C3 for depositary method of payment . (Check ▶ ☐ if Form 2220 is attached. See instruction D.) ▶ $_____	33	702
34	OVERPAYMENT (subtract line 31 from line 32)	34	
35	Enter amount of line 34 you want: Credited to 1982 estimated tax ▶ _____ Refunded ▶	35	

Please Sign Here

Under penalties of perjury, I declare that I have examined this return, including accompanying schedules and statements, and to the best of my knowledge and belief, it is true, correct, and complete. Declaration of preparer (other than taxpayer) is based on all information of which preparer has any knowledge.

Signature of officer: *J. Builder*   Date 5/17/82   Title President

Paid Preparer's Use Only

Preparer's signature ▶ X _Beancounter_	Date 5/10/82	Check if self-employed ▶ ☐	Preparer's social security no.
Firm's name (or yours, if self-employed) and address ▶ Berry, Beancounter & Co. Last Street, Anywhere, Cal.		E.I. No. ▶ 23–9173716	ZIP code ▶ 93521

Form 1120 (1981)   **Schedule A**   **Cost of Goods Sold** (See Instructions for Schedule A)   **Page 2**

1 Inventory at beginning of year	167,946
2 Merchandise bought for manufacture or sale	698,427
3 Salaries and wages	178,400
4 Other costs (attach schedule)	374,463
5 Total—Add lines 1 through 4	1,419,236
6 Inventory at end of year	372,914
7 Cost of goods sold—Subtract line 6 from line 5. Enter here and on line 2, page 1	1,046,322

8 (a) Check all methods used for valuing closing inventory: (i) ☒ Cost (ii) ☐ Lower of cost or market as described in Regulations section 1.471–4 (see instructions) (iii) ☐ Writedown of "subnormal" goods as described in Regulations section 1.471–2(c) (see instructions)

   (b) Did you use any other method of inventory valuation not described above? . . . . ☐ Yes ☒ No

      If "Yes," specify method used and attach explanation ▶ ....

   (c) Check if the LIFO inventory method was adopted this tax year for any goods (If checked, attach Form 970.) . . . . . . ☐

   (d) If the LIFO inventory method was used for this tax year, enter percentage (or amounts) of closing inventory computed under LIFO . . . .

   (e) If you are engaged in manufacturing, did you value your inventory using the full absorption method (Regulations section 1.471–11)? . . . . ☐ Yes ☐ No

   (f) Was there any substantial change in determining quantities, cost, or valuations between opening and closing inventory? . . . ☐ Yes ☒ No
      If "Yes," attach explanation.

Schedule C   **Dividends and Special Deductions** (See instructions for Schedule C)

	(A) Dividends received	(B) %	(C) Special deductions: multiply (A) × (B)
1 Domestic corporations subject to 85% deduction		85	
2 Certain preferred stock of public utilities		59.13	
3 Foreign corporations subject to 85% deduction		85	
4 Wholly-owned foreign subsidiaries subject to 100% deduction (section 245(b)) .		100	
5 Total—Add lines 1 through 4. See instructions for limitation			
6 Affiliated groups subject to the 100% deduction (section 243(a)(3))		100	
7 Other dividends from foreign corporations not included in lines 3 and 4 . . .			
8 Income from controlled foreign corporations under subpart F (attach Forms 3646) .			
9 Foreign dividend gross-up (section 78)			
10 DISC or former DISC not included in line 1 (section 246(d))			
11 Other dividends			
12 Deduction for dividends paid on certain preferred stock of public utilities (see instructions)			
13 Total dividends—Add lines 1 through 11. Enter here and on line 4, page 1 ▶			
14 Total deductions—Add lines 5 through 12. Enter here and on line 29(b), page 1 ▶			

Schedule E   **Compensation of Officers** (See instruction for line 12)

1. Name of officer	2. Social security number	3. Time devoted to business	Percent of corporation stock owned		6. Amount of compensation	7. Expense account allowances
			4. Common	5. Preferred		
J. Builder	211-32-9113	100%	100		25,600	None
Total compensation of officers—Enter here and on line 12, page 1						

Schedule F   **Bad Debts—Reserve Method** (See instruction for line 15)

1. Year	2. Trade notes and accounts receivable outstanding at end of year	3. Sales on account	Amount added to reserve		6. Amount charged against reserve	7. Reserve for bad debts at end of year
			4. Current year's provision	5. Recoveries		
1976						
1977						
1978						
1979						
1980						
1981						

Form 1120 (1981)   Page **3**

Schedule J **Tax Computation** (See instructions for Schedule J on pages 7 and 8)

Note: *Fiscal year corporations, see instructions on pages 10 and 11. Omit line 1, complete line 2(a) and, if applicable, line 2(b), and enter on line 3, the amount from line 44, Part III, of the fiscal year worksheet provided on page 11 of the instructions.*

1 Taxable income (line 30, page 1) . . . .

2 (a) Are you a member of a controlled group? . . . . ☐ Yes ☒ No

   (b) If "Yes," see instructions and enter your portion of the $25,000 amount in each taxable income bracket:

      (i) $............................. *(ii)* $............................. *(iii)* $............................. *(iv)* $.............................

3 Income tax (see instructions to figure the tax; enter this tax or alternative tax from Schedule D, whichever is less). Check if from Schedule D ▶ ☐ **702**

4 (a) Foreign tax credit (attach Form 1118) . . . .

   (b) Investment credit (attach Form 3468) . . . .

   (c) Work incentive (WIN) credit (attach Form 4874) . . . .

   (d) Jobs credit (attach Form 5884) . . . .

   (e) Other credits (see instructions—attach forms and schedule) . . . .

5 Total—Add lines 4(a) through 4(e) **702**

6 Subtract line 5 from line 3 . . . .

7 Personal holding company tax (attach Schedule PH (Form 1120)) . . . .

8 Tax from recomputing prior-year investment credit (attach Form 4255) . . . .

9 Minimum tax on tax preference items (see instructions—attach Form 4626) . . . .

10 Total tax—Add lines 6 through 9. Enter here and on line 31, page 1 . . . . **702**

Additional Information (See page 8 of instructions)

	Yes	No
G Did you claim a deduction for expenses connected with:		
(1) Entertainment facility (boat, resort, ranch, etc.)?		X
(2) Living accommodations (except employees on business)? . .		X
(3) Employees attending conventions or meetings outside the North American area? (See section 274(h))		X
(4) Employees' families at conventions or meetings? . . .		X
If "Yes," were any of these conventions or meetings outside the North American area? (See section 274(h))		
(5) Employee or family vacations not reported on Form W–2? . .		X

H (1) Did you at the end of the tax year own, directly or indirectly, 50% or more of the voting stock of a domestic corporation? (For rules of attribution, see section 267(c).) . . . . | | X

If "Yes," attach a schedule showing: (a) name, address, and identifying number; (b) percentage owned; (c) taxable income or (loss) (e.g., if a Form 1120: from Form 1120, line 28, page 1) of such corporation for the tax year ending with or within your tax year; (d) highest amount owed by you to such corporation during the year; and (e) highest amount owed to you by such corporation during the year.

(2) Did any individual, partnership, corporation, estate or trust at the end of the tax year own, directly or indirectly, 50% or more of your voting stock? (For rules of attribution, see section 267(c).) If "Yes," complete (a) through (e) . . . . | | X

(a) Attach a schedule showing name, address, and identifying number.

(b) Enter percentage owned ▶ ....

(c) Was the owner of such voting stock a person other than a U.S. person? (See instructions) . . . .

If "Yes," enter owner's country ▶ ....

(d) Enter highest amount owed by you to such owner during the year ▶

(e) Enter highest amount owed to you by such owner during the year ▶ ....

(Note: For purposes of H(1) and H(2), "highest amount owed" includes loans and accounts receivable/payable.)

I If you were a member of a controlled group subject to the provisions of section 1561, check the type of relationship:

(1) ☐ parent-subsidiary (2) ☐ brother-sister

(3) ☐ combination of (1) and (2) (See section 1563.)

J Refer to page 9 of instructions and state the principal:

Business activity Building contractor

Product or service Homes

	Yes	No
K Were you a U.S. shareholder of any controlled foreign corporation? (See sections 951 and 957.) If "Yes," attach Form 3646 for each such corporation		X
L At any time during the tax year, did you have an interest in or a signature or other authority over a bank account, securities account, or other financial account in a foreign country (see instructions)?		X
M Were you the grantor of, or transferor to, a foreign trust which existed during the current tax year, whether or not you have any beneficial interest in it?		X
If "Yes," you may have to file Forms 3520, 3520–A or 926.		
N During this tax year, did you pay dividends (other than stock dividends and distributions in exchange for stock) in excess of your current and accumulated earnings and profits? (See sections 301 and 316)		X
If "Yes," file Form 5452. If this is a consolidated return, answer here for parent corporation and on Form 851, Affiliations Schedule, for each subsidiary.		
O During this tax year was any part of your tax accounting records maintained on a computerized system?		X

Form 1120 (1981)   Page **4**

Schedule L — Balance Sheets

	Beginning of tax year		End of tax year	
ASSETS	(A)	(B)	(C)	(D)
1 Cash		10,751		1,658
2 Trade notes and accounts receivable	2,358		4,793	
(a) Less allowance for bad debts		2,358		4,793
3 Inventories		167,946		372,914
4 Gov't obligations: (a) U.S. and instrumentalities .				
(b) State, subdivisions thereof, etc.				
5 Other current assets (attach schedule)		1,537		3,721
6 Loans to stockholders		500		1,500
7 Mortgage and real estate loans				
8 Other investments (attach schedule)				
9 Buildings and other depreciable assets	95,031		101,791	
(a) Less accumulated depreciation	28,706	66,325	33,252	68,539
10 Depletable assets				
(a) Less accumulated depletion				
11 Land (net of any amortization)		6,000		6,000
12 Intangible assets (amortizable only)				
(a) Less accumulated amortization				
13 Other assets (attach schedule)		14,500		3,500
14 Total assets		269,917		462,625
LIABILITIES AND STOCKHOLDERS' EQUITY				
15 Accounts payable		19,207		2,703
16 Mtges, notes, bonds payable in less than 1 year . .		153,644		351,780
17 Other current liabilities (attach schedule) . . .		3,266		5,227
18 Loans from stockholders				
19 Mtges, notes, bonds payable in 1 year or more . .		54,726		63,347
20 Other liabilities (attach schedule)		8,000		5,000
21 Capital stock: (a) Preferred stock				
(b) Common stock		10,000		10,000
22 Paid-in or capital surplus				
23 Retained earnings—Appropriated (attach sch.) . .				
24 Retained earnings—Unappropriated		21,074		24,568
25 Less cost of treasury stock	(	)	(	)
26 Total liabilities and stockholders' equity		269,917		462,625

Schedule M–1 — Reconciliation of Income Per Books With Income Per Return

1 Net income per books	3,494	7 Income recorded on books this year not included in this return (itemize)	
2 Federal income tax	702	(a) Tax-exempt interest $............	
3 Excess of capital losses over capital gains			
4 Income subject to tax not recorded on books this year (itemize)............			
		8 Deductions in this tax return not charged against book income this year (itemize)	
5 Expenses recorded on books this year not deducted in this return (itemize)		(a) Depreciation . . . $............	
(a) Depreciation . . . . $............		(b) Contributions carryover . $............	
(b) Contributions carryover . . $............			
		9 Total of lines 7 and 8	
6 Total of lines 1 through 5	4,196	10 Income (line 28, page 1)—line 6 less 9 . .	4,196

Schedule M–2 — Analysis of Unappropriated Retained Earnings Per Books (line 24 above)

1 Balance at beginning of year	21,074	5 Distributions: (a) Cash	
2 Net income per books	3,494	(b) Stock	
3 Other increases (itemize)		(c) Property	
		6 Other decreases (itemize)	
		7 Total of lines 5 and 6 . . .	
4 Total of lines 1, 2, and 3	24,568	8 Balance at end of year (line 4 less 7) . . .	24,568

☆U.S. GOVERNMENT PRINTING OFFICE: 1981-343-117 E.I. 43-0787287

Form 4562
(Rev. September 1981)
Department of the Treasury (0)
Internal Revenue Service

Depreciation

▶ See separate instructions.
▶ Attach this form to your return.

OMB No. 1545-0172
Expires 12/31/82

Name(s) as shown on return

Custom Home Builders

Identifying number
24-5671234

▶ Generally, you must use the Accelerated Cost Recovery System of depreciation (ACRS) for all assets you placed in service after December 31, 1980. Report these assets in Part I, lines 1(a) through 1(f).

▶ You may elect to exclude certain property. Report this property in Part I, line 2.

▶ Use Part II for assets you placed in service before January 1, 1981, and certain other assets for which you cannot use ACRS.

▶ Filers of Schedule C (Form 1040), Schedule E (Form 1040) and Form 4835 should see the instructions for those forms before completing Form 4562.

Part I Assets placed in service after December 31, 1980

A. Class of property	B. Date placed in service	C. Cost or other basis	D. Recovery period	E. Method of figuring depreciation	F. Percentage	G. Deduction for this year
1 Accelerated Cost Recovery System (ACRS) (See instructions for grouping assets):						
(a) 3-year property						
(b) 5-year property						
(c) 10-year property						
(d) 15-year public utility property						
(e) 15-year real property—low-income housing						
(f) 15-year real property other than low-income housing						
2 Property subject to section 168(e)(2) election (see instructions):						
3 Totals (add amounts in columns C and G) . . .						0

4 Depreciation from Part II, line 3 10,106

5 Total (add column G, lines 3 and 4). Enter this amount on the depreciation expense line (where it applies) of your return 10,106

See Paperwork Reduction Act Notice on page 1 of the separate instructions.   Form **4562** (Rev. 9–81)

Form 4562 (Rev. 9–81)   Page 2

Part II   Assets placed in service before January 1, 1981 and other assets not qualifying for ACRS

A. Description of property	B. Date acquired	C. Cost or other basis	D. Depreciation allowed or allowable in earlier years	E. Method of figuring depreciation	F. Life or rate	G. Depreciation for this year
1 Class Life Asset Depreciation Range (CLADR) System Depreciation . . . . ▶						
2 Other depreciation (for grouping assets, see instructions for Part II):						
Buildings	1978	15,400	1,457	SL	20	770
Furniture and fixtures . .	1978	2,820	923	SL	7	410
Transportation equipment	1980	13,400	1,946	SL	3	4,365
Machinery and other equipment	Various	70,171	18,820	Var.	Var.	4,561
Other (specify)						
3 Total (add amounts in column G). Enter here and in Part I, line 4						10,106

☆ U.S. GOVERNMENT PRINTING OFFICE: 1981—O-343-455 58-040-1110

Custom Home Builders, Inc.

ID #24-5671234

SUPPLEMENTAL SCHEDULES

Page 1 - Line 26 - Other Deductions

Commissions to brokers	$ 16,370
Insurance	11,319
Utilities	3,182
Miscellaneous supplies	2,961
Legal and accounting	1,785
Miscellaneous other expenses	486
	$ 36,103

Page 2 - Schedule A - Line 4 - Other Costs

Subcontractors	$ 327,619
Payroll taxes	13,197
Equipment rentals	11,107
Employee traveling cost	9,147
Miscellaneous other expenses	13,393
	$ 374,463

Page 4 - Schedule L

Line 5 - Other current assets	
Prepaid expenses	$ 3,721
Line 13 - Other assets	
Land deposits	3,500
Line 17 - Other current liabilities	
Payroll taxes	3,619
Accrued expenses	1,608
	$ 5,227
Line 20 - Other liabilities	
Customer deposits	$ 5,000

Comments

A first reading of Custom Home Builders' tax return should tell us that, for some reason, the bank has allowed the situation to get completely out of hand. Using the organized approach to statement reading that we have developed, let's turn now to page four and review the balance sheet.

We see that the company's equity is very small, less than $35,000. Compare this with more than $400,000 of debt. The bank officer who showed such generosity ought to look up Webster's definition of "sharing."

The assets of the company are divided between inventory and fixed assets. We have a general idea of the nature and age of the fixed assets from the depreciation schedule which is attached to the return. (Form 4562.) What of the inventory? Do we know anything about it?

The liabilities consist mainly of outside notes, both short- and long-term. How does this debt break down? To whom are these notes payable?

Can we review and analyze this statement without knowing how inventory and liabilities break down? If your answer is no, then progress is being made. Tables 11.2 and 11.3 are breakdowns of the inventory and debt figures. Review them now and then return to the balance sheet.

With inventory and liability figures now broken down, we can begin our analysis. Some of the thoughts and questions which should occur to you follow.

The breakdown shows $303,000 of homes with $277,000 of mortgages: Are the estimates good? Has the bank maintained a continuing inspection program?

The job number coding appears to reflect years. Are some of the homes really three years old? If so, why aren't they selling and how could the bank have allowed this situation to continue? Last year's inventory was less than half of this year's.

What is the reason for having $70,000 of material on hand? That's enough for three or four homes.

The liabilities show a mortgage loan and an equipment loan totaling $48,000. There is $100,000 of equipment and building. The company has little equity. How was the balance financed?

The depreciation schedule shows a slow retirement of machinery. What is the reason for this?

A quick check with the note window reveals that our line of credit has not been paid out in some time. One doesn't have to be an expert to see

Table 11.2 Inventory analysis of Custom Home Builders, Inc. (March 31, 1982)

Job Number	Estimated sales price	Estimated cost at completion	Estimated percentage of completion	Cost assigned
79-07	$45,000	$36,000	100%	$36,000
79-41	42,500	31,600	95%	30,000
80-23	57,000	50,000	90%	45,000
81-09	34,000	26,000	50%	13,000
81-13	38,000	29,000	80%	23,200
81-27	36,500	31,500	90%	28,350
81-31	52,000	41,000	100%	41,000
81-38	58,000	45,000	50%	22,500
81-41	68,000	57,500	20%	11,500
81-42	39,700	35,200	50%	17,500
81-43	45,000	36,000	50%	18,000
			Sub total	$303,450
			Building supplies on hand	69,464
			Total	$372,914

Table 11.3 Debt analysis of Custom Home Builders, Inc.

Short-term notes payable	
Current portion of loan term	$ 15,280
Demand note payable	60,000
Construction mortgages	276,500
	$351,780
Long-term notes/mortgages payable	
Mortgage	$ 10,217
Equipment loans	37,419
Auto loans	4,247
Term loan payable	11,467
	$ 63,347

that these borrowed funds, either directly or indirectly, were used to buy some equipment.

Even though the mortgage and fixed loans are relatively small, how are the fixed payments going to be met on the profit the company is generating?

The income statement portion of this return contains a number of interesting but obvious items requiring no lengthy discussion. The company is spending $22,000 a year for interest. That's more than 20 percent of its gross profit, and another indication of the need for equity. Travel expense is heavy. The company has too many jobs to begin with. Why travel away for more? Despite an overabundance of equipment, rental payments on equipment are quite high. Why?

The conclusion we draw from the income statement is that profit is too low. The company does pay a reasonable salary to the president; but your bank is not doing itself any favors. The client's comment that he always pays his interest on time just adds to the hopelessness of the situation.

Exaggerated as this case is, it was presented in order to make three very significant points.

1. A tax return can yield as much information as a full financial statement (assuming both are prepared by reputable people).
2. Just because a client has a good piece of collateral to offer doesn't mean that a loan based on that collateral will be good. The measurement of quality is in repayment ability. Looking at the inventory list suggests that the cost of completing the houses, especially in a crisis, would be catastrophic. A balance between debt and equity is a standard which cannot be abused.
3. Lines of credit to contractors, even if approved on a general basis, need scrutiny with each request for a draw. The funds advanced here were "frozen" because they were made without knowing where the funds were going and how repayment was to be made.

Analysis of the statement, or at least awareness in this case, plus adherence to the basic rules of lending, would have avoided what is certainly a classified loan.

Part IV The Statement of Change in Financial Position

12 Measuring Changes in Working Capital

The fourth portion of the financial statement is the statement of change in financial position. It is also referred to as the source and application of funds statement or the cash flow statement. In order to avoid confusion and aid understanding of the concept, we will refer to the statement by its most common name, the source and application statement. It is without question the most important tool available to a lending officer in the analysis of a statement.

The primary purpose of the source and application statement is to explain differences in working capital as they appear from statement to statement. It tells us where cash funds were generated and where they were spent. This is important for the lending officer, who must determine how a company will use the loan it is requesting and how the loan will be repaid.

This chapter is devoted to developing a *banker's* approach to source and application of funds. A minimal amount of mechanics will be discussed. A series of illustrations will show how the numbers flow and what they mean.

Working Capital — The Common Denominator

Working capital is a term with which we have become very familiar. It has been used many ways and on many occasions. By definition it is the difference between current assets and current liabilities. It is the net cash or equivalent (cash tied up in semiliquid assets such as receivables and inventory) which the company has available to spend.

We know that a balance sheet has six major groupings, and in the interest of simplicity we could say that working capital represents one-third of the balance sheet, net fixed assets another third, and equity the final third. Table 12.1 illustrates this concept.

Table 12.1   Major groupings of the balance sheet

Six parts of balance sheet		Short form
Current assets	Current liabilities	Working capital
Fixed assets	Long-term debt	Net fixed & other assets
Other assets	Equity	Equity

The source and application of funds statement monitors transactions that change the amount of working capital. This kind of change is not the same thing as what happens when an account receivable is collected and the figures for both total cash and receivables are changed. You now have cash instead of its equivalent, but the *amount* of working capital has not changed with the transaction. Such transactions do not receive primary attention in the source and application statement. If the cash were used to purchase a new truck however, then working capital (as well as fixed assets) would change and this transaction which used working capital would be clearly shown on the source and application statement.

The transactions just given as examples are illustrated in Table 12.2 which summarizes four balance sheets. Balance sheet *A* represents the company before the transactions. *B* represents the company after it has collected $6,000 of accounts receivable. *C* represents a new wrinkle, the payment of $3,000 of accounts payable. *D* represents the purchase of the truck. Study them carefully.

This illustration demonstrates that the collection of receivables and the payment of bills do not change working capital because the changes in cash and its equivalent are contained in the working capital section. When working capital is used to purchase a fixed asset, or for that matter to affect anything beyond its own area, then a change in financial position occurs.

Table 12.2 Balance sheet comparison (in thousands of dollars)

	A		B Collection		C Payment		D Purchase
Cash	$ 20	+$6	$ 26	−$3	$ 23	−$10	$ 13
Other current assets	70	−$6	64		64		64
Total current assets	$ 90		$ 90		$ 87		$ 77
Fixed assets	60		60		60	+$10	70
Total assets	$150		$150		$147		$147
Current liabilities	$ 30		$ 30	−$3	$ 27		$ 27
Long-term debt	60		60		60		60
Equity	60		60		60		60
Total liabilities & equity	$150		$150		$147		$147
Working capital	$ 60		$ 60		$ 60	−10	$ 50

If the truck were purchased with a short-term note, we would have balance sheet *E*, as shown in Table 12.3. This is not drastically different from *D* which is shown alongside *E* for comparison. In both cases working capital was used to purchase the truck, and thus working capital was reduced in both.

Table 12.3 Balance sheet comparison

	C		E Purchase by short-term note	D Result of purchase by cash
Cash	$ 23		$ 23	$ 13
Other current assets	64		64	64
Total current assets	$ 87		$ 87	$ 77
Fixed assets	60	+$10	70	70
Total assets	$147		$157	$147
Current liabilities	$ 27	+$10	$ 37	$ 27
Long-term debt	60		60	60
Equity	60		60	60
Total liabilities & equity	$147		$157	$147
Working capital	$ 60	−$10	$ 50	$ 50

Let's take our illustration one step further. Assume the truck was purchased with a long-term note, a note payable next year. We now have balance sheet *F,* summarized in Table 12.4. Working capital has not changed

Table 12.4   Balance sheet comparison

	C		F *Long-term note*	E *Short-term note*	D *Cash purchase*
Cash	$ 23		$ 23	$ 23	$ 13
Other current assets	64		64	64	64
Total current assets	$ 87		$ 87	$ 87	$ 77
Fixed assets	60	+$10	70	70	70
Total assets	$147		$157	$157	$147
Current liabilities	$ 27		$ 27	$ 37	$ 27
Long-term debt	60	+$10	70	60	60
Equity	60		60	60	60
Total liabilities & equity	$147		$157	$157	$147
Working capital	$ 60		$ 60	$ 50	$ 50

because we have not spent cash or its equivalent; instead we found a new source of funds in long-term borrowing. The net difference between fixed assets and liabilities is also unchanged. We did increase one non-current asset, however, and this change in our financial position is reflected on the statement.

Those who refer to the change in financial position or source and application of funds statement as a cash flow statement are not completely correct. The primary purpose of this statement is to measure the *changes in working capital* — their causes and effects. In the sense that working capital is cash equivalent, the assumption implied in the term cash flow is correct. However, as balance sheet *F* in Table 12.4 demonstrates, other changes may be shown as well. Our interest then is also directed to changes that occur outside of working capital. As we saw in our first example, simple collections and payments do not affect working capital, therefore in the source and application of funds statement, our attention is focused on transactions that are out of the ordinary.

Before reviewing a series of such transactions, let's summarize what we have said in this chapter so far. If the flow of cash is from one form of current item to another it is of no concern to us — not at this point. (See Table 12.5.)

Table 12.5 Transactions not resulting in change in financial position

Current assets	Current liabilities
Fixed assets	Long-term debt
Other assets	Equity

When working capital either increases or decreases because of a change in one of the noncurrent portions of the statement, we have a change in financial position. (See Table 12.6.)

Table 12.6 Transactions resulting in change in financial position

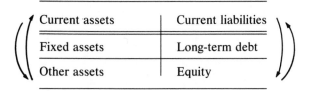

Current assets	Current liabilities
Fixed assets	Long-term debt
Other assets	Equity

Defining Source and Application

Let's look at a series of transactions, one at a time, and decide what is the source of funds, and what is the application. Table 12.7 shows the status of a company at the beginning of its fiscal year.

Let's assume the company buys a $10,000 piece of machinery. For the sake of the example, let us also assume that the company obtained 100 percent financing and that no portion of this is payable for one year. The source of the funds is your loan; the application is the machinery. The

Table 12.7 Sample statement —
status of a company at the beginning
of its fiscal year

Current assets	$10
Fixed assets	23
Other assets	2
Total assets	$35
Current liabilities	$ 5
Long-term debt	10
Net worth	20
Total liabilities & equity	$35

Table 12.8 Sample statement — $10,000 purchase

	Opening	Transaction	A
Current assets	$10		$10
Fixed assets	23	+ $10	33
Other assets	2		2
Total assets	$35		$45
Current liabilities	$ 5		$ 5
Long-term debt	10	+ $10	20
Net worth	20		20
Total liabilities & equity	$35		$45

source and application statement would reflect this transaction as in Table 12.8.

That was simple enough. Let's try another. The company issues $10,000 of capital stock. They have long needed the cash it generates. The source is the equity issue and the application is the working capital (cash) generated. Our statement now is as shown in Table 12.9.

Table 12.9   Sample statement — $10,000 capital stock issue

	A	Transaction	B
Current assets	$10	+ $10	$20
Fixed assets	33		33
Other assets	2		2
Total assets	$45		$55
Current liabilities	$ 5		$ 5
Long-term debt	20		20
Net worth	20	+ $10	30
Total liabilities & equity	$45		$55

Assume $3,000 of the new money retires some current payables. What effect will this have on the statement? (See Table 12.10.)

Table 12.10   Sample statement — $3,000 retires current payables

	B	Transaction	C
Current assets	$20	− $3	$17
Fixed assets	33		33
Other assets	2		2
Total assets	$55		$52
Current liabilities	$ 5	− $3	$ 2
Long-term debt	20		20
Net worth	30		30
Total liabilities & equity	$55		$52

What effect has this last transaction had on working capital? Working capital on statement B was $15,000 ($20,000 current assets − $5,000 current liabilities) and it is still $15,000 ($17,000 current assets − $2,000 current liabilities) on statement C. The numbers on the statement changed, but there was no change in financial position in the sense we are using that term. We are seeking only those items which affect working capital or one of the noncurrent balance sheet categories.

Let's look at two more transactions. The company sells a used piece of equipment for $15,000 and with the proceeds they retire $5,000 of long-term loans outstanding against it. The effect on the statement is shown in Table 12.11. Both transactions changed the cash balance. The sources were first the sale and then the *reduction* of working capital to retire the debt. This latter transaction raises a point we have not discussed yet. A portion of working capital may become the source of funds, and not just the result of transactions. You have taken cash (working capital) and reduced term debt (nonworking capital).

Table 12.11 Sample statement — sale of used equipment and retiring debt

	C	Transaction		D
Current assets	$17	+ $15	− $5	$27
Fixed assets	33	− $15		18
Other assets	2			2
Total assets	$52			$47
Current liabilities	$ 2			$ 2
Long-term debt	20		− $5	15
Net worth	30			30
Total liabilities & equity	$52			$47

The applications in these two transactions were, first, the increase in working capital by proceeds of the sale, and second, the decrease in long-term liability by the $5,000 payment.

Let's complete our series of illustrations with two more transactions. The company sells certain items over a particular period and reflects a profit of $6,000. Secondly, they pay $1,000 to increase the cash-surrender value of officers' life insurance. The effects of these transactions are shown in Table 12.12.

Here the two sources were profit and working capital. The application was first of profits to working capital and then of working capital to life insurance.

Table 12.12 Sample statement — profit for period and increase in cash-surrender value

	D	Transaction		E
Current assets	$27	+ $6	− $1	$32
Fixed assets	18			18
Other assets	2		+ $1	3
Total assets	$47			$53
Current liabilities	$ 2			$ 2
Long-term debt	15			15
Net worth	30	+ $6		36
Total liabilities & equity	$47			$53

This is all a bit confusing. And to add to the confusion, remember that during the course of a year there literally are hundreds of such transactions. It is impossible to follow each and every one. If, however, we could know the total of funds from all sources and then know where the funds have gone, we would be in an excellent position to understand the company. We would be following Kramer's Law (know where the funds go and how they are going to be repaid), but following it in reverse.

If you are going to know anything at all about your client, you should know where he got his cash and what he is doing with it. To see how this is learned, let's return to our example and compare the first balance sheet with the last. They are presented together in Table 12.13. For our purposes we can assume that we are comparing two year-end statements.

To determine the net change in financial position (or the net source and application of funds) requires that you isolate the changes which have occurred between the balance sheet dates and list each change as either a source or an application. The first step is to calculate the net change in working capital, as shown in Table 12.14.

Now that we know how much working capital has changed, we begin to determine why it has changed. The next step is to make a chart that lists and classifies the change in each item, as shown in Table 12.15. The first two columns show the balance sheets at the different dates. Each difference between them is listed as either a change in working capital or as a net source or a net application of funds. What we ask ourselves when classifying

Table 12.13   Comparison of first and last balance sheets
(Tables 12.7 and 12.12)

	Opening	Closing
Current assets	$10	$32
Fixed assets	23	18
Other assets	2	3
Total assets	$35	$53
Current liabilities	$ 5	$ 2
Long-term debt	10	15
Net worth	20	36
Total liabilities & equity	$35	$53

Table 12.14   Calculating working capital differences

	Opening	Closing
Current assets	$10	$32
Current liabilities	5	2
Working capital	$ 5	$30
		5
Net increase for period		$25

these changes is whether funds were required to make the change or whether funds were generated by the change.

We see that the source funds total $26,000, of which $16,000 was equity, $5,000 was from a decrease in fixed assets (an asset was sold, therefore cash must have been generated), and the remaining $5,000 was from an increase in long-term debt (borrowed money). The application of these funds is also evident. It is the $1,000 purchase of life insurance which appears as an increase in other assets. The balance of the source funds ($25,000) represents the increase in working capital that we had calculated earlier.

Table 12.15 Listing and classification of changes

				Changes	
	Opening	Closing	Working capital	Sources	Application
Current assets	$10	$32	$22		
Fixed assets	23	18		$ 5	
Other assets	2	3			1
Total assets	$35	$53			
Current liabilities	$ 5	$ 2	3		
Long-term debt	10	15		5	
Net worth	20	36	—	16	—
Total liabilities & equity	$35	$53	$25	$26	1

Now that we have summarized these changes, we can prepare a net source and application of funds statement, as shown in Table 12.16.

This simplified statement measures the changes from one year to the next. It tells us where the funds came from (source of funds) and where they went (application of funds).

Table 12.16 Summary of changes

XYZ COMPANY
Change in Financial Position
For Year Ended December 31, 19X5

Source of funds:		
Net increase in equity	$16,000	
Net increase in long-term debt	5,000	
Net decrease in fixed assets	5,000	
Total source of funds		26,000
Application of funds:		
Net increase in other assets	1,000	
Total application of funds		1,000
Net increase in working capital		$25,000

When preparing the actual statement, the accountant will analyze in detail each and every non–working capital account. The accountant's statement will not list the changes at net as in our example, but instead will show the whys and wherefores of the changes. Our purpose is not to learn how to prepare such a statement, but because we do know which transactions are behind the changes, let's take a look at how a competent accountant would prepare the statement.

The heading and bottom line ($25,000) of the accountant's source and application statement would be the same as in our simplified version. We listed net increase in equity as the first source of funds, but the accountant lists the transactions that actually comprised this source — the issue of stock and the profit on sales.

> Source of funds
> Net profit from operations $ 6,000
> Proceeds from issuance of stock   10,000

The third source of funds we listed was a net decrease in fixed assets. We classified it as a source because, looking only at the opening and closing statements, it appeared to be a sale only. From the series of transactions in our example, we know that there was both a sale (source) and a purchase (application).

The accountant would list them accordingly. Under source:

> Proceeds from the sale of equipment $15,000

Under application of funds:

> Purchase of machinery $10,000

Each of these transactions had a corresponding transaction. The first was the retirement of a debt and the second was a creation of one. Some accountants would reflect these at net, but that would not yield a complete picture. In this example, our accountant will list each transaction individually.

On our simplified statement we listed increase in other assets as the only application of funds. The accountant presents a more detailed picture and tells us exactly what the increase in other assets is.

The accountant's statement of change in financial position now is complete, and it appears as shown in Table 12.17. The net result of this statement is the same as in our simpler version — a $25,000 increase in working

Table 12.17 Accountant's statement of change in financial position

XYZ COMPANY
Change in Financial Position
For Year Ended December 31, 19X5

Source of funds:		
Net income for the year	$ 6,000	
Issuance of capital stock	10,000	
Sale of machinery & equipment	15,000	
Proceeds of loan	10,000	
Total source of funds		$41,000
Application of funds:		
Purchase of machinery & equipment	$10,000	
Decrease in long-term debt	5,000	
Increase in CSV — officers life insurance	1,000	
Total application of funds		$16,000
Increase in working capital		$25,000

capital — and the only difference between them is in the amount of detail presented.

Summary

The statement of change in financial position is the *most important part* of a financial statement. It tells you, the banker, what changes have occurred in a company, and also what funds are available for debt service. If this statement is not part of the data you are reviewing, then you must create your own statement of change and think in terms of source and application of funds.

13 Classifying Changes in Working Capital

In the previous chapter, we discussed by way of example only a few of the transactions that could occur during the year. The purpose of this chapter will be twofold: first, to summarize the majority of transactions that can find their way into our statement, and second, to define the role of depreciation in cash flow. We will direct most of our attention to this latter point — depreciation as a source of funds.

To summarize the transactions that affect the source and application statement is much simpler than one would expect. Just remember the two key guidelines established in the previous chapter: 1) At this point our only interest is in measuring changes in working capital. We calculate the net change before we start and then we reconcile each of the individual changes with that figure. 2) The balance sheet has six parts (Table 13.1) and only transactions which affect any of the four non – working capital sections can cause a change in working capital. Our principal task is to decide whether a change (an increase or decrease) in one of these sections indicates a source or an application of funds.

For example, if fixed assets increased during the year, was the increase from funds spent or from funds received? Obviously, additional units had to be purchased in order to increase the total. If fixed assets had dropped, then something would have had to be sold. Table 13.2 summarizes the meaning of an increase or decrease in fixed assets.

Table 13.1 Six parts of a balance sheet

Current assets	Current liabilities
Fixed assets	Long-term debt
Other assets	Equity

Table 13.2 Summarizing a change in assets on the balance sheet

Current assets	Current liabilities
Fixed assets (+) application (−) source	Long-term debt
Other assets	Equity

Similarly, to increase other assets one would have to spend funds (an application). To decrease it would require a sale, making it a source.

Liabilities would work the opposite way. If one increased the loans outstanding, it would mean that funds, the proceeds of the loan, were brought into the company. If the loans decrease, it would mean funds had been expended (an application).

Equity changes in the same manner as liabilities. To increase equity requires an infusion of funds. The source could be profits or new capital. If equity has decreased, it means that funds were spent. The application could be dividends paid or treasury stock purchased. If a company loses money, the loss is an application. In effect, the company is spending cash to pay for bills that are larger than its receipts.

All of these changes and their meaning are summarized in Table 13.3. It is interesting to note that although we may have known before what these changes meant, we probably had not thought of them in these terms until now.

Table 13.3 Summarizing changes on the balance sheet

Current assets	Current liabilities
Fixed assets +application −source	Long-term debt +source −application
Other assets +application −source	Equity +source −application

Noncash Expenses

We have used the term working capital quite freely. It has, for our purposes, meant the same thing as cash. Working capital actually is cash equivalent. There is a distinction which we will discuss more fully later. We also have seen how profit is a generator of funds, a source of funds. That is a simple enough idea. Profit is the reason why companies are in business. However, noncash expenses, particularly depreciation, are not so simple to understand.

In the course of business a company purchases certain pieces of physical property. By usage, the value of these items decreases, and at a certain point, they are valueless. The measurement of such attrition from the first day to the last day is termed depreciation. Many assets, however, especially buildings, actually increase in value while the company continues to depreciate their worth on the statement. We are aware of this contradiction, and as bankers we use both measurements of worth to determine the value we place on such an asset.

How does all this relate to source and application statements? Simply this way: If a company is showing a profit of $10,000, then we say it has $10,000 available to spend. This profit is a source of funds. If we analyze the income statement and find that the profit is after a deduction of $6,000 for depreciation, then we know that there really was $16,000 in cash to expend. No cash was spent in conjunction with the $6,000 depreciation deduction. The company does not make out a check for depreciation as it would for office supplies.

Cash is what we measure in the source and application statement; because no cash was spent on depreciation, both the profit and the noncash expenses are sources of funds and they are treated as such on the statement.

Source of funds	
Net profit for period	$10,000
Add: Expenses not requiring the outlay of working capital during the period — depreciation	6,000
Total funds from operation	$16,000

If a company had a loss for the period instead, we would have an application of funds because funds were spent from the company's reserve to make up the loss. Assume that the loss is $10,000 and that this is after the same $6,000 depreciation expense. The statement would show:

Application of funds	
Net loss for the period	$10,000
Less: Expenses not requiring the outlay of working capital during the period — depreciation	6,000
Total funds used in operations	$ 4,000

This adjustment on the statement of financial change leads many to think of depreciation as a "repayer of loans," but it really isn't. The adjustment simply reflects the reality — that the profit is larger (or the loss smaller) on a cash basis. In the profit example, there is $16,000 of cash, generated by cash profits, that the company may spend in any manner it chooses, including debt reduction. In the loss example, the company does *not* have $6,000 of cash (depreciation) with which to reduce loans. What the company has is $6,000 less that it must make up. There still is a $4,000 cash drain caused by the loss.

Depreciation is a noncash expense. A noncash expense is added to profit in order to determine cash profit. In this sense, depreciation may be part of the cash available to service debt.

To aid our understanding of the two topics discussed in this chapter — the classification of changes in noncurrent assets and the role of depreciation as a noncash expense — let's construct a source and application of funds statement. Table 13.4 presents a comparative year-end statement for the

Table 13.4 Sample statements

HORN COMPANY
Comparative Balance Sheets
As of December 31, 19X5 and 19X4

ASSETS

	19X5	19X4
Current assets		
Cash	$ 125,000	$ 65,000
Accounts receivable	350,000	225,000
Inventory	200,000	190,000
Prepaid expense	25,000	20,000
Total current assets	$ 700,000	$ 500,000
Fixed assets		
Property, plant & equipment	$ 500,000	$ 425,000
Less: Reserve for depreciation	125,000	75,000
Net fixed assets	$ 375,000	$ 350,000
Other assets		
Goodwill	$ 25,000	—
Total assets	$1,100,000	$ 850,000

LIABILITIES AND EQUITY

	19X5	19X4
Current liabilities		
Notes payable	$ 160,000	$ 110,000
Accounts payable	290,000	175,000
Accrued expenses	25,000	20,000
Current portion of long-term debt	20,000	20,000
Total current liabilities	$ 495,000	$ 325,000
Long-term debt		
Mortgage payable	$ 200,000	$ 220,000
Term-loan payable	75,000	—
Total	$ 275,000	$ 220,000
Less: Portion listed as current	20,000	20,000
Net long-term debt	$ 255,000	$ 200,000
Total liabilities	$ 750,000	$ 525,000
Equity		
Common stock	$ 50,000	$ 50,000
Paid in surplus	250,000	250,000
Retained earnings	50,000	25,000
Total equity	$ 350,000	$ 325,000
Total liabilities and equity	$1,100,000	$ 850,000

Table 13.4 — continued

HORN COMPANY
Income Statement
For Year Ended December 31, 19X5

Sales	$1,300,000
Cost of sales*	1,000,000
Gross profit	$ 300,000
Operating expenses	260,000
Profit before taxes	$ 40,000
Taxes on income	15,000
Net profit from operations	$ 25,000
Retained earnings — beginning	25,000
Retained earnings — end of period	$ 50,000

* Includes depreciation of $50,000

Horn Company as of 19X4 and 19X5, and an income statement for the year just ended. Take a few moments to read the data.

After reading the statement we begin to get a feel for the company. The balance sheet shows reasonable equity; there has been no change in capital, but retained earnings have increased as a result of profitability throughout the past year. Liabilities are somewhat higher than they were, and some leverage does exist. The equity appears to be evenly distributed between current and fixed assets, working capital is $205,000 and net fixed assets are $120,000 (a 60 – 40 split).

The income statement presents an equally well-balanced picture. The ratios (we are thinking of these in general terms) are reasonable.

To reconcile the differences between the two year-end statements requires that we construct a source and application statement. The first step is to calculate the net difference that we seek to reconcile, the change in total working capital. This calculation is presented in Table 13.5.

During the year the company generated $30,000 of additional working capital. This does not mean that other transactions did not occur. The $30,000 increase is the net result of all of the transactions that had an effect on working capital.

With this point of reference established, we begin to examine the funds

Table 13.5 Calculating a change in working capital for the Horn Company

	19X5	19X4
Current assets	$700,000	$500,000
Current liabilities	495,000	325,000
Total working capital	$205,000	$175,000
	175,000	
Net increase	$ 30,000	

that were available to the company and how they were spent (source and application). We will begin with the equity portion of the balance sheet (see Table 13.6).

Table 13.6 Equity portion of the Horn Company balance sheet

	19X5	19X4
Equity		
Common stock	$ 50,000	$ 50,000
Paid in surplus	250,000	250,000
Retained earnings	50,000	25,000
Total equity	$350,000	$325,000

There has been no issue of new stock; the increase in equity is due strictly to the increase in retained earnings which, as the income statement clearly shows, is a result of net profit. This information gives us the first line of our source and application statement.

        Source of funds
            Net profit for the period $25,000

We also saw on the income statement that the company incurred depreciation expenses of $50,000. This is a noncash expense that must be added to the profit figure before we can know the total funds provided by operations. The first part of the source section of the statement now will read:

Source of funds
    Net profit for the period $25,000
    Add: Expenses not requiring the outlay
         of working capital during the
         period — depreciation   50,000
            Total funds provided by $75,000
            operations

The second major source of funds is new borrowings. Therefore, we turn our attention to the long-term debt section (see Table 13.7).

Table 13.7 Long-term debt section of the Horn Company statement

	19X5	19X4
Long-term debt		
Mortgage payable	$200,000	$220,000
Term loan payable	75,000	—
Total	$275,000	$220,000
Less: Portion listed as current	20,000	20,000
Net long-term debt	$255,000	$200,000

The total debt has increased by $55,000, but close examination reveals that there was a decrease as well as an increase in borrowings. The mortgage has been reduced by $20,000, the normal payment due; this is an application of funds. A term loan was obtained during the year. At this point, we are not as interested in the purpose of the loan as much as in the fact that the funds were made available. (If we were familiar with the account, we would know the reason for the loan.) The two items listed under long-term debt will be listed separately on the source and application statement. The term loan is listed under sources.

Proceeds of term loan $75,000

The mortgage reduction is listed under applications.

Reduction in long-term debt $20,000

The liability and equity side of the balance sheet now is complete, and so we now look at fixed assets.

	19X5	19X4
Fixed assets	$500,000	$425,000
Less: Reserve for depreciation	125,000	75,000
Net fixed assets	$375,000	$350,000

Here we have two changes. The first is the increase in fixed assets, which we assume is the result of a purchase. There could have been sales as well as purchases of fixed assets, but we only know the net change between years. The accountant would review this account in detail.

Any asset purchased would be an application of funds because money was spent (regardless of the source) to get the items. The transaction is reflected as such under applications.

Purchase of fixed assets $75,000

The depreciation reserve was taken care of when we added it as a noncash expense to profits. In this case the opening depreciation plus the current expense equals the year-end balance ($75,000 + $50,000 = $125,000). There are many reasons why these figures may not always reconcile. For example, the trade-in of a used item or even the sale of one would cause a change in the reserve account. The charge-off of an antiquated unit would also change the balance. These areas are the domain of the accountant, not the banker, but you can call the accountant or the client in order to reconcile these differences if they are significant.

The final portion of the statement is other assets.

	19X5	19X4
Other assets		
Goodwill	$25,000	—
Total other assets	$25,000	—

At this point, we do not know why or how such an item came about. We will know before the interview is finished however. What we do know is that the company expended funds to create this asset, therefore it is listed on the source and application statement under application.

Increase in goodwill $25,000

Now all balance sheet items have been examined and classified as a source or application of funds. When we add the items in each group together we will know how much was available to the company (and from where) and how the company decided to spend it. Table 13.8 presents this completed statement of change.

Table 13.8   Completed statement of change in financial position for Horn Company

HORN COMPANY
Statement of Change in Financial Position
For the Year Ended December 31, 19X5

Source of funds	
Net profit for the period	$ 25,000
Add: Expenses not requiring the outlay of working capital during the period — depreciation	50,000
Total funds provided by operations	$ 75,000
Proceeds from term loan	75,000
Total source of funds	$150,000
Application of funds	
Purchase of fixed assets	$ 75,000
Increase in goodwill	25,000
Reduction in mortgage payable	20,000
Total application of funds	$120,000
Net increase in working capital	$ 30,000

Reading the statement, we see that the company had, from cash profit and new borrowings, $150,000 to spend. We can tell that part of these funds were used to acquire certain assets and retire certain debt, and that the balance was used to increase working capital. Clearly, the statement of financial change is an impressive tool. In the next chapter we will examine the role this statement plays in the lending function.

Exercise 9

The comparative balance sheets of the Dixon Company for the past two fiscal years and an income statement for the current year follow. Review these statements and prepare a statement of change in financial position. If your first several efforts are unsuccessful, you may use as a worksheet the form that follows the statements. At the end of this exercise section you will find the completed statement of change and the executed worksheet.

It is not important that you be an exacting accountant. Before you learn to use this crucial tool, however, you must develop a feeling for the flow of funds.

Before beginning, you may be interested to know that the company was shut down during a portion of the year because management moved their operation to a new facility. Management points out to you that, even though the year has been disappointing, your loans are well secured. The new mortgage/term loan of $115,000 is covered by buildings worth at least $300,000. The line of credit is covered better than two to one by accounts receivable and inventory. They can't understand your uneasiness.

Problem

DIXON COMPANY *(A Partnership)*
Balance Sheet
As of June 30, 19X8 and 19X7

ASSETS

	19X8	19X7
Current assets		
Cash	$ 70,000	$ 60,000
Accounts receivable	140,000	155,000
Inventories	120,000	105,000
Prepaid expenses	20,000	5,000
Total current assets	$350,000	$325,000
Property, plant & equipment		
Land	$ 10,000	$ 10,000
Buildings	115,000	65,000
Equipment	100,000	45,000
Total	$225,000	$120,000
Less: Reserve for depreciation	85,000	40,000
Net property, plant & equipment	$140,000	$ 80,000
Other assets		
Cash surrender value — officers life insurance	$ 10,000	$ 6,000
Total other assets	$ 10,000	$ 6,000
Total assets	$500,000	$411,000

LIABILITIES AND EQUITY

	19X8	19X7
Current liabilities		
Notes payable	$100,000	$ 10,000
Accounts payable	100,000	40,000
Accrued expenses	55,000	30,000
Current portion of long-term debt	10,000	5,000
Total current liabilities	$265,000	$ 85,000
Long-term debt		
Term loan payable	$115,000	$ 60,000
Less: Current portion	10,000	5,000
Net long-term debt	$105,000	$ 55,000
Total liabilities	$370,000	$140,000
Partnership equity		
Partners capital — July 1, 19X7	$271,000	$208,000
Add: Profit for the period	(81,000)	123,000
Less: Partners drawings	60,000	60,000
Total partnership equity — June 30, 19X8	$130,000	$271,000
Total liabilities and partnership equity	$500,000	$411,000

DIXON COMPANY (A Partnership)
Income Statement
For the Year Ended June 30, 19X8

Sales	$850,000
Cost of sales*	410,000
Gross profit	$440,000
Operating expenses	521,000
Net loss from operations	($ 81,000)

* Include depreciation of $45,000.

Sample format and worksheet

	19X8	19X7
Working capital change		
Current assets		
Current liabilities		
Total working capital		
Net increase/decrease in working capital		

Item	19X8	19X7	Change	Source	Application
Fixed assets					
Other assets					
Long-term debt					
Equity					
Profit/loss					
Depreciation					
Partners drawings					
Total					

Solution

DIXON COMPANY (A Partnership)
Statement of Change in Financial Position
For Year Ended June 30, 19X8

Source of funds		
Increase in long-term debt		$ 50,000
Total source of funds		$ 50,000
Application of funds		
Net loss for the period	$81,000	
Less: Expenses not requiring the outlay of working capital during the period — depreciation	45,000	
Plus: partners' drawings	60,000	
Net application of funds from operations		$ 96,000
Purchase of fixed assets		105,000
Increase in CSV — officers life insurance		4,000
Total application of funds		$205,000
Net decrease in working capital		$155,000

Executed worksheet

	19X8	19X7
Working capital change		
Current assets	$350,000	$325,000
Current liabilities	265,000	85,000
Total working capital	$ 85,000	$240,000
		85,000
Net increase/decrease in working capital		$155,000

Item	19X8	19X7	Change	Source	Application
Fixed assets					
Building	$115,000	$65,000	$50,000		$ 50,000
Equipment	100,000	45,000	55,000		55,000
Other assets					
CSV — life insurance	10,000	6,000	4,000		4,000
Long-term debt					
Term loan	105,000	55,000	50,000	$50,000	
Equity					
Profit/loss	(81,000)		81,000		81,000
Depreciation	45,000		45,000	45,000	
Partners drawings	60,000		60,000		60,000
Total				$95,000	$250,000
					95,000
Net change in working capital					$155,000

Comment

The Dixon Company has many problems. We can tell this readily from the balance sheet and income statement. The equity of the company dropped drastically as the result of the sizeable operating loss.

Why, then, the need for a source and application of funds statement? What additional information did we learn as a result of putting together the statement?

One thing we learned is that the company purchased $105,000 of fixed assets but borrowed only $50,000 of new funds in order to make the purchase. Fifty-five thousand dollars is a good example of an adequate down payment, *but* where did the funds come from?

The company sustained a loss, a sizeable one. The funds designated as depreciation offset a part of this loss, but the cash loss still totaled $36,000 ($81,000 net loss minus $45,000 depreciation). The partners' drawings of $60,000 (which would be salary in a corporate return) are added to this loss figure for a total cash drain of $96,000. Where did these funds originate?

We are raising some very important questions. So far we have answered them by saying that the funds were generated from working capital, which is correct. The working capital of the company did decrease by $155,000, but this is only half the picture. What did the company have to do to generate such working capital to make up the difference between the sources of funds available to them ($50,000) and the application of funds ($205,000)? Where did these funds ($155,000 net outflow) come from?

In the next chapter we'll discuss the second half of the source and application of funds statement, the reconciliation of changes in current assets and liabilities; what we learn should help us to answer questions such as the ones we raise here.

14   Reconciling Changes in Working Capital

The statement of change in financial position is used first to see how the flow of funds affects working capital and then to examine the individual assets and liabilities that are affected by or are the cause of these changes. Until now, we have focused on the changes in working capital and looked at all other changes only as they affected this item. In the majority of cases, we can achieve adequate insight into the flow of a company's funds this way. Now that the general flow of funds is understood, however, we can go on to the second part of the statement which reconciles the changes in working capital.

Let's re-examine the Horn Company's statements which were reviewed in Table 13.4. In preparing the source and application, we stopped at the net increase in working capital. But where did this increase come from? (Or where did a decrease go?) Answering this question is the job of the second part of our statement.

The net increase in working capital was $30,000. We calculated this before we began to develop the statement. It was the net difference between the working capital figures of the past two years. Let's review the current assets and current liabilities and decide which items have changed and then classify each change as an increase or decrease, just as we did for noncurrent assets and liabilities.

The current assets as of the two year-ends were as shown in Table 14.1

Table 14.1   Current assets of the Horn Company

	19X5	19X4
Cash	$125,000	$ 65,000
Accounts receivable	350,000	225,000
Inventory	200,000	190,000
Prepaid expense	25,000	20,000
Total current assets	$700,000	$500,000

and the current liabilities in Table 14.2. Our $30,000 increase in working capital was calculated as shown in Table 14.3.

Following this calculation, the changes in the individual items are reconciled to the total change of $30,000. First we calculate the changes in

Table 14.2   Current liabilities of the Horn Company

	19X5	19X4
Notes payable	$160,000	$110,000
Accounts payable	290,000	175,000
Accrued expenses	25,000	20,000
Current portion of long-term debt	20,000	20,000
Total current liabilities	$495,000	$325,000

Table 14.3   Calculating increase in the working capital of the Horn Company

	19X5	19X4
Current assets	$700,000	$500,000
Current liabilities	495,000	325,000
Working capital	$205,000	$175,000
	175,000	
Net Increase in working capital	$ 30,000	

assets as shown in Table 14.4, and then we calculate the changes in liabilities as shown in Table 14.5. The difference between the $200,000 of asset changes and the $170,000 of liability changes represents the $30,000 net working capital increase.

Table 14.4   Changes in assets of the Horn Company

	19X5	19X4	Change
Cash	$125,000	$ 65,000	+$ 60,000
Accounts receivable	350,000	225,000	+ 125,000
Inventory	200,000	190,000	+ 10,000
Prepaid expenses	25,000	20,000	+ 5,000
Total	$700,000	$500,000	+$200,000

Table 14.5   Change in liabilities of the Horn Company

	19X5	19X4	Change
Notes payable	$160,000	$110,000	+$ 50,000
Accounts payable	290,000	175,000	+ 115,000
Accrued expenses	25,000	20,000	+ 5,000
Current portion of long-term debt	20,000	20,000	
Total	$495,000	$325,000	+$170,000

The second part of the source and application statement shows this. The statement in its entirety is presented in Table 14.6.

This part of the statement could be as revealing, if not more so, than the first part. It tells us a number of things. We know the company had a profit of $25,000. The cash available to the company was this profit plus noncash expenses and bank borrowings (long-term). The funds were used to purchase certain fixed assets, accumulate goodwill (acquisition or merger), and retire certain debt. The balance increased working capital.

But that is only half the picture. The company increased cash by $60,000. It also had a major increase in accounts receivable (some $125,000). Obviously, the $30,000 of increased working capital didn't produce all this.

Table 14.6   Horn Company statement with changes in working capital reconciled

HORN COMPANY
Statement of Change in Financial Position
For the Year Ended December 31, 19X5

Source of funds:		
Net profit for the period		$ 25,000
Add: Expenses not requiring the outlay of working capital during the period — depreciation		50,000
Total funds provided by operations		$ 75,000
Proceeds of term loan		75,000
Total source of funds		$150,000
Application of funds:		
Purchase of fixed assets		$ 75,000
Increase in goodwill		25,000
Reduction in mortgage payable		20,000
Total application of funds		$120,000
Net increase in working capital		$ 30,000
Changes in working capital:		
Increase (decrease) in current assets:		
Cash	$ 60,000	
Accounts receivable	125,000	
Inventory	10,000	
Prepaid expenses	5,000	
Total		$200,000
Increase (decrease) in current liabilities:		
Notes payable	$ 50,000	
Accounts payable	115,000	
Accrued expenses	5,000	
Total		$170,000
Net increase in working capital		$ 30,000

What happened is that the company borrowed $50,000 from the bank on a short-term basis and did not pay suppliers (accounts payable increased $115,000). If you were requested to increase the line of credit in order to reduce the accounts payable (context of the request), would you spot the major increase in receivables and realize that this is the cause of the problem? That's what this statement should show.

The statement is as complete a picture as you can get of what happened to the company last year. It is a summary of what you, the banker, seek to find when you analyze the statement.

The Dixon Case

In Exercise 9 (page 251) we reviewed the statements of the Dixon Company. When we completed the source and application statement we learned that the company had used $155,000 of working capital to do certain things. Primarily it absorbed a substantial loss (including partners' drawings) of $96,000 and it purchased fixed assets of $105,000. It borrowed $50,000 to aid in meeting these ends. But where did the $155,000 come from? The company spent this much; it must have a source.

This question can be answered only by the second part of the source statement. Review the Dixon balance sheet and the first part of the change in financial position; then review the reconciliation of the change in Dixon's working capital. You are now in a position to prepare the entire source and application statement.

The current assets were as shown in Table 14.7, and the liabilities were as shown in Table 14.8.

Table 14.7 Current assets of the Dixon Company

	19X8	19X7
Cash	$ 70,000	$ 60,000
Accounts receivable	140,000	155,000
Inventories	120,000	105,000
Prepaid expenses	20,000	5,000
Total current assets	$350,000	$325,000

Table 14.8 Current liabilities of the Dixon Company

	19X8	19X7
Notes payable	$100,000	$10,000
Accounts payable	100,000	40,000
Accrued expenses	55,000	30,000
Current portion of long-term debt	10,000	5,000
Total current liabilities	$265,000	$85,000

We calculated the change in working capital in advance by subtracting the current working capital of $85,000 from the previous working capital of $240,000. This yielded the net decrease of $155,000. The individual changes in the current assets and current liabilities are shown in Table 14.9. We add this information to our statement and get the complete picture of the flow of funds as shown in Table 14.10.

We are now in a position to make some keen observations. The gifted and experienced analyst would have gotten the essence of the comments that follow by reading only the balance sheet and income statement. He or she is the rare exception however. Such an analyst is able to relate the change in the balances and tie in the contributions of the income statement.

Table 14.9 Changes in current assets and current liabilities of the Dixon Company

Cash	$ 10,000
Accounts receivable	(15,000)
Inventory	15,000
Prepaid expenses	15,000
Total	$ 25,000
Notes payable	$ 90,000
Accounts payable	60,000
Accrued expenses	25,000
Current portion of long-term debt	5,000
Total	$180,000

Table 14.10   Completed statement of change in financial position for Dixon Company

DIXON COMPANY (A Partnership)
Statement of Change in Financial Position
For Year Ended June 30, 19X8

Source of funds:		
Increase in long-term debt		$ 50,000
Total source of funds		$ 50,000
Application of funds:		
Net loss for the period	$ 81,000	
Less: Expenses not requiring the outlay of working		
capital during the period — depreciation	45,000	
Plus: Partner's drawings	60,000	
Net application of funds from operations		$ 96,000
Purchase of fixed assets		105,000
Increase in CSV — officers life insurance		4,000
Total application of funds		$205,000
Net decrease in working capital		$155,000
Changes in working capital:		
Increase (decrease) in current assets		
Cash	$ 10,000	
Accounts receivable	(15,000)	
Inventory	15,000	
Prepaid expenses	15,000	
Total		$ 25,000
Increase (decrease) in current liabilities		
Notes payable	$ 90,000	
Accounts payable	60,000	
Accrued expenses	25,000	
Current portion of long-term debt	5,000	
Total		$180,000
Net decrease in working capital		$155,000

The majority of analysts would not grasp the total picture until they had seen the change in position statement.

We have already reviewed the first part of that picture. The company had a sizable cash loss and they acquired certain pieces of equipment. They funded these needs from working capital for the most part.

Their need to consume working capital was small. The increase in inventory offset an equal decrease in receivables. Cash increased slightly, and some funds were tied up in prepaid expenses.

The majority of the working capital that was used came from the increase in payables (loans plus trade). In fact, $90,000 was generated by short-term borrowing and $85,000 from not paying payables. At this point we do not know whether this increase in payables is due to higher purchases caused by the increase in volume.

What the source and application statement tells an experienced analyst is that the company used its line of credit and backed up its payables in order to finance the purchase of some new assets as well as carry a substantial deficit year of operation. (How will this short-term loan be paid off?) A problem loan is forming.

The statement has served its purpose. It told you exactly what was done with the funds the company had available to use and it showed how the funds were generated.

Exercise 10

You have just received the annual financial statement of Richard Enterprises, Inc., from Mr. Jim Brace, the company's president. Oddly enough,
Mr. Brace called to ask if he could stop by this afternoon to review that
statement with you. Brace seemed quite perplexed. He told you that the
statement was the best his company had ever had, and that profits are
higher than they had ever been before, yet he finds himself unable to meet
his ninety-day note which is due next week. He reminds you that you have
already renewed it twice and that at the last meeting you said you would
not renew again.

Review the financial statement prior to Brace's arrival. Be in a position
to explain in your discussion with him the reason for his cash backup.

RICHARD ENTERPRISES

BALANCE SHEET

AS OF JULY 31, 19X7 and 19X6

	19X7	19X6
ASSETS		
Current Assets		
Cash	$ 23,500	$ 18,500
Accounts Receivable	51,000	46,000
Inventory	34,000	32,000
Prepaid items	7,500	7,000
Total Current Assets	116,000	103,500
Fixed Assets		
Machinery and Equipment	17,000	10,000
Leasehold Improvements	19,000	5,000
Automotive Equipment	11,000	11,000
Total	47,000	26,000
Less Accumulated Depreciation	19,000	14,000
Total Fixed Assets	28,000	12,000
Other Assets - Net	1,000	1,500
Total Assets	$145,000	$117,000
LIABILITIES AND EQUITY		
Current Liabilities		
Notes payable - bank	$ 35,000	$ 15,000
Accounts payable	21,000	24,000
Accrued taxes and expenses	14,000	11,000
Current portion of debt	6,000	6,000
Total Current Liabilities	76,000	56,000
Long Term Debt		
Notes payable - bank	15,000	21,000
Less current portion	6,000	6,000
Total Long Term Debt	9,000	15,000
Total Liabilities	85,000	71,000
STOCKHOLDERS' EQUITY		
Capital Stock	25,000	25,000
Retained Earnings	35,000	21,000
Total Equity	60,000	46,000
Total Liabilities and Equity	$145,000	$117,000

RICHARD ENTERPRISES

INCOME STATEMENT

FOR THE YEAR ENDED JULY 31, 19X7

Sales			$295,000
Cost of Sales			
Material		$ 75,000	
Labor		25,000	
Overhead			
Rent	$ 12,000		
Depreciation	5,000		
Other	24,000	41,000	
Total Cost of Sales			141,000
Gross Profit			154,000
Operating Expenses			
Officer salaries		30,000	
Selling expenses		46,000	
Administrative expenses		56,000	
Total Operating Expenses			132,000
Profit Before Taxes			22,000
Reserve For Taxes			8,000
Profit After Taxes			14,000
Retained Earnings August 1, 19X6			21,000
Retained Earnings July 31, 19X7			$ 35,000

Comments

Your initial review of the financial statement confirmed everything that Brace had said. Sales were $295,000 and profitability was quite good. The company now has total footings of $145,000 and equity of $60,000. Total liabilities of $85,000 are reasonable in light of the $60,000 equity figure. In general, you feel that the statement is the best the company ever had. If there is a problem, it is that, as of the statement date, $35,000 of notes payable to the bank represent the maximum amount of Brace's line. (The balance has been reduced to $15,000 at present. It is this amount that is now due.) Brace is right. There does not seem to be adequate working capital to allow for the promised reduction at this time.

Because the statement does not include a source and application of funds statement, you decide to prepare one yourself. (If you have not already done so now is the time to prepare such a statement. The sample statement on page 269 shows you what it should look like.) The answer to Brace's question has to be contained in this particular statement. For the current year the company shows profitability of $14,000, plus depreciation of $5,000. The reduction of other assets contributed another $500 of noncash expense, yielding a total of $19,500 with which to pay debt. Against this the company purchased $21,000 of fixed assets and reduced its long-term debt by $6,000. This $27,000 total expense meant a $7,500 reduction in working capital ($27,000 − $19,500). To generate this working capital, the company increased its notes payable by $20,000. Some of that $20,000 was used to increase the levels of receivables and inventory which were caused by the increases in sales. The balance, of course, is the deficit working capital of $7,500.

We conclude that Brace used all of his cash profits plus borrowings on your line (a) to increase receivables and inventory, and (b) to purchase $21,000 worth of fixed assets. It's an oversimplification, but in effect the company has increased its notes payable by $20,000 and has purchased fixed assets with the proceeds. This is why the line of credit has not been cleaned up and why the notes will come due without there being a source of repayment for them. The correct approach would have been for the company to use the profit and depreciation to increase the receivables and inventory and to make a reasonable down payment on the new equipment. The balance would be financed by some type of term note — not by a line of credit.

RICHARD ENTERPRISES

STATEMENT OF CHANGE IN FINANCIAL POSITION

FOR YEAR ENDED JULY 31, 19X7

Source of Funds		
Net Profit from Operation	$ 14,000	
Plus: expense not requiring cash - depreciation	5,000	
Reduction of other assets	500	
Total Source of Funds		$ 19,500
Application of Funds		
Purchase of fixed assets	21,000	
Reduction of long term debt	6,000	
Total Application of Funds		27,000
Net Decrease In Working Capital		$ 7,500
Changes In Working Capital:		
Increase in current assets:		
Cash	5,000	
Accounts receivable	5,000	
Inventories	2,000	
Other	500	
Total increase		12,500
Increase in current liabilities:		
Notes payable	20,000	
Accounts payable	(3,000)	
Accrued taxes	3,000	
Total increase		20,000
Net Decrease In Working Capital		$ 7,500

In your discussion with Jim Brace, you decide to offer a financing package which would include financing for the fixed assets already acquired; the proceeds would be used to reduce the line of credit. The important thing is to educate Brace as to the proper use of short-term and long-term financing, or asset-conversion financing and profitability financing.

If you pour a cup of water into a bucket already nearly full of water, can you point to the water you just poured in? You can't of course, because it is indistinguishable from the rest of the water. So it is with cash. You cannot say where the working capital went. You only can say that it went somewhere in the pot. By eliminating and combining certain related transactions (a fixed-assets increase and long-term debt increase, for example), you can follow the general flow of funds and, in particular, see where the working capital is being used.

What you do know with some certainty, and what can be clearly seen in this source and application statement, is that the company has used short-term funds to acquire long-term assets.

Whether or not the company can continue to grow at the rate it has grown during the past year is the key issue in your analysis of the statement. The growth rate may require increases in assets that appear to outstrip the company's ability to generate funds. Repayment ability seems strong; with the structure of fixed-asset acquisitions recast, the credit line will be used to fund only seasonal needs and, it is hoped, convert itself during the normal business cycle.

15 Conclusion

The purpose of this book has been to help you feel comfortable with a financial statement. By knowing what a statement is capable of telling you, as well as what advantages you have as a lending officer when reading one, you should be able to make the statement part of your arsenal of tools. Use it. If you have questions, ask. No financial analyst has all the answers. Know your strength and limitations and act accordingly.

Learn to think in terms of statements. Your interview with the client is the best way to learn what makes up the *content* of the statement. Go through the balance sheet in your mind while talking with your client. Be certain you cover all the major items. Use the client's most recent report as a checklist.

Once you have established the framework, go past the numbers. Dig deep into their content. Learn enough to make a decision.

If you have no statement, prepare one. No matter how inexact it may be, it will at least provide you with a benchmark. Review the statement as the client presents his or her request. All statement analysis becomes more meaningful when it is done with a specific request in mind.

Finally, learn to know the real causes and effects of certain changes. You should question the purpose of each loan that is requested as well as the source of repayment. You should understand the overall flow of funds through the company. Where did funds originate and where were they expended?

Remember, "You can't make a loan solely on the basis of a good financial statement; by the same token, you can't make a good loan without any statement." There is wisdom in that financial maxim.

Learn to use your most valuable tool.

271

Exercise 11

Dingman Excavating Co. has been a client of yours for many years. Its association with your bank is eighteen years old, ever since Mr. Henry, the former president of the bank, financed Dingman's first equipment loan.

Chris Dingman, the firm's president and founder, is still active at sixty-three. His son Scott runs the day-to-day operations, and Scott has called for an appointment to see you this afternoon.

The firm is small and its basic goal is to earn a profit sufficient to allow the company to pay the principals a reasonable salary. Its reputation and quality is without question. Your bank enjoys the personal business of all the employees and your trust department has various trust and pension accounts of the firm.

On the basis of your past association, you know that almost any reasonable request by Chris Dingman will be given fair consideration. Your association with Scott is just beginning, and based on what he said when he called to make the appointment, it appears Scott will be taking over the financial end of the business. He also mentioned that they need a new back hoe.

The company is a sole proprietorship with all assets owned by Chris Dingman. Dingman has considered incorporating on a number of occasions but hasn't done so because he feels that the company would lose the confidence of its clients by incorporating.

As the loan officer in charge of the accounts, you want your relationship with the client to continue smoothly in spite of the change in ownership. You should take the opportunity afforded by Scott's visit to discuss the overall bank-client relationship and to review Scott's long-term goals.

Whenever a banker meets a client for the first time, even if that client is already a customer of the bank, the banker must develop and explain his philosophy with the client. Without being overbearing, explain to Scott the guidelines that the bank must follow when making a loan. Take a few moments to list the key points you think should be made during the interview and then read the model interview that follows.

Model Interview

John Jones, Banker
Scott Dingman, Dingman Excavating Co.

Jones: Hi Scott. Good to see you.
Dingman: Good morning, it was nice of you to see me this morning.
Jones: The pleasure is mine. I've wanted us to get together for some time. I realize you've taken over the day-to-day operation, and banking is of course a big part of any operation.
Dingman: That's why I wanted to see you. Dad has always done the banking, and frankly he's quite conservative. I think he's never really expanded as he should. There are half a dozen firms in town with much larger contracts than we handle. I see these guys once in a while, and they tell me about the big lines of credit they have. I don't even know if we have a line.
Jones: Well your firm has always had a friend at this bank and although we don't have a formal line, we have made funds available to you in the past.
Dingman: But how much can we borrow?
Jones: That depends on a lot of things. If the reasons are good, then almost any amount you need. We've always financed your equipment — and at reasonable rates. Some of those others you mentioned are paying some dear rates for that extra equipment.
Dingman: Hold on, you're going too quickly. Let's start from the beginning. What do we borrow now?
Jones: Let's review your loans. As you already know, your firm owes about $40,000 on term loans and $10,000 on demand loans. This does not include your dad's personal mortgage.
Dingman: Why do we have two different loans — a term did you say? and one on demand?
Jones: The reason is quite simple. Let's take the demand loan first. There are occasions during the year when funds due to you don't come on time or perhaps you need to purchase some special supplies in advance of a job. In these cases we give you a short-term note. When whatever it was that caused the need for borrowing corrects itself, then you have funds to pay back

	the debt. When you get that check or use those supplies then, as we say, you converted the assets and funds are available.
Dingman:	What if I still needed funds for a different reason? Do I have to pay you off?
Jones:	Yes, you should. If you have need for other funds, then we'll talk about them. In practice we don't always do it that way. Instead, we establish a line of credit which is really a pre-approval. You use funds as you need them and pay off as you have excess funds available. Then at the end of the year we see how you did and then we discuss renewing it for the next year.
Dingman:	Is it possible that I might always need your loan?
Jones:	If that situation exists, then you really don't need my loan — you need more capital. That's one thing banks try not to do — lend capital.
Dingman:	I'm not sure I follow you.
Jones:	We bankers are very interested in being part of your picture — but only part. In our shop we say we want to *share* in your opportunity. That means just what it says — you invest something and we invest something.
Dingman:	How much is enough?
Jones:	That depends on many things. Let's look at your term loans.
Dingman:	Excuse me, but what is a term loan?
Jones:	It's a loan which you pay out over a period of time.
Dingman:	Is that the only difference?
Jones:	No, the philosophy behind such a loan is different. In the short-term, time, or demand note, the repayment comes from conversion of certain assets into cash.
	In a term loan, repayment comes from the return on the assets and not from its sale. Let's take the truck your dad financed last year. He felt he needed the truck in his business, and he felt that he could make money by having it.
	With a term loan, a portion of the money he received in profits is given to us to retire the debt.
Dingman:	How much return is enough?
Jones:	It has to be a reasonable return which means it pays enough to make it worthwhile for you to own the asset plus allow for the retirement of the loan.
Dingman:	Then the important thing before I decide to purchase new

equipment is to determine how much profit can be generated.

Jones: Exactly.

Dingman: What about things like down payments? Do we have to do that?

Jones: The purpose of a down payment is to give the lender some equity in the asset. If you pay $4,000 against a $16,000 truck and I finance the balance, then should a problem ever arise, I have some negotiating room to sell the equipment and retire the debt.

Dingman: So if I have good equipment and have some down payment, then I've got no problem borrowing.

Jones: Not entirely. Collateral is one part of a loan. Ability to repay is more critical.

Dingman: I guess that's where I don't understand banks. If you have good collateral and a nice down payment, how can you go wrong?

Jones: Let me answer you with a question. If an employee of yours, who makes $20,000 a year, came to me with a $40,000 deposit on a $200,000 house, would it be wise to finance the residence for him?

Dingman: He couldn't afford the payments. I see, it's the same with the truck. I have to have enough income to pay the loan.

Jones: That's what commercial lending is all about.

Dingman: There is one final area I'd like to discuss. That's about expansion and money to do it.

              There are some really big jobs that we haven't bid on before, but if we had more funds, we could. Does the bank help us with that?

Jones: Your dad and I looked at a number of these contracts and he did bid some. In most cases, it wasn't worth the gamble.

Dingman: I guess I disagree. Could you be more specific?

Jones: Remember the Omega job? It would have taken nine months to complete. Your dad had a good bid but the company that was putting up the building wasn't too solid. The progress payment schedule wasn't adequate, and the mortgage that the developer had wasn't sufficient. The potential profit wasn't there and, even if it were, the interest expense of carrying the job would have taken most of the profit.

Dingman: But there were other contracts.

Jones: Yes there have been. But just as I have to ask you how you are going to be able to pay back a loan, you have got to make sure you know how you're going to be paid. Check with your client's bank. Ask who has the construction mortgage. You invest a lot of money on these jobs; one mistake and it's over.

Dingman: If we find a good contract, will the bank help us?

Jones: Certainly — that's why we're here. But you shouldn't need a lot of money to get the job done. You should be paid as you go and have enough equity to exist between payments. When you have a good contract, let's talk about it.

Dingman: Before I leave, I want to talk about a new back hoe. We presently have two that are fully depreciated which will be traded in for one larger unit. We will save labor cost and increase capacity at the same time.

Jones: I see no real problem. How many dollars, after the trade in, will the unit cost?

Dingman: We're getting a good deal. The model we need sells for $45,000. Our price, net of everything, is $32,000. We'd like to borrow that much.

Jones: Over five years that would mean payments of about $8,000 a year. Will the new unit help to increase sales?

Dingman: Yes. We see a number of new areas we can get into — especially sewer work on a greater scale. The efficiency alone will save half a man a year. We see a good return on the unit.

Jones: Your dad's tax return showed that the company made $48,000 last year. About $36,000 of that went to him for salary and taxes. This left a real profit of $12,000. The company also had $16,000 of depreciation. That gives $28,000 of cash profit.

Dingman: Hold on, what about depreciation and cash profit?

Jones: Well Scott, the profit is easy to understand. That's the difference between what you receive and what you spend. On the tax return there is a list of expenses. One of them is depreciation. By definition this is a reserve for the use or attrition of the capital asset.
              Unlike all of the other expenses, you don't pay for depreciation. You don't write a check for it as you do for office supplies.
              In this sense it is cash available for you to spend. It should be used to help retire the loan on the unit which is depreciating.

Dingman: I see.

Jones: Getting back to the statement, you have sufficient funds available to meet your present debt plus handle unforeseen working capital needs. I see no problem with a new payment.

Dingman: Fine.

Jones: Why not call me when the unit is ready for delivery. I'll prepare the papers in advance, and the transfer can be easily made.

Dingman: Thank you for your time. I think I'm beginning to understand.

Jones: Thank you for letting us serve you. Say hello to the family for me.

Exercise 12

Throughout the book we have referred to the Example Company, Inc. We have spread the company's statements, compared the statement with consecutive year-end figures, and finally compared it with the averages established by the RMA.

The entire company has been commented on at various stages, but a complete, independent, and observant review by a credit department was not performed.

The following data should be reviewed for two reasons. First, for the report of the analyst (and follow-up memo of the loan officer) and secondly, to learn a different spread sheet format and method of analysis. In particular, please note the extensive use of ratios in determining the viability of the company.

Take full advantage of this exercise by preparing your own credit write-up after reviewing the Example Company statement (Exhibit 10.1) and the spread sheets (Exhibit 10.4).

FIRST COMMERCIAL BANK
of ANYWHERE, N.A.
Post Office Box 000
Anywhere, USA 00001
Telephone 888-987-6543

M E M O R A N D U M

TO: ROBERT KNIGHTLEY - VICE PRESIDENT

FROM: WILLIAM VOLE - CREDIT DEPARTMENT

SUBJECT: EXAMPLE COMPANY, INC. AND SUBSIDIARIES

DATE: MARCH 31, 19X6

The Credit department has spread and analyzed the audited financial statements of Example Company, Inc. and Subsidiaries for the two fiscal years ending 12-31-X4 and 12-31-X5. A clean opinion was issued by the CPA firm on both sets of statements. The company manufactures small metal parts for various industries and has approximately 300 customers nationwide. Industry averages are available through Robert Morris Associates.

Liquidity:	FYE X4	FYE X5	
Net Working Capital	$ 719M	$ 829M	+15.3%

A $110,000 increase in net working capital during FYE X5 was primarily attributable to more than adequate cash generated from operations, new equity investment during 19X5, and new long-term debt. All three of these sources of funds offset the following uses of cash, namely payment of $360,000 in dividends and payments made against long-term debt.

Cash	$ 135M	$ 207M	+53.3%
Accounts Receivable—Trade	637	890	+39.7%
Inventories	725	822	+13.4%
Total Current Assets	1547	1969	+27.3%
Bank Loans—Short Term	100	400	+300%
Accounts Payable—Trade	444	386	-13.1%
Accrued Income Tax	181	218	+20.4%
Total Current Liabilities	828	1140	+37.7%
			RMA
Current Ratio	1.87	1.73	1.70
Quick Ratio	.99	1.01	.80

The resulting decrease in the current ratio from 1.87 to 1.73 suggests a slight increase in dependence on short-term credit to finance accounts receivable. The available RMA industry average was 1.70. Example Company carried an increased percentage of its total assets in trade accounts receivable for FYE X5 reaching 31%, while the RMA. industry average was only 27%. The quality of these receivables has weakened as the number of days for collection of trade receivables rose from 57 to 70. Average companies in this industry collect receivables within 43 days. Inventory, the other major component of the company's liquidity structure, turned over in almost 100 days while the industry average is only 50.

Capitalization:	FYE X4	FYE X5
Capital Structure	66%	60%
Financial Structure		
Stockholders' Equity	68%	70%
Long-term Debt	32%	30%

The capital structure (stockholders' equity and long-term debt) decreased as a percentage of the financial structure (total debt and stockholders' equity) due to a greater use of short-term borrowing. It is also evident that a larger proportion of permanent risk has been taken by stockholders during FYE X5, placing permanent creditors in a more secure position. Example Company covered each dollar of current maturities of its long-term obligations with almost $10.00 of cash generated from operations (net profit after tax and depreciation). Interest charges were also well covered from funds generated through normal operations.

Profitability:	FYE X4	FYE X5	
Net Sales	$4,022M	$4,561M	+13.4%
Cost of Sales	2,880	3,222	+11.8%
			Ind.
Operating Profit	19%	19%	10%
Net Profit Before Tax/Sales	19%	19%	6%
Net Profit After Tax/Sales	9%	8%	N.A.
Net Profit Before Tax/Tangible Worth	70%	72%	30%
Net Profit Before Tax/Total Assets	31%	30%	12%

The company continues to hold operating expenses around 11% which remains better than the industry average. A profitable return was achieved against 19X5 sales even after the extraordinary loss of $36,740 resulting from earthquake destruction of its plant in Lawrence, Massachusetts last March.

Summary:

The company increased net working capital after generating more than adequate earnings from operations and funding expansion and paying dividends primarily from this source. Extra attention needs to be given to improvement in collectibility of trade accounts receivable. Stronger credit policies and use of discounts may be the immediate answer.

Example Company now offers more protection to its long-term creditors as stockholders' increased their investment in the company through new paid-in-capital and retained earnings. A strong profitability was observed, and this is a credit to good management of resources and planning.

```
                    HISTORICAL BALANCE SHEET
EXAMPLE COMPANY, INC. & SUBSIDIARIES

   CONSOLIDATED        AMOUNTS IN THOUSANDS        SIC CODE =
=================================================================
SOURCE OF STATEMENT    AUDITED   AUDITED
        DATE          12/31/x4  12/31/x5
-----ASSETS------------------------------------------------------
 1 CASH                   135       207
 2 TEMP INVESTMENTS        50        50
 3 ACCTS REC-NET          637       890
 4 INVENTORIES            725       822
 5 OTHER CURR ASSETS
 6
 7    CURRENT ASSETS    1,547     1,969
 8 NET PROPERTY           579       557
 9 INVESTMENTS            161       186
10 INTANGIBLES
11 OTHER NONCUR ASSETS
12 PREPDS & OTH ASSETS    146       129
-----------------------------------------------------------------
13    TOTAL ASSETS      2,433     2,841
=================================================================
--LIABILITIES & NET WORTH----------------------------------------
14 BANK LOANS-S/T         100       400
15 CURR MAT L/T LIABIL     22        44
16 OTHER NOTES PAYABLE
17 ACCTS PAYABLE          444       386
18 ACCRUED INCOME TAX     181       218
19 OTHER CURRENT LIAB
20 ACCRUED EXPENSES        81        92
21    CURRENT LIABIL.    828     1,140
22 BANK LOANS-L/T                   160
23 MORTGAGE LOANS          38        34
24 DEFERRED INCOME TAX     91       125
25 OTHER L/T LIABIL
26 EQUIP LEASE OBLGTNS     48        42
27 SUBORDINATED LIABIL    334       150
-----------------------------------------------------------------
28    TOTAL LIABILITIES 1,339     1,651
-----------------------------------------------------------------
29 SUSPENDED ITEMS
30 MINORITY INTEREST
-----------------------------------------------------------------
31 PREFERRED STOCK        215       270
32 COMMON STOCK           143       145
33 CAPITAL SURPLUS        177       206
34
35 RETAINED EARNINGS      569       584
36 (TREAS STOK DEDUCT)   - 10      - 15
-----------------------------------------------------------------
37  TOTAL LIAB&NT WRTH  2,433     2,841
=================================================================
38  NT WORKING CAPITAL    719       829
39  TANGIBLE NET WORTH  1,094     1,190
40 CURRENT RATIO         1.87      1.73
41 TANG WORTH/TOT LIAB   0.82      0.72
42 SALES/RECEIV-DAYS    57.02     70.25
43 COST SALES/INV-DAYS  90.63     91.84
44 GROSS PROPERTY         744       755
45 CONTINGENT LIAB
   INITIALS OF ANALYST:   CMH       CMH
```

```
EXAMPLE COMPANY, INC. & SUBSIDIARIES
 OPERATING DATA FOR    12 MONTHS 12 MONTHS
                       12/31/x4  12/31/x5
===============================================================
46 NET SALES              4,022    4,561
47 LESS:COST OF SALES     2,880    3,222
---------------------------------------------------------------
48    GROSS PROFIT        1,142    1,339
49    % OF NET SALES      28.39%   29.36%
50 LESS:OPERATING EXP.      400      497
51 AFL INCOME EXP(INC)     - 19     - 25
52 DEPRECIATION&DEPLET
---------------------------------------------------------------
53    OPERATING PROFIT      761      867
54    % OF NET SALES      18.92%   19.01%
55 ADD:OTHER INCOME          28       19
56 LESS:OTHER EXPENSE
57       INTEREST EXP.       28       28
58
---------------------------------------------------------------
59    NET PROF BEF TAX      761      858
60    % OF NET SALES      18.92%   18.81%
61 LESS INCOME TAX          395      446
62 % OF PROFIT B4 TAX     51.91%   51.98%
63
---------------------------------------------------------------
64 PROFIT AFTER TAX         366      412
65 % OF NET SALES          9.10%    9.03%
66 AFTER TAX INC(EXP)                - 37
---------------------------------------------------------------
67    NET PROFIT(LOSS)      366      375
68    % OF NET SALES       9.10%    8.22%
69    CASH PREFERRED         11       14
70    CASH COMN/WTHDRLS     289      346
71    STOCK DIVIDENDS
---------------------------------------------------------------
72 NET AFTER DIVIDENDS       66       15
73 ADD:BEG RET  EARN        503      569
74 PLUS OTHER ADDITION
75 LESS OTHER DEDUCT.
76 ENDING RET EARNINGS      569      584
77 EARN/SHARE (A PRFD)
---------------------------------------------------------------
===SOURCE & APPLICATION OF FUNDS===============================
78 NET PROFIT               366      375
79 DEPRECIATION&DEPL         53       51
80  CASH GENERATION         419      426
81 DEC-OTHR NONC ASSTS                17
82 INC-L/T LIABILITIES              194
83 INC-SUSPENDED ITEMS
84 INC-OTHER EQUITY                  86
---------------------------------------------------------------
85   TOTAL SOURCES                  723
---------------------------------------------------------------
86 CASH DIV.&WITHDRWLS              360
87 INDICATED CAP EXPEN               29
88 INC-OTHR NONC ASSTS               25
89 DEC-L/T LIABILITIES             194
90 DEC-SUSPENDED ITEMS
91 DEC-OTHER EQUITY                   5
---------------------------------------------------------------
92 TOTAL APPLICATIONS              613
93 INC(DEC)-WORK. CAP.             110
```

```
                 COMMON SIZE HISTORICAL SPREAD SHEET
EXAMPLE COMPANY, INC. & SUBSIDIARIES
```

CONSOLIDATED			SIC CODE = 3411
SOURCE OF STATEMENT DATE	AUDITED 12/31/x4	AUDITED 12/31/x5	IND. AVG. RMA
-----ASSETS----			
1 CASH	5.55%	7.29%	6.00%
2 TEMP INVESTMENTS	2.06	1.76	
3 ACCTS REC-NET	26.18	31.32	27.30
4 INVENTORIES	29.79	28.93	27.50
5 OTHER CURR ASSETS	-	-	3.30
6			
7 CURRENT ASSETS	63.58	69.31	64.10
8 NET PROPERTY	23.80	19.61	25.70
9 INVESTMENTS	6.62	6.55	-
10 INTANGIBLES	-	-	.10
11 OTHER NONCUR ASSETS			
12 PREPDS & OTH ASSETS	6.00	4.54	10.00
13 TOTAL ASSETS	100.00	100.00	100.00
--LIABILITIES & NET WORTH----			
14 BANK LOANS-S/T	4.11	14.08	11.40
15 CURR MAT L/T LIABIL	0.90	1.55	.90
16 OTHER NOTES PAYABLE			
17 ACCTS PAYABLE	18.25	13.59	19.60
18 ACCRUED INCOME TAX	7.44	7.67	
19 OTHER CURRENT LIAB	-	-	4.80
20 ACCRUED EXPENSES	3.33	3.24	8.70
21 CURRENT LIABIL.	34.03	40.13	45.30
22 BANK LOANS-L/T		5.63	
23 MORTGAGE LOANS	1.56%	1.20%	
24 DEFERRED INCOME TAX	3.74	4.40	
25 OTHER L/T LIABIL			9.60
26 EQUIP LEASE OBLGTNS	1.97	1.48	
27 SUBORDINATED LIABIL	13.73	5.28	
28 TOTAL LIABILITIES	55.03	58.11	
29 SUSPENDED ITEMS			
30 MINORITY INTEREST			
31 PREFERRED STOCK	8.84	9.50	
32 COMMON STOCK	5.88	5.10	
33 CAPITAL SURPLUS	7.27	7.25	
34			45.10
35 RETAINED EARNINGS	23.39	20.56	
36 (TREAS STOK DEDUCT)	-0.41	-0.53	
37 TOTAL LIAB&NT WRTH	100.00	100.00	100.00
38 NT WORKING CAPITAL	29.55	29.18	
39 TANGIBLE NET WORTH	44.97	41.89	45.10
40 CURRENT RATIO	1.87	1.73	
41 TANG WORTH/TOT LIAB	0.82	0.72	
42 SALES/RECEIV-DAYS	57.02	70.25	
43 COST SALES/INV-DAYS	90.63	91.84	
44 GROSS PROPERTY	30.58	26.58	
45 CONTINGENT LIAB			
INITIALS OF ANALYST-	CMH	CMH	

```
                COMMON SIZE OPERATING DATA
         PERIOD COVERED  12 MONTHS 12 MONTHS    RMA
                          12/31/x4  12/31/x5
=======================================================================
46 NET SALES              100.00%   100.00%   100.00%
47 LESS:COST OF SALES      71.61     70.65     77.80

-----------------------------------------------------------------------
48    GROSS PROFIT         28.39     29.36     22.20
50 LESS:OPERATING EXP.      9.95     10.90     11.90
51 AFL INCOME EXP(INC)     -0.47     -0.55
52 DEPRECIATION&DEPLET

-----------------------------------------------------------------------
53    OPERATING PROFIT     18.92     19.01     10.30
55 ADD:OTHER INCOME         0.70      0.42
56 LESS:OTHER EXPENSE
57      INTEREST EXP.       0.70      0.61
58

-----------------------------------------------------------------------
59    NET PROF BEF TAX     18.92     18.81      6.30
61 LESS INCOME TAX          9.82      9.78
63

-----------------------------------------------------------------------
64    PROFIT AFTER TAX      9.10      9.03
66 AFTER TAX INC(EXP)                -0.81

-----------------------------------------------------------------------
67    NET PROFIT(LOSS)      9.10      8.22
69    CASH PREFERRED        0.27      0.31
70    CASH COMN/WTHDRLS     7.19      7.59
71    STOCK DIVIDENDS

-----------------------------------------------------------------------
72 NET AFTER DIVIDENDS      1.64      0.33
74 PLUS OTHER ADDITION
75 LESS OTHER DEDUCT.
77    CASH GENERATION      10.42      9.34

-----------------------------------------------------------------------
===SOURCE & APPLICATION OF FUNDS=======================================
78 NET PROFIT                        51.88%
79 DEPRECIATION&DEPL                  7.05
80    CASH GENERATION                58.92
81 DEC-OTHR NONC ASSTS               2.35
82 INC-L/T LIABILITIES              26.83
83 INC-SUSPENDED ITEMS
84 INC-OTHER EQUITY                 11.89

-----------------------------------------------------------------------
85    TOTAL SOURCES                 100.00

-----------------------------------------------------------------------
86 CASH DIV.&WITHDRWLS              49.79
87 INDICATED CAP EXPEN               4.01
88 INC-OTHR NONC ASSTS               3.46
89 DEC-L/T LIABILITIES              26.83
90 DEC-SUSPENDED ITEMS
91 DEC-OTHER EQUITY                  0.69

-----------------------------------------------------------------------
92 TOTAL APPLICATIONS               84.79
93 INC(DEC)-WORK. CAP.              15.21
```

```
                          RATIO ANALYSIS
          EXAMPLE COMPANY, INC. & SUBSIDIARIES

                CONSOLIDATED                    SIC CODE=  3411
          =====================================================================
          SOURCE OF STATEMENT     AUDIT  AUDIT   WT  INDUS.
          DATE                    1231x4 1231x5  AVG. AVG.
          =====================================================================
          LIQUIDITY RATIOS
          ---------------------------------------------------------------------
           1 QUICK RATIO          0.993  1.006   1.001   .800
           2 CURRENT RATIO        1.868  1.727   1.798  1.700
           3 SALES/RECEIVABLES    6.314  5.125   5.621  8.500
           4 SALES/RECEIV-DAYS    57.016 70.248  63.632    43.000 days
           5 COST OF SALES/INVENT 3.972  3.920   3.944  7.300
           6 SALES/WORKING CAPIT  5.594  5.502   5.545 10.500
          =====================================================================
          CAPITAL RATIOS
          ---------------------------------------------------------------------
           7 TOTAL LIAB/TANG WRTH 1.224  1.387   1.309  1.300
           8 TANG WRTH/TOTAL LIAB 0.817  0.721   0.764
           9 TANG WRTH/L/T LIABIL 2.141  2.329   2.235
          10 NET WRTH/CAPITALIZ   0.682  0.700   0.691
          11 L/T LIAB/CAPITALIZ   0.318  0.300   0.309
          12 SEN L/T LIAB/CAPITAL 0.110  0.212   0.163
          13 SUBORD LIAB/CAPITALZ 0.208  0.088   0.146
          14 NET PROPER/TANG WRTH 0.529  0.468   0.497   .600
          =====================================================================
          COVERAGE RATIOS
          ---------------------------------------------------------------------
          19 PROF B4 INT&TX/INT   28.179 31.643  29.911  9.900
          20 CSHFL B4 INT&TAX/INT 30.071 33.464  31.768
          21 CSHFLO/CURR MAT-L/T  19.045  9.682  12.803  9.500
          =====================================================================
          PROFITABILITY RATIOS
          ---------------------------------------------------------------------
          23 N SALES/NET PROPERTY 6.946  8.189   7.555 12.100
          24 N SALES/TOT ASSETS   1.653  1.605   1.627  2.300
          25 NET SALES/TANG WRTH  3.676  3.833   3.758
          26 OP PROF/NET SALES    0.189  0.190   0.190
          27 PROF B4 TX/N SALES   0.189  0.188   0.189
          28 NET PROF/NET SALES   0.091  0.082   0.086
          29 PROF B4 TAX/WORTH    0.696  0.721   0.709   .297(29.7%)
          30 PROF B4 TAX/ASSETS   0.313  0.302   0.307   .122(12.2%)
          31 NET PROF/TANG WORTH  0.335  0.315   0.324
          32 NET PROF/CAPITALIZ   0.228  0.220   0.224
          33 NET PROF/TOT ASSETS  0.150  0.132   0.141
```

M E M O R A N D U M

**FIRST COMMERCIAL BANK
of ANYWHERE, N.A.**
Post Office Box 000
Anywhere, USA 00001
Telephone 888-987-6543

TO: WILLIAM VOLE — CREDIT DEPARTMENT

FROM: ROBERT KNIGHTLEY

SUBJECT: EXAMPLE COMPANY, INC.

DATE: APRIL 5, 19X6

The recent credit analysis performed on the above listed company was received and reviewed this date. Please see to it that the following items are given further review:

1. The company continues to grow but shortages of working capital coupled with overuse of bank lines are in evidence. The basic problem seems to rest with the dividend policy and to a lesser degree with the receivable back-up you mention in your report. A field audit of receivables may well be in order. Certainly a current aging is needed.

2. Please summarize the conditions contained in the convertible debenture. In particular, the footnotes show that restrictions exist regarding the maintenance of working capital and payment of cash dividends. Include restatement of and compliance with these restrictions, in all future write-ups.

3. The subordinate debt is subordinated only to senior debt (term debt) but has status equal to other unsecured creditors, including the bank. Future analysis should not list it as subordinated debt but as term debt.

When time permits, it would be wise to review the rules of equity vs. cost reporting of affiliate investments. The current earnings from this source are minor but may be significant in the future.

Exercise 13

You are an analyst in your bank's credit department and have been asked by a senior lending officer to prepare an analytical report on the Empire Manufacturing Company. She gave you the copy of the current year-end statement that follows and told you she expects to meet with the company in the next few days. The company is not a client of your bank at present and the lending officer has no idea of what its request will be.

You do not know the request and you will not be able to discuss the contents of the listed items. Your normal advantage as a banker will not be available to you. What then should be the goal of your report?

Primarily your goal should be to highlight the key points for the lending officer. You will prepare a spread and perform certain mechanical measurements. She can read, so don't merely repeat a series of numbers to her. Digest the statement and outline the good and the bad. Compare your remarks with those of the analyst whose report appears following the statement.

EMPIRE MANUFACTURING COMPANY

DECEMBER 31, 19X8

EMPIRE MANUFACTURING COMPANY

DECEMBER 31, 19X8

CONTENTS

To the Directors and Shareholders
Empire Manufacturing Company
42 Shore Road
Wilkes-Barre, Pennsylvania

We have examined the balance sheet of EMPIRE MANUFACTURING
COMPANY as of December 31, 19X8 and the related statements of
income and retained earnings and changes in financial position
for the year then ended. Our examination was made in accordance
with generally accepted auditing standards and accordingly
included such tests of the accounting records and such other
auditing procedures as we considered necessary in the circumstances.

In our opinion, the accompanying financial statements
present fairly the financial position of EMPIRE MANUFACTURING
COMPANY at December 31, 19X8 and the results of its operations
and the changes in its financial position for the year then
ended, in conformity with generally accepted accounting
principles applied on a basis consistent with that of the
preceding year.

Kingston, Pennsylvania
February 19, 19X9

EMPIRE MANUFACTURING COMPANY

BALANCE SHEET - DECEMBER 31, 19X8

ASSETS

Current Assets:			
Cash			$ 7,156
Accounts receivable (Note 1)	$360,614		
Less: Allowance for doubtful accounts	3,606		357,008
Accounts receivable, miscellaneous			5,959
Inventories, cost, first-in, first-out			
(Note 1):			
Raw materials	$ 65,638		
Containers and supplies	115,322		
Finished goods	191,392		372,352
Marketable securities, cost, (which			
approximates market value) (Note 2)			1,289
Travel advance			5,630
Prepaid expenses			7,110
Total current assets			$ 756,504
Property and Equipment - At Cost:			
Land		$ 31,000	
Buildings and improvements	$490,951		
Machinery and equipment	197,294		
Office furniture and fixtures	8,883		
	$697,128		
Less: Accumulated depreciation			
(Note 1)	76,138	620,990	$ 651,990
Other Assets:			
Cash, construction escrow account		$ 5,699	
Organization expense, net of			
amortization		9,887	
Prepaid expenses, net of current portion		1,975	
			17,561
			$ 1,426,055

See notes to financial statements

EMPIRE MANUFACTURING COMPANY

BALANCE SHEET - DECEMBER 31, 19X8

Current Liabilities:

Notes payable, revolving line of credit (Note 3)		$ 400.347
Notes payable, bank (Note 4)		47.764
Mortgage payable, bank, current maturities (Note 5)		20,807
Equipment obligation		590
Accounts payable		127.742
Withheld and accrued payroll taxes		2.865
Accrued salaries and expenses		46.941
State income tax payable (Note 7)		2,555
Total current liabilities		$ 649.611

Long Term Debt:

Note payable, bank (Note 4)	$ 25,225	
Note payable, subordinated (Note 6)	105,400	
Mortgages payable, bank, net of current maturities (Note 5)	390,384	$ 521,009

Deferred Credit:

Deferred credit arising from sale and leaseback of property (Note 8)		13.950

Shareholders' Equity:

Common stock - par value $10; authorized, issued and outstanding 14,170 shares	$141,700	
Additional paid-in capital	82,336	
Retained earnings	17,449	$ 241.485
		$ 1,426,055

See notes to financial statements

EMPIRE MANUFACTURING COMPANY

STATEMENT OF RETAINED EARNINGS

YEAR ENDED DECEMBER 31, 19X8

Balance, January 1, 19X8	$ 11,359
Net Income	6,090
Balance, December 31, 19X8	$ 17,449

See notes to financial statements

EMPIRE MANUFACTURING COMPANY

STATEMENT OF INCOME

YEAR ENDED DECEMBER 31, 19X8

Sales	$1,923,190
Less: Sales returns and allowances	13,879
	$1,909,311
Cost of Goods Sold	1,396,166
Gross Profit	$ 513,145
Operating Expenses:	
Selling and delivery	250,948
General and administrative	142,287
	$ 393,235
Net Operating Profit	$ 119,910
Other Income and (Deductions):	
Interest expense	($ 101,915)
Bad debt expense	(20,520)
Miscellaneous income	9,526
	($ 112,909)
Net Income Before Income Taxes	$ 7,001
Federal and State Income Taxes (Note 7)	911
Net Income	$ 6,090
Earnings Per Common Share (Note 1)	$ .43

See notes to financial statements

EMPIRE MANUFACTURING COMPANY

STATEMENT OF CHANGES IN FINANCIAL POSITION

YEAR ENDED DECEMBER 31, 19X8

Source of Funds:
  Operations:
    Net income .... $ 6,090
    Add and deduct items not requiring outlay of working
      capital:
      Depreciation 42,704
      Amortization 3,977
      Deferred credits .... (1,644)
  Total funds provided from operations 51,127
  Reduction of cash construction escrow account 121,216
  Proceeds from sale and leaseback 93,000

                                                            $265,343

Application of Funds:
  Additions to property and equipment $155,325
  Reduction in long term debt 59,735
  Increase in working capital 50,283

                                                            $265,343

Changes in Working Capital:
  Increase (decrease) in current assets:
    Cash .... ($ 6,733)
    Accounts receivable 160,457
    Accounts receivable, miscellaneous 1,810
    Stock subscriptions receivable .... (77,500)
    Inventories 73,133
    Marketable securities 1,289
    Travel advance 4,421
    Prepaid expenses .... (822)

                                                            $156,055

  Increase (decrease) in current liabilities:
    Notes payable, revolving line of credit $156,006
    Notes payable, bank .... (25,164)
    Note payable, other, current maturities .... (28,520)
    Mortgage payable, bank, current maturities 15,616
    Equipment obligation .... (99)
    Accounts payable .... (22,055)
    Withheld and accrued payroll taxes 362
    Accrued salaries and expenses 7,914
    State income tax payable 1,712

                                                            $105,772

Increase in Working Capital .... $ 50,283

See notes to financial statements

EMPIRE MANUFACTURING COMPANY

NOTES TO FINANCIAL STATEMENTS

YEAR ENDED DECEMBER 31, 19X8

1. Summary of Significant Accounting Policies:

   A. Inventories - Inventories are valued at cost. The cost
      of these inventories are determined on the first-in,
      first-out method.

   B. Receivables - The allowance for doubtful accounts
      represents one per cent of customer accounts receivable
      at year end. The company has a credit insurance
      policy covering certain accounts with a primary loss
      not less than $5,598 and a 10% co-insurance clause.

   C. Depreciation - Depreciation is computed principally
      using the straight-line method for financial reporting
      and the declining balance method for machinery and ·
      equipment for income tax purposes. The depreciation
      is provided for in amounts sufficient to relate the
      cost of depreciable assets to operations over their
      estimated service lives.

   D. Investment Credit - Investment tax credits are accounted
      for on the "flow through" method, which recognizes the
      benefit in the year in which the assets which gave rise
      to the credit are placed in service. This is consistent
      with the treatment for income tax purposes. The
      alternative method would allocate the credit over the
      depreciable lives of the related assets.

   E. Earnings Per Common Share - Earnings per common share were
      computed on the basis of the weighted average number of
      shares outstanding during the year. The common stock
      equivalents were not considered in the computation since
      the average market price of the common stock obtainable
      upon exercise, did not exceed, the exercise price of the
      option.

   F. Bad Debt Expense - The company uses the reserve method of
      accounting for doubtful accounts.

2. Marketable Securities:

   104 shares XYZ Company $ 1,289

EMPIRE MANUFACTURING COMPANY

NOTES TO FINANCIAL STATEMENTS

YEAR ENDED DECEMBER 31, 19X8

3. Notes Payable, Revolving Line of Credit:

   Notes payable, revolving line of credit, represents an
   obligation in the amount of $400,347 with interest computed
   at 7½% above the prime interest rate. These obligations
   are secured by accounts receivable and inventory. All
   collections of accounts receivable are remitted to the
   lender and advances are made to the company as requested.

4. Notes Payable, Bank:

	Rate	Amount	Collateral
Demand Note	10%	$37,200	Unsecured
Amortized note	8%	35,789	Guaranty of stockholder
		$72,989	

5. Mortgage Payable, Bank:

	Rate	Amount	Maturity Date
	7 3/4%	$411,191	19X3

6. Note Payable, Subordinated:

   The note payable, subordinated represents an obligation to
   a shareholder in the amount of $105,400 at 6% interest. No
   provision has been made for payment of principal as of the
   balance sheet date.

7. Income Taxes:

   The company's federal income tax liability was offset by a
   net operating loss carryforward and an investment credit. A
   reconciliation between the income tax expense computed by
   applying the statutory rate to income, the actual tax expense
   and the amount reported for financial statement purposes is
   as follows:

Provision for income taxes at statutory rate	$5,355
State corporate tax	2,555
Benefit from net operating loss carryforward	(416)
Amortization of investment tax credit	(4,939)
Actual tax expense	$2,555
Amortization of prior year deferred income tax credit	(1,644)
Tax expense financial reporting	$ 911

EMPIRE MANUFACTURING COMPANY

NOTES TO FINANCIAL STATEMENTS

YEAR ENDED DECEMBER 31, 19X8

8. Leases and Commitments:

On June 18, 19X8 the company entered into a sale and leaseback
arrangement for certain machinery and equipment. The equipment
was sold for $93,000 and leased back for five years at an annual
rental of $25,445. The sale resulted in a gain for financial
reporting of $15,500 of which $13,950 has been deferred and will
be amortized as a reduction of rent expense over the term of
the lease for financial statement purposes. A total of $1,550
has been amortized in the current year. The company has other
long term leases covering a period of five years for equipment.
The aggregate annual rental payment for all of the above leases
is $31,051. The total amount of rental expense charged to
operations for the current year is $14,783.

EMPIRE MANUFACTURING COMPANY

REPORT ON SUPPLEMENTAL FINANCIAL INFORMATION

The financial statements of EMPIRE MANUFACTURING COMPANY referred to in the opinion on page 1 are set forth in the preceding pages of this report. Other data and comments included in the following pages of this report, although not considered necessary for a fair presentation of financial position and results of operations are presented primarily for supplemental and analysis purposes. This additional information relative to the year ended December 31, 19X8 has been subjected to the audit procedures applied in the examination of the basic financial statements, and is, in our opinion, fairly stated in all material respects in relation to the basic financial statements taken as a whole.

Kingston, Pennsylvania
February 18, 19X9

EMPIRE MANUFACTURING COMPANY

COST OF GOODS MANUFACTURED AND SOLD

YEAR ENDED DECEMBER 31, 19X8

Raw Materials and Supplies:		
Inventory, beginning		$ 138,224
Purchases	$1,214,607	
Less: Purchase discounts	19,155	1,195,452
Freight-in		10,482
		$1,344,158
Less: Inventory, ending		180,960
Cost of Raw Materials and Supplies		$1,163,198
Factory Overhead:		
Salaries and wages	$ 139,466	
Supplies and general factory expense	8,787	
Repairs and maintenance	14,505	
Heat, light and power	14,666	
Payroll taxes	9,982	
Insurance	16,335	
Group insurance	2,492	
Real estate taxes	2,724	
Equipment leasing	14,783	
Depreciation - machinery and equipment	21,585	
Depreciation - building and improvements	18,039	
		263,364
Cost of Goods Manufactured		$1,426,562
Add: Finished goods inventory, beginning		160,996
		$1,587,558
Less: Finished goods inventory, ending		191,392
Cost of Goods Sold		$1,396,166

EMPIRE MANUFACTURING COMPANY

OPERATING EXPENSES

YEAR ENDED DECEMBER 31, 19X8

Selling and Delivery:
Trade shows and convention expense	$ 7,460
Salaries, sales	12,091
Payroll taxes	785
Commissions	75,131
Advertising	8,405
Travel and selling expense	30,706
Freight-out	113,498
Collection expense	272
Catalog expense	2,600
	$250,948

General and Administrative:
Officers' salaries	$ 51,801
Office salaries	27,883
Payroll taxes	2,902
Group insurance	2,492
Insurance, general	3,894
Real estate taxes	2,724
Telephone	9,894
Professional services	12,293
Office supplies and expenses	7,767
Miscellaneous expenses	1,035
Postage	1,385
Pennsylvania corporate loans tax	200
Pennsylvania capital stock tax	27
Dues and subscriptions	1,070
Equipment leasing	6,729
Officers' life insurance	3,331
Contributions	293
Depreciation, furniture and fixtures	1,076
Depreciation, buildings and improvements	2,005
Amortization, organization expense	3,486
	$142,287
	$393,235

Statement Analysis Report

TO: J. Smith, Vice President
RE: Empire Manufacturing Company
FROM: J. Purlat, Credit Department
DATE: August 22, 19X9

The Empire Manufacturing Company audit was performed by a reputable firm. They issued a clean opinion; the statement presented was complete and it contains supplementary schedules on income and expenses.

The footnotes reveal that the company has entered into a variety of financing agreements. When taken as a group, these agreements suggest that the company has had severe cash problems. This conclusion is based on both the type and cost of these various loans.

The company generates cash flow by factoring its accounts receivable. It presently pays a very high rate of interest (7¼ percent over prime) for its money. The line is secured by both receivables and inventory. The company also borrows $75,000 on a short-term basis from its bank. Half of this amount is secured by the guarantee of a stockholder. Long-term debt consists of a mortgage of $412,000 due in twenty years. Finally, a stockholder has advanced to the company on a subordinated basis a total of $105,000 at a nominal rate of interest with no set principal reduction.

In addition to these four loans the company entered into a sale-leaseback on certain machinery and equipment. The company generated some cash by doing this, but the effective rate for this borrowing is high.

The balance sheet confirms the tight cash position. Of $1.4 million of assets, cash represents only $7,000. With the loans being secured by inventory, receivables, physical plant and equipment, there are no significant "free" assets.

The liabilities comprise the previously listed loans and a sizeable accrued-expense and account-payable balance. Taxes appear to be paid current.

The equity of the company totals $240,000 with the majority of that being cash invested. The debt to equity ratio is quite high (1185:241 or 4½ to 1 without subordination, and 1080:350 or 3 to 1 when subordinated debt is considered as capital.)

As the ratios show, the company has little working capital, a fair receivable turnover, and a poor inventory turnover. Comparison with industry figures will be made after you have completed the preliminary interview. Prior-year statements should also be requested at that time.

The income statement shows a poor net profit of $6,000 on sales of $1.9 million. Cost of sales totals 71 percent of sales. The supplemental data show two large expenses that seem to make the selling expenses quite high. The first is freight delivery of $114,000 (6 percent of sales) and the second is commissions totaling $75,000 (4 percent of sales). Officers' salaries of $52,000 are in line with the sales volume, and depreciation of $42,000 has not had any significant effect on the numbers. The major operating expense, as expected, is interest expense which totals over $100,000.

The change in financial position statement reveals that profit and depreciation generated sufficient cash to meet long-term debt requirements. The company completed a building and the funds came mainly from a cash escrow account. The remaining source of funds for the building came from a sale and leaseback, which created the increase in working capital.

The majority of working capital was used to increase inventory by $75,000. Receivables increased by $160,000; this increase was not supported by the company's working capital but by additional funding from the accounts receivable factor. The company did receive $75,000 of new capital, and it appears that these funds were used to reduce both accounts and notes payable.

CONCLUSION: The company appears quite new. This assumption is based on low depreciation reserve and low accumulated earnings. Management has entered into a series of expensive financing arrangements to make up for its inadequate capital base. This has cost them profitability and has tied up all assets.

Growth of the company will require additional working capital, but at present the company appears to have no means of getting it. Any additional burden will seriously impair an already unsatisfactory fixed debt retirement.

The key to success for this company must be to improve on its current assets. Receivables and inventory must be reduced and/or new working capital injected. Participation by a new bank without taking over the existing credits is neither possible nor attractive.

Please contact me if you have need for further discussion.

(Spread sheet attached.)

FIRST EASTERN BANK, N. A.
COMPARISON STATEMENT

000's Omitted

NAME   Empire Manufacturing Company

	ASSETS Date	12/31/X8				
1	Cash	7				
2	Marketable Securities — C/D's					
3	Receivable — Trade (Net)	357				
4						
5	Inventories	372				
6						
7						
8	All Other Current					
9	TOTAL CURRENT ASSETS	736				
10	Fixed Assets — Net	652				
11						
12						
13	Investments					
14						
15	All Other Noncurrent (Incl. Prepaid)	38				
16	TOTAL NONCURRENT ASSETS	690				
17	TOTAL ASSETS	1,426				
	LIABILITIES					
18	Notes Payable — Banks	48				
19	Notes Payable — Other	400				
20						
21	Current Maturities of L. T. Debt	21				
22	Accounts Payable — Trade	128				
23						
24	Interest & Other Accruals	50				
25	Taxes Payable	4				
26						
27						
28	All Other Current					
29	TOTAL CURRENT DEBT	651				
30	Mortgage Payable	390				
31	Long Term Debt	25				
32	Subordinated Notes Payable	105				
33	All Other Noncurrent	14				
34	TOTAL NONCURRENT DEBT	534				
35	TOTAL LIABILITIES	1,185				
36	Capital	224				
37	Retained Earnings	17				
38						
39	NET WORTH	241				
40	TOTAL LIABILITIES&NET WORTH	1,426				
41						
42	NET WORKING CAPITAL (9-29)	85				
	RATIOS					
43	Quick	.56 to 1				
44	Current	1.13 to 1				
45	Total Debt/Working Capital	1185/85				
46	Total Debt/Net Worth	1185/241				
47	Receivable Turnover Days	69 days				
48	Inventory Turnover Days	100 days				
49	% Profit bef. Taxes/Net Worth	2.9%				
50	% Profit bef. Taxes/Total Assets	.5%				
51						
52	Statement by					
53	Type of Statement	Unqualified				
54	Spread by	JP				
55	Contingent Liabilities					
56						

FORM 18-1

FIRST EASTERN BANK, N. A.

NAME   Empire Manufacturing Company

OPERATIONS	Date	12/31/X8	%		%		%		%		%
101 Net Sales		1,909	100								
102 Cost of Sales		1,356	71								
103 Gross Profit		553	29								
104 Operating Expenses		499	26								
105 Net Profit before Depreciation		54	3								
106 Depreciation		47	3								
107 Profit from Operations		7									
108 Extraordinary Items											
109											
110 Profits Before Taxes		7									
111 Income Taxes		1									
112											
113 NET PROFIT AFTER TAXES		6	.3								
RECONCILIATION OF NET WORTH											
114 Net Worth — Beginning		340									
115 Add: Net Profit After Taxes		6									
116											
117											
118 Less: Net Loss											
119 Dividend Paid											
120											
121											
122 Net Worth — Ending		346									
SOURCE & APPLICATION OF FUNDS											
Source of Funds:											
123 Net Profit		6									
124 Depreciation, Amort., Depletion		45									
125 Increase Long Term Debt											
126 Reduction in Escrow Acct.		121									
127 Proceeds of Sale/Lease		93									
128 Other Noncurrent Accounts — Net											
129 TOTAL SOURCES		265									
Application of Funds:											
130 Net Loss											
131 Dividends Paid											
132 Purchase of Fixed Assets		155									
133 Reduction Long Term Debt		60									
134											
135											
136 Other Noncurrent Accounts — Net											
137 TOTAL APPLICATIONS		215									
138 INC./DEC. OF WORKING CAPITAL		+50									
RECONCIL. OF W/C CHANGES											
139 Cash		(7)									
140 Accounts Receivable		162									
141 Inventory		73									
142 Other		5									
143 Stock Subscription Rec.		(78)									
144 Notes Payable—Revolving Cr.		156									
145 Accounts Payable		(22)									
146 Current Maturities — L.T. Debt		(13)									
147 Other		9									
148 Notes Payable—Other		(25)									
149 Inc/Dec W/C (139-143) − (144-148)		+50									

COMMENTS:

Exercise 14

The following pages contain highlights of a dialogue between George Smith, an experienced commercial officer, and Jim Walters, a prospective client. The two have never met before. The interview occurred spontaneously; Walters did not ask in advance for an appointment.

Put yourself in the place of his lending officer. Judge his approach both to the request as well as to the financial statements. What questions would you have asked? What areas could have been developed more fully?

Interview

Walters: Hello, I'm Jim Walters. We've never met before, but I believe that you know my brother Harry. You financed a building for him a few years ago. His company is Giant Steel Company.

Smith: Oh, certainly. I remember Harry quite well; I haven't seen him for some time. I think we had a problem with rates and he changed banks. How is Harry?

Walters: He's fine. Actually, it is Harry who suggested I see you. He says if I can be helped, and I know I can, you're the man to do it.

Smith: I had hopes Harry would return to this bank. How's his business doing?

Walters: Quite well. He has so much work, he's subcontracting a portion to me. I work part-time for him and devote the rest of my time to my business. It keeps the money in the family and saves taxes at the same time.

Smith: I'm glad to hear of Harry's success. What's the name of his company? I remember he had a knack for forming new corporations every other day. And I'm especially glad to hear he's subcontracting. Harry's capital was always marginal. To use subs in steel erection requires a lot of cash. Those boys want to get paid but quick.

Walters: He now does work under Structural Steel, Inc. and Erection Unlimited. One's for union and the other nonunion jobs. The industry does have its short-term problems and that's got some cash tied up, but generally both of us, Harry and I, are okay. When you gotta give, you gotta give.

Smith: Well, that's enough of Harry. Tell me about you. What is your business?

Walters: I've been working most of my life. I'm getting toward middle age and I really don't have a lot to show for it. That's when Harry mentioned he was subcontracting out some of his work. To make a long story short, I took all I had, mortgaged the house and started A. B. Enterprises. That was two years ago. I started on a mere $10,000 of capital and have built a reputable business. We specialize in industrial air equipment. From air conditioning to exhaust fans. If it blows around, we're involved.

Smith: I see. And to whom do you sell?

Walters: To a lot of people in a lot of ways. We're not proud! No job is too small. Just last week, we did a $200 attic fan for a little old lady. A few months ago, we did a $15,000 job at the new college gym. Sometimes we work for Harry. Usually we do the installation — especially if the union's on his back. They want the cash escrowed before their boys go on the job. They don't think highly of my brother. We've got a better relationship with them than Harry does.

Smith: And what is it that our bank can help you with?

Walters: What I need is a line of credit. I think that's what it is called. When I need money, I need it. Not three weeks from now when the committee meets. You know, a preapproval.

Smith: And how much do you think you may need?

Walters: I'd like $10,000. I really don't ever expect to use all of it, but I'd like the backup to be there.

Smith: And how would you like to pay us back?

Walters: Wouldn't the line be on demand?

Smith: The line can be on a demand note. That doesn't mean it doesn't have to be paid. If you need the funds for a purpose, then as the purpose is completed, you pay us back.

Walters: What I need it for may vary. Right now my receivables are backed up a little. When they get paid I could pay you.

Smith: We'll come back to that in a bit. Do you have an accountant?

Walters: Yes, I use Joseph Henry Associates. All I really do is have him prepare my tax return. I understand he's quite good.

Smith: He certainly is. Do you have the tax return with you?

Walters: Yes, it's here somewhere. Oh yes, here it is.

(Walters presents the return that is shown on the following page to Smith. Review it at the same time Smith does.)

Form **1120**	**U.S. Corporation Income Tax Return**	OMB No. 1545–0123
Department of the Treasury Internal Revenue Service	For calendar year 1981 or other tax year beginning ...., 1981, ending ...., 19...... ▶For Paperwork Reduction Act Notice, see page 1 of the instructions	**1981**

Check if a—	Use IRS label. Other- wise please print or type.	Name	D. Employer identification number
A. Consolidated return ☐		A. B. Enterprises, Inc.	24-2888028
B. Personal Holding Co. ☐		Number and street	E. Date incorporated
C. Business Code No. (See page 9 of Instructions) 1711		7000 Sundown Avenue	2/1/80
		City or town, State, and ZIP code	F. Total assets (see Specific Instructions)
		Last Town, Utah 84321	$ 21,525

Gross Income	1 (a) Gross receipts or sales $ .... (b) Less returns and allowances $ .... Balance ▶	**1(c)**	33,650
	2 Cost of goods sold (Schedule A) and/or operations (attach schedule)	**2**	
	3 Gross profit (subtract line 2 from line 1(c))	**3**	33,650
	4 Dividends (Schedule C)	**4**	
	5 Interest on obligations of the United States and U.S. instrumentalities	**5**	
	6 Other interest	**6**	
	7 Gross rents	**7**	
	8 Gross royalties	**8**	
	9 (a) Capital gain net income (attach separate Schedule D)	**9(a)**	
	(b) Net gain or (loss) from Form 4797, line 11(a), Part II (attach Form 4797)	**9(b)**	
	10 Other income (see instructions—attach schedule)	**10**	
	11 TOTAL income—Add lines 3 through 10	**11**	33,650
Deductions	12 Compensation of officers (Schedule E)	**12**	9,200
	13 (a) Salaries and wages .... 13(b) Less WIN and jobs credit(s) .... Balance ▶	**13(c)**	10,100
	14 Repairs (see instructions)	**14**	750
	15 Bad debts (Schedule F if reserve method is used)	**15**	
	16 Rents	**16**	2,950
	17 Taxes	**17**	1,350
	18 Interest	**18**	400
	19 Contributions (not over 5% of line 30 adjusted per instructions)	**19**	
	20 Amortization (attach schedule)	**20**	
	21 Depreciation from Form 4562 (attach Form 4562) .... less depreciation claimed in Schedule A and elsewhere on return .... Balance ▶	**21**	25
	22 Depletion	**22**	
	23 Advertising	**23**	
	24 Pension, profit-sharing, etc. plans (see instructions)	**24**	
	25 Employee benefit programs (see instructions)	**25**	
	26 Other deductions (attach schedule)	**26**	5,150
	27 TOTAL deductions—Add lines 12 through 26	**27**	29,925
	28 Taxable income before net operating loss deduction and special deductions (subtract line 27 from line 11)	**28**	3,725
	29 Less: (a) Net operating loss deduction (see instructions—attach schedule) . **29(a)** 4,200		
	(b) Special deductions (Schedule C) . **29(b)**	**29**	4,200
	30 Taxable income (subtract line 29 from line 28)	**30**	NONE
Tax	31 TOTAL TAX (Schedule J)	**31**	
	32 Credits: (a) Overpayment from 1980 allowed as a credit		
	(b) 1981 estimated tax payments		
	(c) Less refund of 1981 estimated tax applied for on Form 4466 . ( )		
	(d) Tax deposited: Form 7004 .... Form 7005 (attach) .... Total ▶		
	(e) Credit from regulated investment companies (attach Form 2439)		
	(f) Federal tax on special fuels and oils (attach Form 4136 or 4136–T)	**32**	
	33 TAX DUE (subtract line 32 from line 31). See instruction C3 for depositary method of payment . (Check ▶ ☐ if Form 2220 is attached. See instruction D.) ▶ $..............	**33**	NONE
	34 OVERPAYMENT (subtract line 31 from line 32)	**34**	
	35 Enter amount of line 34 you want: Credited to 1982 estimated tax ▶ .... Refunded ▶	**35**	

Please Sign Here	Under penalties of perjury, I declare that I have examined this return, including accompanying schedules and statements, and to the best of my knowledge and belief, it is true, correct, and complete. Declaration of preparer (other than taxpayer) is based on all information of which preparer has any knowledge.
	▶ *James G Watters* 2/14/82▶ President
	Signature of officer Date Title

Paid Preparer's Use Only	Preparer's signature ▶ *Joseph Henry*	Date 2/10/82	Check if self-em-ployed ▶ ☐	Preparer's social security no.
	Firm's name (or yours, if self-employed) and address ▶ Joseph Henry Associates Last Town, Utah		E.I. No. ▶ ZIP code ▶	24 ┊ 2870083 84321

Form 1120 (1981)   **Schedule A**   Cost of Goods Sold (See Instructions for Schedule A)   Page **2**

1 Inventory at beginning of year . . . .
2 Merchandise bought for manufacture or sale . . . .
3 Salaries and wages . . . .
4 Other costs (attach schedule) . . . .
5 Total—Add lines 1 through 4 . . . .
6 Inventory at end of year . . . .
7 Cost of goods sold—Subtract line 6 from line 5. Enter here and on line 2, page 1 . . . .
8 (a) Check all methods used for valuing closing inventory: (i) ☐ Cost (ii) ☐ Lower of cost or market as described in Regulations section 1.471–4 (see instructions) (iii) ☐ Writedown of "subnormal" goods as described in Regulations section 1.471–2(c) (see instructions)
   (b) Did you use any other method of inventory valuation not described above? . . . . ☐ Yes ☐ No
       If "Yes," specify method used and attach explanation ▶ ....
   (c) Check if the LIFO inventory method was adopted this tax year for any goods (If checked, attach Form 970.) . . . . . . ☐
   (d) If the LIFO inventory method was used for this tax year, enter percentage (or amounts) of closing inventory computed under LIFO . . . .
   (e) If you are engaged in manufacturing, did you value your inventory using the full absorption method (Regulations section 1.471–11)? . . . . ☐ Yes ☐ No
   (f) Was there any substantial change in determining quantities, cost, or valuations between opening and closing inventory? . . . ☐ Yes ☐ No
       If "Yes," attach explanation.

Schedule C   Dividends and Special Deductions (See instructions for Schedule C)

	(A) Dividends received	(B) %	(C) Special deductions: multiply (A) × (B)
1 Domestic corporations subject to 85% deduction		85	
2 Certain preferred stock of public utilities		59.13	
3 Foreign corporations subject to 85% deduction		85	
4 Wholly-owned foreign subsidiaries subject to 100% deduction (section 245(b)) .		100	
5 Total—Add lines 1 through 4. See instructions for limitation			
6 Affiliated groups subject to the 100% deduction (section 243(a)(3))		100	
7 Other dividends from foreign corporations not included in lines 3 and 4			
8 Income from controlled foreign corporations under subpart F (attach Forms 3646) .			
9 Foreign dividend gross-up (section 78)			
10 DISC or former DISC not included in line 1 (section 246(d))			
11 Other dividends			
12 Deduction for dividends paid on certain preferred stock of public utilities (see instructions)			
13 Total dividends—Add lines 1 through 11. Enter here and on line 4, page 1 ▶			
14 Total deductions—Add lines 5 through 12. Enter here and on line 29(b), page 1 ▶			

Schedule E   Compensation of Officers (See instruction for line 12)

1. Name of officer	2. Social security number	3. Time devoted to business	Percent of corporation stock owned 4. Common	5. Preferred	6. Amount of compensation	7. Expense account allowances
James G. Walters	998-87-000	80%	100		9,200	
Total compensation of officers—Enter here and on line 12, page 1					9,200	

Schedule F   Bad Debts—Reserve Method (See instruction for line 15)

1. Year	2. Trade notes and accounts receivable outstanding at end of year	3. Sales on account	Amount added to reserve 4. Current year's provision	5. Recoveries	6. Amount charged against reserve	7. Reserve for bad debts at end of year
1976						
1977						
1978						
1979						
1980						
1981						

Form 1120 (1981)   Page **3**

Schedule J Tax Computation (See instructions for Schedule J on pages 7 and 8)

Note: *Fiscal year corporations, see instructions on pages 10 and 11. Omit line 1, complete line 2(a) and, if applicable, line 2(b), and enter on line 3, the amount from line 44, Part III, of the fiscal year worksheet provided on page 11 of the instructions.*

1 Taxable income (line 30, page 1) . . . .

2 (a) Are you a member of a controlled group? . . . . ☐ Yes ☐ No

    (b) If "Yes," see instructions and enter your portion of the $25,000 amount in each taxable income bracket:

      (i) $............................. *(ii)* $......................... *(iii)* $............................ *(iv)* $.........................

3 Income tax (see instructions to figure the tax; enter this tax or alternative tax from Schedule D, whichever is less). Check if from Schedule D ▶ ☐ . . . .

4 (a) Foreign tax credit (attach Form 1118) . . . .

    (b) Investment credit (attach Form 3468) . . . .

    (c) Work incentive (WIN) credit (attach Form 4874) . . . . . .

    (d) Jobs credit (attach Form 5884) . . . .

    (e) Other credits (see instructions—attach forms and schedule) . . . .

5 Total—Add lines 4(a) through 4(e) . . . .

6 Subtract line 5 from line 3 . . . .

7 Personal holding company tax (attach Schedule PH (Form 1120)) . . . .

8 Tax from recomputing prior-year investment credit (attach Form 4255) . . . .

9 Minimum tax on tax preference items (see instructions—attach Form 4626) . . . .

10 Total tax—Add lines 6 through 9. Enter here and on line 31, page 1 . . . .

Additional Information (See page 8 of instructions)

	Yes	No
G Did you claim a deduction for expenses connected with:		
(1) Entertainment facility (boat, resort, ranch, etc.)?		X
(2) Living accommodations (except employees on business)? . .		X
(3) Employees attending conventions or meetings outside the North American area? (See section 274(h))		X
(4) Employees' families at conventions or meetings?		X
If "Yes," were any of these conventions or meetings outside the North American area? (See section 274(h))		
(5) Employee or family vacations not reported on Form W–2? . .		X
H (1) Did you at the end of the tax year own, directly or indirectly, 50% or more of the voting stock of a domestic corporation? (For rules of attribution, see section 267(c).)		X
If "Yes," attach a schedule showing: (a) name, address, and identifying number; (b) percentage owned; (c) taxable income or (loss) (e.g., if a Form 1120, line 28, page 1) of such corporation for the tax year ending with or within your tax year; (d) highest amount owed by you to such corporation during the year; and (e) highest amount owed to you by such corporation during the year.		
(2) Did any individual, partnership, corporation, estate or trust at the end of the tax year own, directly or indirectly, 50% or more of your voting stock? (For rules of attribution, see section 267(c).) If "Yes," complete (a) through (e).		X
(a) Attach a schedule showing name, address, and identifying number.		
(b) Enter percentage owned ▶		
(c) Was the owner of such voting stock a person other than a U.S. person? (See instructions)		
If "Yes," enter owner's country ▶		
(d) Enter highest amount owed by you to such owner during the year ▶		

	Yes	No
(e) Enter highest amount owed to you by such owner during the year ▶		
(Note: For purposes of H(1) and H(2), "highest amount owed" includes loans and accounts receivable/payable.)		
I If you were a member of a controlled group subject to the provisions of section 1561, check the type of relationship:		
(1) ☐ parent-subsidiary (2) ☐ brother-sister		
(3) ☐ combination of (1) and (2) (See section 1563.)		
J Refer to page 9 of instructions and state the principal:		
Business activity Building contractor		
Product or service air conditioning		
K Were you a U.S. shareholder of any controlled foreign corporation? (See sections 951 and 957.) If "Yes," attach Form 3646 for each such corporation		X
L At any time during the tax year, did you have an interest in or a signature or other authority over a bank account, securities account, or other financial account in a foreign country (see instructions)?		X
M Were you the grantor of, or transferor to, a foreign trust which existed during the current tax year, whether or not you have any beneficial interest in it?		X
If "Yes," you may have to file Forms 3520, 3520–A or 926.		
N During this tax year, did you pay dividends (other than stock dividends and distributions in exchange for stock) in excess of your current and accumulated earnings and profits? (See sections 301 and 316).		X
If "Yes," file Form 5452. If this is a consolidated return, answer here for parent corporation and on Form 851, Affiliations Schedule, for each subsidiary.		
O During this tax year was any part of your tax accounting records maintained on a computerized system?		X

Form 1120 (1981)   Page **4**

Schedule L	Balance Sheets	Beginning of tax year		End of tax year	
		(A)	(B)	(C)	(D)
	ASSETS				
1	Cash		5,800		3,065
2	Trade notes and accounts receivable		12,725		13,250
	(a) Less allowance for bad debts				
3	Inventories				
4	Gov't obligations: (a) U.S. and instrumentalities .				
	(b) State, subdivisions thereof, etc.				
5	Other current assets (attach schedule)		2,500		2,500
6	Loans to stockholders				
7	Mortgage and real estate loans				
8	Other investments (attach schedule)				
9	Buildings and other depreciable assets	250		250	
	(a) Less accumulated depreciation	15	235	40	210
10	Depletable assets				
	(a) Less accumulated depletion				
11	Land (net of any amortization)				
12	Intangible assets (amortizable only)				
	(a) Less accumulated amortization				
13	Other assets (attach schedule)				
14	Total assets		21,260		21,525
	LIABILITIES AND STOCKHOLDERS' EQUITY				
15	Accounts payable		500		4,000
16	Mtges, notes, bonds payable in less than 1 year . .		10,000		2,000
17	Other current liabilities (attach schedule) accruals		460		1,500
18	Loans from stockholders		4,500		4,500
19	Mtges, notes, bonds payable in 1 year or more . .				
20	Other liabilities (attach schedule)				
21	Captial stock: (a) Preferred stock				
	(b) Common stock	10,000	10,000	10,000	10,000
22	Paid-in or capital surplus				
23	Retained earnings—Appropriated (attach sch.) . .				
24	Retained earnings—Unappropriated		(4,200)		(475)
25	Less cost of treasury stock	( )	( )	( )	( )
26	Total liabilities and stockholders' equity . . .		21,260		21,525

Schedule M-1	Reconciliation of Income Per Books With Income Per Return		
1 Net income per books	3,725	7 Income recorded on books this year not included in this return (itemize)	
2 Federal income tax		(a) Tax-exempt interest $...............	
3 Excess of capital losses over capital gains . . .			
4 Income subject to tax not recorded on books this year (itemize) _____			
_____		8 Deductions in this tax return not charged against book income this year (itemize)	
5 Expenses recorded on books this year not deducted in this return (itemize)		(a) Depreciation . . . $...............	
(a) Depreciation . . . . $...............		(b) Contributions carryover . $...............	
(b) Contributions carryover . . $...............			
_____		9 Total of lines 7 and 8	None
6 Total of lines 1 through 5	3,725	10 Income (line 28, page 1)—line 6 less 9 . .	3,725

Schedule M-2	Analysis of Unappropriated Retained Earnings Per Books (line 24 above)		
1 Balance at beginning of year	(4,200)	5 Distributions: (a) Cash	
2 Net income per books	3,725	(b) Stock	
3 Other increases (itemize) _____		(c) Property	
_____		6 Other decreases (itemize) _____	
_____		_____	
_____		7 Total of lines 5 and 6	
4 Total of lines 1, 2, and 3	(475)	8 Balance at end of year (line 4 less 7) . . .	(475)

✩ U.S. GOVERNMENT PRINTING OFFICE: 1981-343-117 E.I. 43-0787287

Form **4562**
(Rev. September 1981)
Department of the Treasury
Internal Revenue Service (O)

Depreciation
▶ See separate instructions.
▶ Attach this form to your return.

OMB No. 1545-0172
Expires 12/31/82

Name(s) as shown on return	Identifying number
A. B. Enterprises, Inc.	24-2888028

▶ Generally, you must use the Accelerated Cost Recovery System of depreciation (ACRS) for all assets you placed in service after December 31, 1980. Report these assets in Part I, lines 1(a) through 1(f).

▶ You may elect to exclude certain property. Report this property in Part I, line 2.

▶ Use Part II for assets you placed in service before January 1, 1981, and certain other assets for which you cannot use ACRS.

▶ Filers of Schedule C (Form 1040), Schedule E (Form 1040) and Form 4835 should see the instructions for those forms before completing Form 4562.

Part I   Assets placed in service after December 31, 1980

A. Class of property	B. Date placed in service	C. Cost or other basis	D. Recovery period	E. Method of figuring depreciation	F. Percentage	G. Deduction for this year
1 Accelerated Cost Recovery System (ACRS) (See instructions for grouping assets):						
(a) 3-year property						
(b) 5-year property						
(c) 10-year property						
(d) 15-year public utility property						
(e) 15-year real property—low-income housing						
(f) 15-year real property other than low-income housing						
2 Property subject to section 168(e) (2) election (see instructions):						
3 Totals (add amounts in columns C and G) . . .						0
4 Depreciation from Part II, line 3						25
5 Total (add column G, lines 3 and 4). Enter this amount on the depreciation expense line (where it applies) of your return						25

See Paperwork Reduction Act Notice on page 1 of the separate instructions.

Form **4562** (Rev. 9-81)

Form 4562 (Rev. 9–81)   Page **2**

Part II Assets placed in service before January 1, 1981 and other assets not qualifying for ACRS

A. Description of property	B. Date acquired	C. Cost or other basis	D. Depreciation allowed or allowable in earlier years	E. Method of figuring depreciation	F. Life or rate	G. Depreciation for this year
1 Class Life Asset Depreciation Range (CLADR) System Depreciation . . . . ▶						
2 Other depreciation (for grouping assets, see instructions for Part II):						
Buildings						
Furniture and fixtures . .	1980	250	15	SL	10yrs	25
Transportation equipment						
Machinery and other equipment						
Other (specify)....................						
3 Total (add amounts in column G). Enter here and in Part I, line 4						25

☆ U.S. GOVERNMENT PRINTING OFFICE: 1981—O-343-455 58-040-1110

```
A. B. Enterprises, Inc.

ID #24-2888023

SUPPLEMENTAL SCHEDULES


Page 1 - Line 17 - Taxes
     Payroll taxes                            $ 1,350

Page 1 - Line 26 - Other Deductions
     Travel expenses                          $ 1,700
     Management fees                            1,200
     Employees insurance                          900
     Telephone                                    500
     Insurance                                    300
     Parts, supplies, small tools                 300
     Miscellaneous expenses                       250

                                             $ 5,150


Page 4 - Line 5 - Other Current Assets
     Loans receivable                         $ 5,000
```

Before resuming the interview, ask yourself what have you decided about the loan. Will you make it? List the balance sheet items you wish to explore, and the questions you will ask.

Smith: You should be quite proud of the statement. A profit plus a salary to an officer is quite an accomplishment for such a new company. Last year's sales were $34,000. How do you feel about this year?

Walters: Quite comfortable. We've got a big backlog of work. As soon as Harry's job gets settled and he can ship the product to the site, we can get to it. We'll have a good year. Maybe even $50,000.

Smith: Will the bottom line continue?

Walters: Knock on wood. I think so.

Smith: Your balance sheet has a couple of items I don't quite follow. Perhaps you can explain them to me. First, what is this loan receivable all about?

Walters: Don't ask. I feel bad about this. It's money to Harry. He had some problems. That's where my loan — loan to stockholders — came from. I borrowed the money from Mom. She'd die if she knew Harry had it.

Smith: If you feel that bad, why did you increase it?

Walters: I guess blood's thicker than water.

Smith: I also see that you had short-term loans of $10,000 last year?

Walters: Yes, we've paid them down to two grand. Not bad!

Smith: But hasn't this caused your suppliers to back up? Are you current with the vendors?

Walters: I'm okay. Sure, we're tight, but no one is going to panic. That's one of the reasons we want the line. My suppliers say not to borrow from them but to see a bank.

Smith: Speaking of banks, what is your relationship with our competition?

Walters: They renewed the line. Frankly, they just hemmed and hawed too much. I need quick answers. That's why I'm here.

Smith: I guess my final question is the receivables. What makes them up? Do you have a listing?

Walters: My accountant said you might want this. Here's a year-end aging. We're on top of everything.
          (Walters presents the aging shown on the following page).

A B ENTERPRISES INCORPORATED

ACCOUNTS RECEIVABLE AGING

NAME	TOTAL	CURRENT	30-60	60-PLUS	COMMENT
J. Smith	$ 450	450			
Giant Steel	1,100			1,100	Retainage
Howard Industries	900	500	400		
Structual Steel, Inc.	3,100		3,100		Pre job billings
Erection, Unltd.	900			900	Retainage
Giant Steel	750		750		
Mrs. Arnold	200	200			
Erection Unltd.	1,850			1,850	Retainage
Quick Steel	4,000	3,600	400		
TOTAL	$13,250	4,750	4,650	3,850	

Smith: This is really quite surprising. Aren't most of these bills from Harry's companies?

Walters: Some are. They're quite good. As soon as the retainage is paid him, we'll get paid. We always have in the past. This year's a little slow, but we'll be all right.

Smith: Jim, what you're really doing is financing Harry. And if I finance you, I'd really be financing him. Remember what you told me your suppliers said to you. Don't borrow from them, see a bank. Well, that's what Harry's doing to you. You're his banker and that's not fair. Just look at your balance sheet. Between the loans and your investment you have $15,000 in the business. And where is it? $5,000 is a loan to Harry and $7,000 or $8,000 is his accounts receivable. You put all your equity in him.

Walters: I guess I always realized this, but you just drove home the point. Harry and I have got to resolve our problem. Then I'll be back to see you.

Smith: I hope you do come back. We'd be most eager to be part of your company.

Comments

George Smith is an experienced veteran. His questions and answers show this. A less experienced person may have accepted the statement without proper exploration. Smith saw good equity and profitability. He also recognized the need to know what constitutes the key assets. He got to their content.

By following the funds from where they originated to and where they were spent, he was able to understand the events of the past year at a single glance.

As an epilogue, it's worth noting that Harry's problems proved insurmountable. He lost his bonding and his house of cards quickly fell. Jim's commitment was too large and Harry's inability to pay almost destroyed Jim. It will take some time until Jim can return to the strength he had on this year's statement.

Exercise 15

Your associate, Bill Waring, is out of the bank for three weeks. You receive a call from John Quick, president of Superior Oil Company, asking that you consider a request to finance new delivery trucks. Their value, fully-equipped, will be at least 30 percent more than their base cost. He would like to borrow 90 percent of this base cost on a four-year term loan. He estimates his need at $90,000. The equipment of this nature which he presently owns has a life of six years, after which he replaces the unit. The trade-in of old units acquired from the previous owners of the business constitutes his down payment.

Upon receiving the request you reviewed the credit file which contains the interim six-month statement and spread sheets. The statement has been prepared by a highly reputable regional CPA firm. Although it is unaudited, you feel comfortable with the numbers.

Also in the file was a memo your associate wrote prior to making the term loan which is presently the only debt due the bank. You have made loans for inventory which are always paid on time. Your associate is a seasoned veteran and his memo contains all that you need to know to understand your bank's relationship with the company. There is a shorter memo written by him after the annual review of the company's year-end statement. The highlights of this memo are also quite pertinent to understanding the company.

Read the memos on the following pages and, with their content in mind, review the statement and the spread sheets. List the questions you wish to discuss with Mr. Quick on your return phone call. Be prepared to give him an indication on how you feel about his request for $90,000.

If you feel the need for practice, use the statement for spreading and for ratio calculations. Then compare your answer with the analyst's.

SUPERIOR OIL COMPANY, INC.

FINANCIAL STATEMENTS

FOR THE SIX MONTHS ENDED MAY 31, 19X4

TABLE OF CONTENTS

<u>ACCOUNTANTS' REPORT WITHOUT OPINION</u>

Superior Oil Company, Inc.:

In connection with our examination for the year which will end November 30, 19X4, we have performed certain auditing procedures with respect to the financial statements of Superior Oil Company, Inc. as of May 31, 19X4 and for the six months then ended, as listed in the foregoing table of contents. As this is an interim period, such auditing procedures did not include all of the customary audit procedures which we consider necessary for the expression of an opinion on the financial statements.

Accordingly, we do not express an opinion on the accompanying financial statements as of May 31, 19X4 and for the six months then ended; we expect to express an opinion upon the completion of our examination at November 30, 19X4.

July 2, 19X4

- 2 -

SUPERIOR OIL COMPANY, INC.

BALANCE SHEET
MAY 31, 19X4
(UNAUDITED)

A S S E T S

CURRENT ASSETS:
Cash.. $ 36,283
Accounts receivable - trade (net of allowance for doubtful
  accounts of $9,000) (Note 2)............................... 237,123
Inventories (Notes 1 and 2):
  Petroleum products... 41,946
  Burner parts and supplies.................................. 22,175
Prepaid expenses... 4,152

     Total current assets........................ 341,679

EQUIPMENT - At cost (Notes 1 and 2):
  Motor vehicles... 76,193
  Storage tanks and tools.................................... 24,958
  Office equipment... 9,156
   Total.. 110,307
  Less accumulated depreciation.............................. 19,136

     Equipment - net............................. 91,171

OTHER ASSETS:
  Agreements not to compete (Note 1)......................... 203,300
  Organization costs (Note 1)................................ 252
  Goodwill (Note 1).. 1,001
  Deposit - Liquid Fuel Tax Bond............................. 1,024

     Total other assets.......................... 205,577

        TOTAL...................... $638,427

- 3 -   (Continued)

SUPERIOR OIL COMPANY, INC.

BALANCE SHEET
MAY 31, 19X4
(UNAUDITED)

L I A B I L I T I E S   A N D
S T O C K H O L D E R ' S   E Q U I T Y

CURRENT LIABILITIES:
   Current portion of long-term notes payable (Note 2)........... $ 49,967
   Accounts payable - trade..................................... 136,248
   Payroll taxes withheld from employees........................ 2,190
   Sales tax payable.. 437
   Excise taxes payable... 2,136
   Accrued interest... 1,000
   Accrued income taxes... 36,000

        Total current liabilities.................. 227,978

LONG-TERM NOTES PAYABLE (Note 2)............................... 215,114

        Total liabilities..................... 443,092

STOCKHOLDER'S EQUITY:
   Common stock authorized 150,000 shares of $1 par
     value each; 100,000 shares issued and outstanding. $100,000
   Retained earnings.................................   95,335

        Total stockholder's equity............ 195,335

        TOTAL....................... $638,427

See Notes to Financial Statements

- 4 -   (Concluded)

SUPERIOR OIL COMPANY, INC.

STATEMENT OF INCOME AND RETAINED EARNINGS
FOR THE SIX MONTHS ENDED MAY 31, 19X4
(UNAUDITED)

SALES:
Petroleum products............................ $1,274,451
Service and parts - heating and air condition-
ing..   63,814

        Total sales.................................... $1,338,265

COST OF SALES...   1,107,570

GROSS PROFIT..   230,695

OPERATING EXPENSES..   106,146

OPERATING INCOME..   124,549

OTHER EXPENSES:
Amortization of agreements not to compete,
  etc. (Note 1)...............................   24,108
Interest......................................   16,104

        Total other expenses........................   40,212

INCOME BEFORE PROVISION FOR INCOME TAXES....................   84,337

PROVISION FOR INCOME TAXES (Note 1).........................   36,000

NET INCOME..   48,337

RETAINED EARNINGS, BEGINNING................................   46,998

RETAINED EARNINGS, ENDING................................... $ 95,335

NET INCOME PER SHARE OF COMMON STOCK (Note 5)............... $ .46

See Notes to Financial Statements

- 5 -

SUPERIOR OIL COMPANY, INC.

STATEMENT OF CHANGES IN FINANCIAL POSITION
FOR THE SIX MONTHS ENDED MAY 31, 19X4
(UNAUDITED)

WORKING CAPITAL PROVIDED BY:
Net income..	$ 48,337
Add expenses not requiring outlay of working capital in the current period:	
Depreciation..	9,127
Amortization of agreements not to compete, etc...........	24,108
Total working capital provided..................	81,572

WORKING CAPITAL USED FOR:
Reduction in long-term debt.................................	30,000
Equipment purchases...	14,183
Deposit - Liquid Fuel Tax Bond.............................	1,344
Total working capital used......................	45,527

INCREASE IN WORKING CAPITAL..................................	$ 36,045

CHANGES IN COMPONENTS OF WORKING CAPITAL COMPRISED OF:
Increase (decrease) in current assets:
Cash..	$(6,904)
Accounts receivable...	129,719
Inventories...	(29,106)
Prepaid expenses..	(158)
Net increase in current assets..................	93,551

Increase (decrease) in current liabilities:
Notes payable...	857
Accounts payable..	26,317
Payroll taxes withheld......................................	1,725
Sales tax payable...	(2,615)
Excise taxes payable..	1,222
Accrued taxes on income....................................	30,000
Net increase in current liabilities.............	57,506

INCREASE IN WORKING CAPITAL..................................	$ 36,045

See Notes to Financial Statements

- 6 -

<u>SUPERIOR OIL COMPANY, INC.</u>

NOTES TO FINANCIAL STATEMENTS
(UNAUDITED)

1. SUMMARY OF SIGNIFICANT ACCOUNTING POLICIES:

   INVENTORIES - Inventories are stated at the lower of cost or market. Cost is determined on the first-in, first-out method.

   DEPRECIATION - Tangible property is depreciated over the following lives on the straight-line method.

	Useful Lives
Cars	3 years
Light trucks	4-5 years
Heavy trucks	5-7 years
Office equipment	7 years
Tanks	7 years

   Depreciation expense charged to operations for the six months ended May 31, 19X4 was $9,127.

   INTANGIBLE ASSETS:

   AGREEMENT NOT TO COMPETE - The portion of the purchase price of businesses acquired attributable to agreements on the part of the sellers to refrain from competition with the Company is amortized on the straight-line method over the period that the sellers agree to refrain from competition. For the six months ended May 31, 19X4 amortization of the cost of agreements not to compete was $24,108.

   ORGANIZATION COSTS - Amortization is computed over 60 months on the straight-line method.

   PURCHASED GOODWILL - Amounts paid for goodwill are stated at cost. In the opinion of management purchased goodwill has not declined in value.

   INCOME TAXES - Investment tax credits are treated as reduction in the provision for Federal income taxes in the period qualifying. assets are acquired. During the current period investment tax credits of approximately $2,100 have been used as reductions in income taxes.

- 7 -   (Continued)

FIRST EASTERN BANK, N. A.
COMPARISON STATEMENT

000's Omitted

NAME   Superior Oil Company, Inc.   6 Months

	ASSETS Date	11/30/X2	11/30/X3		5/31/X4	
1	Cash	56	43		36	
2	Marketable Securities — C/D's					
3	Receivable — Trade (Net)	87	107		237	
4						
5	Inventories	64	93		64	
6						
7						
8	All Other Current					
9	TOTAL CURRENT ASSETS	207	243		337	
10	Fixed Assets — Net	93	87		91	
11						
12	Agreement not to compete	275	227		203	
13	Investments					
14						
15	All Other Noncurrent (Incl. Prepaid)	5	5		7	
16	TOTAL NONCURRENT ASSETS	373	319		301	
17	TOTAL ASSETS	580	562		638	
	LIABILITIES					
18	Notes Payable — Banks					
19	Notes Payable — Other					
20						
21	Current Maturities of L. T. Debt	41	49		50	
22	Accounts Payable — Trade	94	110		136	
23						
24	Interest & Other Accruals	4	2		1	
25	Taxes Payable	3	9		41	
26						
27						
28	All Other Current					
29	TOTAL CURRENT DEBT	142	170		228	
30	Mortgage Payable					
31	Long Term Debt	275	245		215	
32						
33	All Other Noncurrent					
34	TOTAL NONCURRENT DEBT	275	245		215	
35	TOTAL LIABILITIES	417	415		443	
36	Capital	100	100		100	
37	Retained Earnings	63	47		95	
38						
39	NET WORTH	163	147		195	
40	TOTAL LIABILITIES&NET WORTH	580	562		638	
41						
42	NET WORKING CAPITAL (9-29)	65	73		109	
	RATIOS					
43	Quick	1.01 to 1	.88 to 1		1.19 to 1	
44	Current	2.32 to 1	1.43 to 1		1.48 to 1	
45	Total Debt/Working Capital	395/158	415/73		443/109	
46	Total Debt/Net Worth	395/163	415/147		443/195	
47	Receivable Turnover Days	26 days	20 days		32 days	
48	Inventory Turnover Days	24 days	20 days		10 days	
49	% Profit bef. Taxes/Net Worth	NA	NA		43%	
50	% Profit bef. Taxes/Total Assets	NA	NA		13%	
51						
52	Statement by					
53	Type of Statement	Certified	Certified		Interim	
54	Spread by	TJO	TJO		TJO	
55	Contingent Liabilities					
56						

FORM 18-1

FIRST EASTERN BANK, N. A.

NAME   Superior Oil Company, Inc.

6 Months

OPERATIONS Date	11/30/X2	%	11/30/X3	%		%	5/31/X4	%		%
101 Net Sales	1,713	100	1,917	100			1,338	100		
102 Cost of Sales	1,510	88	1,659	87			1,108	83		
103 Gross Profit	203	12	258	13			230	17		
104 Operating Expenses	154	9	197	10			113	8		
105 Net Profit before Depreciation	49	3	61	3			117	9		
106 Depreciation	17	1	21	1			9	1		
107 Profit from Operations	32	2	40	2			108	8		
108 Extraordinary Items ✻	48	3	48	3			24	2		
109										
110 Profits Before Taxes	(16)		(8)				84	6		
111 Income Taxes										
112							36	3		
113 NET PROFIT AFTER TAXES	(16)		(8)				48	3.6		
RECONCILIATION OF NET WORTH										
114 Net Worth — Beginning	79		63				47			
115 Add: Net Profit After Taxes							48			
116										
117										
118 Less: Net Loss	16		8							
119 Dividend Paid										
120 Adjust. to Prev. Year			8							
121										
122 Net Worth — Ending	63		47				95			
SOURCE & APPLICATION OF FUNDS										
Source of Funds:										
123 Net Profit							48			
124 Depreciation, Amort., Depletion	65		69				33			
125 Increase Long Term Debt										
126										
127										
128 Other Noncurrent Accounts — Net										
129 TOTAL SOURCES	65		69				81			
Application of Funds:										
130 Net Loss	16		8							
131 Dividends Paid										
132 Purchase of Fixed Assets	11		15				14			
133 Reduction Long Term Debt	30		30				30			
134 Adjustment Prior Years			8							
135										
136 Other Noncurrent Accounts — Net	2						1			
137 TOTAL APPLICATIONS	59		61				45			
138 INC./DEC. OF WORKING CAPITAL	+6		+8				+36			
RECONCIL. OF W/C CHANGES										
139 Cash	3		(13)				(7)			
140 Accounts Receivable	(8)		20				130			
141 Inventory	6		29				(29)			
142 Other										
143										
144 Notes Payable										
145 Accounts Payable	(6)		16				26			
146 Current Maturities — L.T. Debt	2		8				1			
147 Other	(1)		4				1			
148 Income Taxes Payable							30			
149 Inc/Dec W/C (139-143) — (144-148)	+6		+8				+36			

COMMENTS:

✻Represents amortization of an agreement not to compete.

M E M O R A N D U M

RE: Superior Oil Company, Inc.

FROM: Bill Waring

DATE: January 27, 19X4

I visited with John Quick to tour his plant and to review his 19X3
statement. The premises were neat and orderly and the operation
appears to be run in a highly efficient manner. The 19X3 statement
was delivered last week and was spread by our credit department.

Sales for 19X3 showed a $200M increase with profits before non-cash
items increasing from $49M to $61M. The bottom line showed a loss
but this was caused by the amortization of the agreement not to compete
plus depreciation. Although these numbers are in line with projections
and budgets, we had hoped that this year's sales would top the $2MM
mark.

The company has landed a major commercial account. They have signed
a two-year contract (with a variable price per gallon based on published
oil head prices). This is expected to put 19X4 sales close to $2.5
million and will create sales during the normally slow summer months.

So far, the company has used all of its cash profits to meet our term
loan. The operating loss has actually reduced the total book equity
as reported by their CPA.

We discussed the possible need for a line of credit some time after
receipt of the 19X4 statement, a year from now. By late spring, we
will be requested to consider financing certain new equipment. Our
decision will have to await an interim statement which must reflect the
ability to meet these additional payments.

M E M O R A N D U M

RE: Quick/ Superior Oil Company, Inc.

FROM: Bill Waring

DATE: July 14, 19X1

Mr. John Quick and his CPA visited with me at the bank today to discuss
Quick's desire to purchase the assets of Superior Oil Company, Inc.
The company is presently owned by Mr. Harry Siles and has been in existence
for 15 years. Mr. Siles has certain real estate investments and plans
to use the sales proceeds and his free time to further these interests.

Mr. Quick has been in the area for some time. His background in the
oil industry is quite extensive and includes a number of years with two
major oil companies plus several years as a private consultant (including
work for Siles). This is how he knew of the pending sale.

Quick has $100,000 of equity which he will invest. The total purchase
price will be $480,000. Siles has agreed to finance $100,000 of this
by acceptance of a note from the company. The balance, $280,000, is
what Quick would like our bank to finance. He would like it payable over
approximately six or seven years. He plans on payments of $4,000 per
month plus interest, but realizes that some summer months may be slow
and principal payments may have to be postponed for short periods.

He has discussed supply with a number of major oil companies, and he
will not need a line of credit at this time. This dealership is a major
consumer in this area, and the competition between various companies
to supply him has been intense. He will sign a four-year supply contract
since he feels the industry will become quite tight over the next three
or four years. A line of credit and equipment loans (on an add-on basis)
were discussed as future needs.

Quick's accountant presented a summary of past statements under Siles'
ownership. He also presented a cash flow forecast for seven years which
looks encouraging.

The accountant presented in great detail how they would handle the
acquisition. The net amount of $480,000 would purchase between 130 and
150 of assets (net of liabilities assumed). The balance will constitute
an agreement not to compete between the new Superior Oil Company, Inc.
and Siles. Because of this classification it would be tax deductible
to Superior and would still provide the tax advantage of being an
installment sale to Siles.

The covenant would be amortized over a five- or seven-year period. The
expense would be substantial, but will save taxes and profit before
this and depreciation will, on a cash basis, allow for reductions in
our loan. Our loan would be secured by all the assets of the new
corporation. I agreed to his request subject to the approval of our
committee.

Comments

The need for credit files and the advantage of well-maintained ones are evident in this case study. Bill Waring set down in a relatively small number of words the background of the case and the reasoning and position of your bank some three years ago. Thus, in his absence, you were able to learn about the company and to understand the make-up of the most important item on the statement, the covenant not to compete. He left you a road map to the *content* of the numbers reflected. You could not really understand the statement without understanding this point about the covenants, and it is possible that his absence and no memo would have left you in an untenable position.

The credit file also showed its value by being the point from which information on the current statement could be gained. With the recent update and the spreads on the six-month statement, you knew all about the company.

What did this memo and these spreads tell us? The starting point is net worth. This dropped to 163 in 19X2 and to 147 in 19X3. That certainly is far from encouraging. Remember those memos. The company is showing a loss due to the charge-off of an, at best, odd item. Is the company any less a company after this charge-off of the noncompetition covenant? Not really. Quick bought a going-concern and paid a premium for it. Is this premium still warranted? That's the key question. If it is, then the expense of writing off a part is academic and not critical to us. If the company isn't worthy of the premium, then your existing loan is in trouble.

Bill Waring's memo expressed his concern that the company, although meeting its plan, was not generating as high a profit as he had hoped. He also thought that an improved picture would be forthcoming. The six-month's profitability figure is confirming his anticipation. This is most encouraging. The profits have increased net worth to $195,000. Sales have increased and the $2.5 million mark seems a possibility.

The remainder of the financial statement has also changed. Receivables are much higher. This is probably a result of the seasonal nature of the business. Residential customers are just beginning to pay their bills for this winter's final deliveries. The new commercial account is also part of this balance. The inventory is lower for the same reason receivables are higher. The remaining numbers seem in line with previous years' results. Payables are up slightly but, once again, these are reflecting the nature of the business cycle.

The income has changed much more drastically. Not only are sales up, but cost of sales has dropped. The gross profit is now 17 percent versus 12 percent and 13 percent for the two previous years. Operating expenses are up on an annual basis ($113 × 2 = $226 as opposed to $197 and $154).

The prime number, profit before noncash expenses, is the key to this analysis. Our existing loan and our present request both depend on profitability for repayment. This is the context of the request we are judging. As of the six-month period, we have $117,000 of profit before depreciation amortization and taxes. This figure compares with $61,000 and $49,000 for the two previous years. Even a "flat" second half would allow for a more than handsome total year.

All of these conclusions we have drawn from changes in the statement are clearly reflected in the change of financial position statement. The company has its profit plus certain expenses available to spend. They total $82,000. The major item is the noncompetition agreement. The firm used these funds to reduce long-term debt and to purchase some equipment. The competition agreement is the source and the long-term debt is the application. Remember the early discussion we had about depreciation as a "repayer of loans." This expense does not pay loans. Cash pays loans. But in this case, the charge is clearly noncash, and therefore, the company's cash profit is higher. This allows for higher loan repayment capability.

The second half of this statement reconciles the various increases and decreases of current asset items. Finally, we have the footnotes. Item 1 summarizes the key accounting premises. There are no major items besides this one.

The review of this statement was done in a different sequence from previous ones. In this case, the letter was read and then the balance sheet. The analyst then reviewed the spread sheet which gave a concise summary of this as well as past years. The same thing was done with the income statement. First, the actual report and then the spread sheets. The analyst concluded by reading the remaining portion of the accountant's statement.

This method differs from the previously suggested approach of the letter first, then the footnotes, and back to the statement. Everyone must develop his own style.

We review statements in the context of a new or existing request. We then go to the content of any and all reported numbers. This sequence is especially important in the Superior Oil Company. We must understand the agreement not to compete. We must read the statement after deciding on how we will treat this item.

Opinions will vary. If the company had paid a premium for the stock, would you, as the banker, feel more comfortable with the statement because the firm would have a larger capital base (it would if the stock was purchased by a new corporation and not an existing one as in our example). If this investment were in the form of equity, the company could not depreciate it. The company's profits, on paper, would be higher, but it would have to pay taxes on those profits and give up precious dollars. The dollars not used to pay taxes have been available for use as part of the company's working capital base — a key reason why the company has not had to borrow on its line of credit.

The loan request is reasonable. We know the background of the company. The interim statement confirms our expectations for the coming year.

The request will be decided on the basis of cash flow. Does the company have a repayment capability sufficient to meet this new request? The answer is yes. There is sufficient cash flow. The source and application statement clearly showed it. Will this capacity continue in the years ahead? You're the loan officer and that decision is yours.

Glossary

The terms in this glossary are, for the most part, contained in the text. A few have been added because their definitions help to clarify other items found in the book.

Words that appear in italic type within the definitions are also defined in the glossary. These entries are cross-referenced to each other and noted with the words *Compare, Contrast, See, See also.*

accountant A firm or individual that keeps, inspects, or audits the business records of a business concern or a firm or individual who prepares *financial statements,* interim reports, and tax returns.

accountant's letter A letter that precedes a financial statement which reports the scope of the examination being done and gives an opinion (if any) on the overall fairness of the data presented in the report.

accounts payable Amounts owed to others, primarily for goods that have been received, and usually evidenced by a bill of sale or an invoice.

accounts receivable Amounts owed to a business concern by others, primarily for goods and services that have been delivered.

accounts receivable turnover The average life of an account receivable; the average amount of time it takes for customers to pay their bills.

accrual basis A method of accounting in which income and expenses are recorded at the time they are earned or incurred, regardless of when the money is actually received or paid. (Contrast: *cash basis.*)

accrued expenses   Amounts owed to others as of the balance sheet data, primarily for services rendered, and usually evidenced by a bill of sale or an invoice.

accrued taxes   Taxes that are owed but not paid as of the balance sheet date.

acid test ratio   The ratio of cash and receivables to current liabilities. This is a stricter form of *current ratio*; like current ratio, it measures a business's liquidity, or ability to meet current obligations. (*Compare: current ratio.*)

affiliate   An individual or business concern that is closely related to another.

aging schedule   A breakdown of accounts receivable according to the length of time each invoice has been outstanding, usually current, 30 – 59 days, 60 – 89 days, and 90 days and over. (*See also: accounts receivable turnover.*)

amortization   1. The *depreciation,* or writing off, of the value of an *asset* (usually intangible, such as *goodwill* or a copyright) over its useful life. 2. The gradual paying off of a debt by making regular equal payments sufficient to cover (a) interest and (b) a reduction in the principal amount owed so that it becomes zero by the end of the loan period.

arm-length or **arm's-length transaction**   A transaction between parties who are not affiliated.

assets   Anything an individual or business concern owns or is owed to it.

asset conversion loan   A loan whose primary source of repayment comes from the successful conversion of an *asset* from one form to another, e.g. from *inventory* to cash or from *receivables* to cash. Asset conversion loans are usually *short-term loans* extended on the basis of the conversion of *current assets.* (Contrast: *profit distribution loan.*)

bad debts   Amounts due on loans or *receivables* that have been deemed to be uncollectable and are therefore no longer considered to be of value; the act of writing off (expensing) amounts previously listed as income.

balance sheet   The part of a *financial statement* that shows the *assets, liabilities,* and *equity* of a company as of a certain date (and only for that date).

balloon loan   A long-term loan that is retired slowly at first but has one large (inflated) payment on maturity.

bankruptcy   The inability of an individual or business concern to meet its financial obligations. Bankruptcy may be sought voluntarily or forced by one's *creditors.* Legal bankruptcy involves a judgment by a court and its assistance in protecting and distributing *assets* to the creditors.

below-the-line expenses   The expenses of doing business, as opposed to the expenses of the item sold. Known as "below-the-line" because such items are listed below the *gross profit line.*

bond   An instrument of debt (basically a loan or an IOU) by which a company promises to pay back the *principal* amount by the end of a specific period, and to pay *interest* in periodic installments.

calendar year   A year that ends on December 31. A company whose activities, taxes, and financial statements, are timed to coincide with the calendar year is said to have a *fiscal year* that coincides with the calendar year.

capacity The ability — based on evidence of sound management, market stability, and past performance, among other factors — of a company to carry out its plans. Capacity is one of the principal ingredients of *credit*. The other two ingredients are *character* and *capital*.

capital The total investment of a company in itself; its *net worth,* as indicated by the difference between its total *assets* and total *liabilities*.

capital asset An *asset* that is held and used over a long period; a *long-term asset* or *fixed asset* as opposed to a *working-capital* asset. Typical capital assets include land and buildings, machinery, furniture, and moving stock.

cash basis A method of accounting in which income and expenses are recorded as they are paid, regardless of when the income was actually earned or the expenses actually incurred. (See also: *accrual basis*.)

cash flow statement A portion of the financial statement which reports the total funds available to the company (net income, non-cash expenditures, loan and investment proceeds) and how the company elected to spend those funds (loan reduction, purchase of fixed assets, increase in working capital). Also called source and application statement and change in financial position statement; a phrase used to refer to the amount of funds available to service debt (company's income plus non-cash expenses such as depreciation and amortization).

cash surrender value The cash value of a life insurance policy, (determined by the payment of a stipulated number of premiums) that will be paid to a policy-holder if he or she cancels (surrenders) the life insurance. Cash surrender value may be used as *collateral* for a loan against a life insurance policy without having to surrender the actual policy.

character The personal traits, such as honesty and observance of business ethics, of a company and its senior management. Character, along with *capacity* and *capital,* is one of the three principal ingredients of *credit*.

charge–off A loan that bank management no longer considers collectable and is therefore written off as a loss. (See: *bad debts*.)

classified loan A loan that has been reviewed and found to be less satisfactory (a greater risk) than ordinary loans.

clean letter The phrase used to describe the accountant's letter when a statement has been audited or certified.

collateral An *asset* or assets that are pledged by a borrower as a secondary source of repayment on a loan. A loan against such collateral is called a *secured loan*.

common-base statement A statement that reduces all figures to a base of 100, thus making comparison with other common-base statements meaningful.

consolidated statement A *financial statement* showing the total *assets, liabilities,* etc., of two or more affiliated companies (such as a parent and its subsidiaries) as if they were a single company.

consolidating statement A financial statement showing the total assets of two or more affiliated companies separately and then as a whole.

contingent liability   An obligation for which one may become liable but only if some other event occurs or fails to occur. For example, the co-signer of a loan will become liable for the debt only if the original borrower defaults.

contra account   An account that offsets an amount payable to a party with an amount receivable from the same party.

conversion time   The length of a normal business cycle during which *current assets* are converted from one form to another (cash to *inventory* to *receivables* to cash).

corporation   A group of shareholders, investors, and professional management that has been granted a legal charter to do business as an entity distinct from its individual members and having its own rights, duties, and liabilities. (Contrast: *partnership*.)

covenant   A condition or stipulation written into or implied by a contract or instrument of debt.

credit   The ability of a person or business concern to borrow money from a lender, based on the lender's confidence that the borrower will be able to repay. The three principal ingredients of credit, are *capacity, capital,* and *character*.

credit file   Records containing a summary of the history of the company, all past loans, inquiries, and *financial statements* of a potential borrower.

creditor   A person or business concern to whom money is owed.

current assets   *Assets,* such as *inventories* and *receivables,* that will be converted into cash within the normal business cycle.

current liabilities   *Liabilities* that are due in the normal business cycle of a company, usually within a year.

current portion of long-term debt   The *principal* portion of a *long-term loan* that is payable within the next twelve months.

current ratio   The ratio of *current assets* to *current liabilities*. The current ratio is a measure of a company's *liquidity* and is sometimes called the *working capital* ratio. (Compare: *acid test ratio*.)

dealer reserve   An account maintained by a bank to hold funds that belong to a dealer but that will not be released until some certain future performance has occurred. The funds are owned by, but not available to, the dealer.

debtor   One who owes money to another.

debt service   The funds needed to meet debt payments during a given period.

debt service ratio   The ratio of a company's total annual debt payments (*principal* and *interest*) to the cash profits (profit before depreciation or amortization) available to service the debt. The ratio is a measure of a company's ability to meet debt payments.

default   The failure to meet an obligation. The term is particularly applied to the failure to pay the *interest* or the *principal* on a *bond,* but may be applied to any loan.

deferred expenses   Expenses incurred during the current period but which are things that will be delivered or used at some future time. Accounting for such expenses is delayed, or "deferred," until that future time period.

deferred income tax   Tax that is not currently due but that will be due in the future. Usually infers that the company has accounted for profit on its books on a basis different from that used for taxes.

demand loan   A loan that does not have a specific *maturity* date but is due on demand of the holder. (Contrast: *single-payment note*; *term loan*; *time loan*.)

depreciation   An accounting term used to reflect the decrease in value of a *long-term* or *capital asset* over its estimated useful life. Depreciation does not represent a cash outlay, but a charge against earnings.

depressed market   A market that is undergoing a sharp decrease in activity and prices and that therefore fails to deliver a reasonable price for the sale of an *asset* or goods and services.

discount   The percentage amount less than its face value for which an instrument sells.

dividend   A portion of the net profits of a *corporation* that is distributed to the shareholders.

documentation   Physical evidence, e.g. a written contract, that sets forth the rights, duties, and responsibilities of each party to a transaction.

double declining balance   A method of calculating *depreciation* of an *asset* that assumes the asset will lose value at an accelerated rate in the early years of its life and at a slower rate in the later years. (Contrast: *straight-line depreciation*; *sum of the years digits*.)

equity   The amount by which the value of a business's assets or property exceeds any claims (*liens*) against it. The difference between total assets and total liabilities.

escrow account   An account maintained by a bank, broker, or trustee on behalf of two parties to hold funds until such time as certain conditions are met. The funds may be owned by or owed to the parties but are not available until the prescribed conditions are satisfied. An example is a tax escrow account into which a homeowner deposits funds and from which real estate tax payments will be made.

external comparison   The comparison of a company's *financial statement* with that of another company in the same industry. (Contrast: *internal comparison*.)

factoring   The selling of one's *accounts receivable* at a *discount* (to an agent called a factor) thereby guaranteeing collectability as compared to borrowing against them from a lender.

fair market value   The amount that would be realized, given adequate time, by an *arm's-length* sale of an *asset*.

FIFO   Acronym for *First In First Out*. A method of valuing *inventory* in which the cost of the oldest goods in inventory is charged against the earnings of goods sold. (Contrast: *LIFO*.)

financial statement   The summary of a company's financial position as of a certain date and for a certain period, prepared by management and reviewed or audited by outside *accountants*.

fiscal year   A twelve-month period for which a company's activities, taxes, plans, and financial statements are organized. The fiscal year may coincide with the *calendar year* or it may be any other twelve-month period.

fixed asset   A long-term or *capital asset*.

fixed dividend   A *dividend* given each year in the same amount regardless of the profit of the company.

float   1. The amount of money represented by checks that are in transit between banks for collection, i.e., that have not been paid yet. 2. The amount of time such checks are in transit.

friendly debt   A slang name for *subordinated debt,* friendly because it is usually an obligation that is due to a *principal* or *equity* holder of a company. Or it can be treated as equity (given certain contractual agreements) thereby aiding the company's borrowing ability.

general expenses   The cost of doing business, as opposed to the cost or expenses of the actual item sold.

going concern basis   An assumption, in valuing and reporting the *assets* of a company, that the company's business is ongoing; that the assets will be used for the purpose for which they were purchased; and that the assets will not have to be sold under duress at lower-than-normal prices.

goodwill   An intangible *asset* having no physical value but based on name, favorable location, prestige, and/or other favorable conditions.

gross profit   The profit from the sale of an item as calculated by subtracting only the actual cost of the item from the amount of money received from its sale (without subtracting selling and administrative costs). (Compare: *net income*.)

guarantee or **guaranty**   A contract by which a third party promises to pay a borrower's debt if the borrower is unable or unwilling to do so.

income statement   The portion of a *financial statement* that shows the cumulative income and expenses of a company for a specific period, e.g. one month, six months, one year.

indenture   A written *note* evidencing proof of indebtedness, typically showing the *maturity* of the note, *interest* rate, and all terms of repayment.

interest   The price paid for the use of someone else's money, usually expressed as a percentage of the *principal* on an annual basis.

internal comparison   The comparison of a company's *financial statement* for one year with the same company's financial statement for another year. (Contrast: *external comparison*.)

inventory   1. In manufacturing, the raw materials, work in process, and finished goods of a business. 2. In retail business, items bought for resale. 3. A detailed list of items in inventory.

inventory turnover   The average amount of time an item remains in *inventory*; the time from physical arrival of product until removal at the point of sale.

leverage   The use of debt to finance investments.

liabilities   The money or other *assets* that a company owes to others. (Compare: *assets*.)

lien   A recorded claim on an *asset* or a company (or both) that gives a *creditor* the right to hold the property as security for payment of a debt or to sell the asset or company in order to pay off the debt.

LIFO   Acronym for *Last In First Out*. A method of valuing *inventory* in which the cost of the most recent incoming goods is charged against the earnings of goods sold. (Contrast: *FIFO*.)

liquid assets   Synonym for *current assets*, called liquid because they "flow" easily from one form to another.

liquidation   1. The conversion of *assets* to cash. 2. The dissolution of a company by conversion of its assets into cash and distribution of the proceeds to its *creditors* in order of preference, with any remainder going to the owners.

liquidity   The degree to which an individual or business concern has cash or can convert *assets* to cash quickly without suffering losses.

long-term asset   A *capital asset*. An asset with a life that exceeds one normal business cycle, usually a life in excess of one year.

long-term loan   A loan that is structured to be repaid from the profits of a company over a period of time (two to seven years), encompassing many normal business cycles. (Compare: *short-term loan*.)

low point   The period of least activity in a company's year or business cycle.

margin   (See: *gross profit*.)

maturity   The date on which an obligation is due, or the period during which an obligation is in force.

net income   The amount by which revenues or net sales exceed all expenses. (Compare: *gross profit*.)

net worth   The net difference between *assets* and *liabilities*. For a business, this represents the owner's *equity*.

non-cash expense   An expense contained in an *income statement* for which no cash was expended, e.g. *depreciation* and *amortization*.

non-expense cash disbursement   The expenditure of cash that is not reflected as an expense on an *income statement*; a payment of *principal,* the purchase of an asset.

note   A written contract promising to pay a debt and indicating the amount owed and the date by which it must be paid.

notes payable   Obligations due to others and evidenced by a written contract.

offset   The act by which a bank takes the deposits of a *debtor* or guarantor and uses them to pay back the debtor's loan.

other assets   *Assets* that cannot be properly listed as *current assets* or *long-term (capital) assets*, e.g., *goodwill*.

overhead expenses   The cost of doing business; operating expenses.

partnership   A grouping of two or more entities or persons organized as co-owners of a business and sharing in its *profits* and losses. Unlike a *corporation*, a partnership needs no legal charter (though a partnership agreement is advisable). (Compare: *proprietorship*.)

peak debt statement   A projection of what the *balance sheet* will reflect at the point when the maximum amount of debt is in use; or at the time of maximum activity during the year.

piecemeal opinion   An opinion in which the auditor identifies the portions of the *financial statement* that have been audited and confirmed (as opposed to an overall opinion, no longer acceptable by the AICPA, American Institute of Certified Public Accountants).

pledge   The contractual commitment of *collateral* to a bank as security for a loan. The pledge gives the *creditor* a right to the *assets* that make up the collateral.

pre-depreciation profit   A statement of profit before the *non-cash expense* of *depreciation* or amortization is reflected.

prime rate   The *interest* rate that a bank offers to its best corporate borrowers for *short-term loans*.

principal   1. The amount of money that is borrowed, lent, or invested, exclusive of *interest* or income generated by it. 2. The person having the primary responsibility in an obligation.

profit   The gain from a business operation after all costs and expenses have been met.

profitability   The degree to which a company, operation, or investment is profitable.

profit distribution loan   A loan whose primary source of repayment comes from a distribution of *profit*. (Contrast: *asset conversion loan*.)

profit to total asset ratio   A measure of a company's *profitability* on the total assets employed; *profits* divided by total *assets*.

profit to net worth ratio   A measure of a company's *profitability* on the total investment by the firm; *profits* divided by *net worth*.

proprietorship   A business owned and managed by one person, without partners and without a legal structure. Also called a sole proprietorship. (Contrast: *corporation*; *partnership*.)

qualitative ratios   *Ratios* that measure the quality of certain company assets by measuring their turnover rates.

quantitative ratios   *Ratios* that measure the quality of the company's overall assets or certain groupings of assets by comparing quantities of those assets to themselves and/or to certain liabilities.

quick cash items   Assets that are readily converted into cash; assets that can be expected to be converted to cash during a normal business cycle. Also called quick assets. An example of a quick cash item is accounts receivable. (Compare: *current assets*. See also: *acid test ratio*; *current ratio*.)

ratio   A measure of the relationship between certain key numbers in a *financial statement*, gotten by dividing one into the other.

recourse   The right to go back for payment to previous endorsers or parties to a negotiable instrument if the first party fails to pay or deliver.

retained earnings   The portion of a company's earnings retained by it to fund future growth (as opposed to earnings not retained — dividend).

sales leaseback   A method of financing in which a company sells its *assets* (such as equipment or buildings) with the explicit requirement that the assets will be leased back to the company.

secured loan   A loan that contains, among other things, a *pledge* of *collateral*.

short-term loan   A loan that is structured to be repaid during the normal business cycle, typically within one year. (Compare: *long-term loan*.)

single payment note   A loan whose principal is due and payable in total in a single payment at *maturity*. (Contrast *demand loan*; *term loan*; *time loan*.)

sinking fund   A separate cash account maintained by a company or its trustee, into which the company places funds at intervals in order to retire a *bond* or other long-term debt.

source and application statement   A name commonly given to the *statement of change in financial position* in a *financial statement*. (See: *cash flow statement*.)

spreading   Transferring a *financial statement* to a concise, simplified form called a spread sheet.

statement of change in financial position   The portion of a *financial statement* that lists the funds available to a company and the manner in which those funds were expended. Sometimes referred to as *source and application statement*. (See: *cash flow statement*.)

statement of retained earnings   The portion of a *financial statement* that lists current *retained earnings* along with the changes that have occurred during the year and the causes of such changes (profit, dividend).

stock   Physical evidence of ownership in a *corporation*. The degree to which a person or other entity has ownership in a corporation is reflected in the relative number of shares of stock owned.

straight line depreciation   A method of calculating *depreciation* of an *asset* that assumes the asset will lose value in an equal dollar amount per year over its estimated life. (Contrast: *double declining balance*; *sum of the years digits*.)

subordinated debt   A debt that, by written contract, will be paid only after other, more senior, debts are satisfied. Sometimes referred to as friendly debt because it is considered a quasi form of capital thereby increasing the company's net worth and the lender's underlying security.

sum of the years digits   A method of calculating *depreciation* of an *asset* that assumes the asset will lose value at an accelerated rate in the early years of its life and at a slower rate in the later years. (Contrast: *double declining balance*; *straight line depreciation*.)

tax lien   A claim against *assets* filed by a taxing authority (e.g. the IRS) for unpaid taxes.

tenant   A person and/or business concern that has possession of, and pays rent for, a facility or building owned by someone else.

term loan   A *long-term loan* that is repaid in regular periodic payments over a period of years (over a number of business cycles). (Contrast *demand loan*; *single payment note*; *time loan*.)

time loan   A loan that is made with a fixed *maturity* (typically 30, 60, 90, or 120 days) or with a series of fixed maturities, (sometimes with *interest* being discounted in advance. (Contrast: *demand loan*; *single-payment note*; *term loan*.)

total debt to net worth ratio   A measure of the relative degree to which *creditors* (debt) and investors (net worth) share in a company's financial structure. The higher the ratio, the more the company's equity is *leveraged*.

total debt to working capital ratio   A measure of a company's *liquidity* and ability to meet its debt payments.

treasury stock   *Stock* that has been issued by a *corporation* and then repurchased by them using funds from the corporation's treasury.

turnover   The degree, time, or speed with which *current assets* are converted from one form to another, e.g. *inventory* to cash.

unaudited opinion   A term used to indicate that a CPA has not audited the *financial statement* and is not rendering an opinion on it.

unearned income   Funds received by a company for which additional work must be done before the funds can be re-classified as sales or income.

unsecured loan   A loan that does not contain a specific *pledge* of *collateral* but is dependent on the overall strength of the borrower.

working capital   The excess of *current assets* over *current liabilities*, available as cash or *quick cash items* for paying for a company's ongoing operations.

Index